TH ... DE
MOVE-ON BLUES
In Search of the New South Africa

Christopher Hope was born in Johannesburg in 1944. He is the author of *Kruger's Alp*, which won the Whitbread Prize for Fiction, *Serenity House*, which was shortlisted for the 1992 Booker Prize, as well as *My Mother's Lovers* and *Shooting Angels*, which were both published to great acclaim. He is a Fellow of the Royal Society of Literature.

THE CAFÉ DE MOVE-ON BLUES

In Search of the New South Africa

CHRISTOPHER HOPE

Atlantic Books
London

First published in Great Britain in 2018 by Atlantic Books,
an imprint of Atlantic Books Ltd.

This paperback edition published in 2019 by Atlantic Books.

Map artwork by Jeff Edwards

10 9 8 7 6 5 4 3 2 1

A CIP catalogue record for this book is available
from the British Library.

Paperback ISBN: 978 1 78649 061 2
E-book ISBN: 978 1 78649 060 5

Printed in Denmark by Nørhaven

Atlantic Books
An imprint of Atlantic Books Ltd
Ormond House
26–27 Boswell Street
London
WC1N 3JZ

www.atlantic-books.co.uk

For Georgie, wherever he may be

Contents

Preface

This is an account of a journey around South Africa. It is a search for understanding of who 'we' are and what we thought we were doing there. People like myself, and those from whom I came: English-speakers, descendants of European settlers, or 'Whites' – to use the weary, inevitable classification, and thus 'South Africans', of a certain sort. It was a search unlikely to succeed because the country is one where the more you know, the less you understand, but that in no way lessens the need to go on looking. It began in April 2015, when a statue of Cecil John Rhodes, the imperial fortune hunter, was attacked on the campus of Cape Town University. I happened to be there at what proved to be the start of the statue wars.

With each passing week, effigies across South Africa were assaulted, strung with placards, toppled, and daubed with paint and other ordures. The variety of statues targeted was surprising. Besides British imperialists and Dutch colonialists, they included Black revolutionaries, an Indian pacifist, KhoiSan icons, several stone elephants, three monarchs, one tiny rabbit and a horse. Not only statues but paintings, photographs, books and libraries were torched, lecture halls trashed, teachers threatened and assaulted. Race came into it, of course – in South Africa it always does. Many, but not all, of the iconoclasts were Black and most, but by no means all, of the statues assaulted depicted Whites.

It was about this time that I came across an account, given in James Fenton's wonderful little book *On Statues*, of an attack that took place on the sacred images and icons of churches in Bruges, during the French Revolution. Fenton quotes an observer:

> The Heads of the statues taken from the Town Hall were brought to the marketplace and smashed to pieces by people who were very angry and embittered. They also burned all traces of the hateful devices that had previously served the Old Law, such as gibbets, gallows and whips. Throughout these events the whole market square echoed to the constant cries of the assembled people: 'Long live the nation! Long live freedom!'
>
> *(John W. Steyaert, Late Gothic Sculpture: The Burgundian*
> *Netherlands, Ghent, 1994)*

Using these mute assaulted statues as navigation pointers on my map, or windows through which to see the forces at work, I travelled the country. South Africa does not allow much realism, it makes itself up as it goes along, is a work in progress, and it demands you read through to the real drama beneath the surface. It is often surreal, sometimes unhinged and always unexpected. The journey took me to most of the provinces in South Africa, and sometimes to places where, though to anyone else there was not much to see, I had lived and worked and where bits of my life lay buried or hiding, waiting to be rediscovered and where memories welled up in me. These were intensely personal memorials, invisible to others but as solid to me as anything in bronze or marble.

A number of people who spoke to me asked me not to use their names; a few asked me not to take notes; and, in one case, I was asked not to remember what I had been told because I was 'an inappropriate repository'. Yet people wished to talk and once started they did not stop. Not since I spent time in the former Soviet Union have I found people switching between two ways of talking: private truth and public pretence; kitchen-table confidences and official fictions. Censorship, once so familiar to many of us under the old regime, was making a comeback. But this time we were doing it ourselves. Ideas, phrases and sentiments were on the banned list once again and words were weaponized. That is why I have altered the names of everyone who spoke to me and, sometimes, their genders.

Above all, I wanted to look again at the people who made me who I am: Whites who settled in South Africa and believed that they were at home there. If ever freedom was won in South Africa, so went the dream of Oliver Tambo and Nelson Mandela in the dark years of racial hatred, the country would at last belong to all who lived there, with no account paid to colour and creed.

What the fallen statues seemed to say was that this dream was dying. A quarter of a century into the new democracy, I found race and colour to be more divisive than ever. The war of words had never felt more violent. Black people were more and more unforgiving; Whites were angry and baffled, redundant or demonized, their choices narrowing to psychic withdrawal, or the Great Trek in reverse, as they faced up to loss not just of power but of meaning and substance, of being slowly but surely moved on, and out.

The truce that followed the accession of Mandela, when the old adversaries love-bombed each other with 'rainbows', was over. We had now a proxy war, where each side attacked the other's sacred idols because these were next best to the real thing. It was a way of getting at those you wanted removed but were not yet quite prepared to attack outright. In that quintessential South

African fashion, we set out to hunt the hostile others, and kept meeting ourselves coming the other way.

Even so, I believed that what I found was so peculiar to ourselves that no one would wish to follow our example. Our statue wars, I believed, were a result of our intense but lonely obsession with graven images of colonial, imperial and, above all, 'White' oppression. Ours had been a long hard night of racial madness where every waking hour was spent reinforcing ethnic difference and distance, ethnic exclusivity, tribalism, partition, separation and apartness. Over decades we built walls and fences and frontiers with the sole aim of keeping others out or ourselves in. But then, surely, we had been crazy – and more than crazy? The old fascination the Nazis held for some of our rulers had been not just horribly cruel, it was so embarrassingly passé. Other people, in other saner countries, would never succumb to such antediluvian racial dementia.

Then it began happening elsewhere. In the United States people supported their president's desire to build a big wall along the Mexican border. In Britain, in the 2016 referendum to leave the European Union, the idea of borders and boundaries and patrols to keep 'them' out carried the day. In Charlottesville, Virginia, apprentice storm troopers, trying hard to march in step, and denouncing Jews, looked like clones of South Africa's very own home-grown neo-fascists, in similar badly designed khakis, and smudgy imitation swastikas on limp flags, led by Eugene Terre'Blanche and his Afrikaner Resistance Movement, way back in the eighties and nineties of the last century. Next, statues of Confederate generals from the Civil War began coming down in what one American commentator described as 'a war against the dead'. From London came a call for the fall of Nelson's Column in Trafalgar Square.

It all seemed suddenly familiar. It also gave me the alarming feeling that what we had tried to do back in the bad old years, and failed at so lamentably, had not been behind the times at all; maybe we had been way ahead of the curve.

Christopher Hope

The experiment of a White race in Africa is by no means assured, and unless we mend our ways, we may go the same way in the South as the Roman and the Greek, the Carthaginian and the Vandal in the North

John X Merriman (1917)

White people have no right to be here and the White man who says he has got a farm here must roll it up, put it in a train and spread it in the land that he comes from

Pastor Ngobeza (1921)

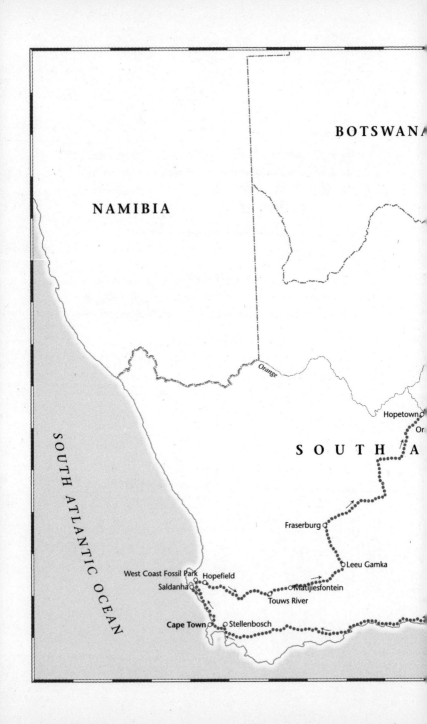

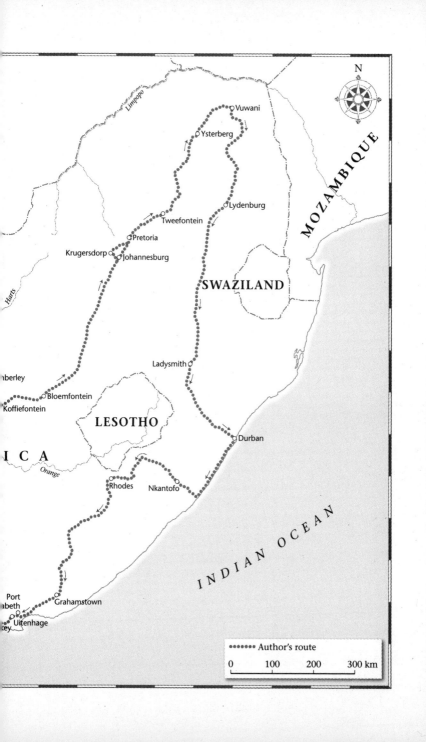

Part 1

EMPIRE OF DREAMS

1

t's not often you watch an angry crowd lynching a statue. But that was what I saw, by chance, one autumn morning in 2015. I was in Cape Town, driving along the boulevard that runs below the main campus of Cape Town University, when traffic ground to a halt and I spotted, high above me, surging crowds on the campus. I left my car on the roadside and walked up the hill to the university, to find squadrons of students mobbing the large statue of a seated man, who seemed to be wearing a mask.

The masked man I knew to be Cecil John Rhodes. He was shown in pensive mode, reminiscent of Rodin's *Thinker*, seated on a plinth, gazing into the distance. I knew something, too, of what lay behind the animated scene. Rhodes had come to be seen by Black students not as genial lord of all he surveyed but as diabolical looter-in-chief.

For weeks there had been demonstrations and threats by demonstrators to unseat the bronze imperialist. His effigy had been jeered, reviled, smeared with human excrement and now the removal truck was on the scene. Behind the wire fence, rigged to protect the memorial from the angry students, workmen in shiny hard hats clambered over the plinth and began securing cables around the statue's base. The crowd chanted, clapped and punched the air in a weird blend of riot and ritual. But then, in

3

South Africa, weird was where we began from, and what started out as crazy often became the new normal. Throughout the tumult the statue remained, as statues will, imperturbable, its eyes fixed on the far horizon.

If you followed Rhodes' line of sight, then, in crucial ways, his gaze traversed, as did his life, the history and the tragedy of South Africa. He looked out, firstly, over the plush green and wooded suburbs, nestled on the skirts of Table Mountain and, for the most part, still home to Whites. Further out lay the dusty Cape Flats, where Coloured people had lived since being banished from the city by the old apartheid regime, in one of its manic spasms of ethnic cleansing. ('Coloured', like 'people of colour', 'mixed race', 'brown people', and recent, and strongly resisted, attempts to label 'Brown' people as 'Black', are deeply suspect terms, hard to define and by no means settled. But they are all we have to go by.) A long way further off, discernible through field glasses, lay the Black African townships, and the sprawling shacks and shanties of the

Rhodes attacked, Cape Town, 9 April 2015

more recent arrivals in the Mother City, often incomers from the Eastern Cape.

The gaze of the seated Rhodes ranged further still, unhindered, all the way to the jagged peaks of the far-away Hottentots Holland mountains, looming gauzy blue as if scissored from the sky itself. There was something proprietorial in his look and that was hardly surprising because Rhodes once owned not only a large chunk of Table Mountain, massed behind him, but huge swathes of Africa to the north and he had designs on the rest of it, from the Cape all the way to Cairo.

Cape Town has always been good at deceiving the traveller and, mostly, the traveller liked being taken in. I think that's because Cape Town has always been good at fooling itself. Among its illusions has been the belief that it was a place apart: liberal, laid-back, ever so slightly superior, beautiful and remote. I once compared it to a ballet shoe on a boxer – a shapely bit of almost-Europe strapped to the foot of not-quite-Africa.

Cape Town was always a city of illusions, a town with form, as well as a string of aliases: it once called itself the 'Tavern of the Seas', and the 'Fairest Cape' – none of these disguises were convincing, except one of the oldest, which is not used any longer: 'The Cape of Slaves'. That last name stung too much to stick for long and it was not to be mentioned in polite company. But that was truly Cape Town, during the great slave period from 1652, with the arrival of the first White colonists, until 1834, when, to the consternation of slave-owning colonists, the practice was abolished by the British. In that period more than sixty thousand slaves were imported from places relatively close like Mozambique, Zanzibar, Madagascar, Angola and Mombasa; and from distant India, the Moluccas, Thailand and Japan.

Cape Town had many faces, many guises: a Dutch fortress, a

5

British colony, and home to a Parliament where every new turn of the apartheid screw was solemnly voted into law. Cape Town called itself 'the bastion' of Western Christian civilization. That was the boast of our old masters and we had the laws to prove it, all of them made in Cape Town by a supine but dedicated band of zealous racists who were not merely pleased with their handiwork, they were noisily proud of it.

I first lived there back in the sixties, an exile from the Highveld, when the city had a quiet and rather dowdy charm, lying as it did under its beautiful, preposterous sawn-off mountain. Capetonians equated topography with virtue; because their mountain was imposing, solid and shapely and they were its disciples, so too must they be saved by living in its shadow. Sacred landmarks and good looks translated into a kind of dreamy superiority.

Coming as I did from 'up North', the rough country beyond the Vaal River, I got the feeling, which was, perhaps, shared by many up-country visitors, that I had fallen among fundamentalists, hill worshippers so proud of 'their' mountain that to hear them talk you'd think that they had built it. Their belief, unstated but pervasive, was that here was God's own capital, together with His holy mountain, and He dwelt on the green slopes in a suitably named suburb of Bishopscourt, spoke only to Capetonians and they spoke only to each other. This was the kind of parochial pantheism that Cecil Rhodes shared, the belief that high mountain places were home to, and reserved for, very special beings.

When I fly into Cape Town I see in the distance the kempt and shapely houses of Constantia, Kenilworth and Newlands climbing the mountain slopes. I glimpse oaks, seashore, whitewashed Cape Dutch gables and vineyards. Table Mountain towers and beyond it, looking out to the Atlantic Ocean, the mansions of Clifton and Camps Bay where the feel is faux-Mediterranean, the villas pure Sorrento, but the sea temperature is Arctic and the south-easterly wind is so pugnacious that I know people who must move into their cellars at night to get some sleep.

And then the plane dips down to the airport and below I see the endless squatter camps and shanty towns of the Cape Flats, where drive-by shootings and gangland slayings are so frequent they rate barely a paragraph in the papers. There is nowhere else I can think of that provides a more dramatic ground-plan of the way things have been, and still are, in South Africa: the rich on the hill, the poor on the flats and, midway between the two, the airport. No matter how often I fly in it's something I never get used to – a city so improbable that it should stand as the primary symbol of a country every bit as improvised, a tale made up as people went along, a story told by a tragedienne with a terrifying sense of humour.

As I watched angry demonstrators assaulting the bronze simulacrum of a Victorian imperialist with their fists, I asked myself why Rhodes, and why now? This brooding figure was so entwined in the history of South Africa that it was impossible to understand the country without knowing something about the man. But familiarity bred forgetfulness. His statue had been such a familiar piece of furniture on the campus for over eighty years that very few passers-by gave it a second thought. He was just there, a permanent presence, unseen, much as Capetonians seldom looked up at the mountain towering over them. But the timing of the attack – and its target – made little sense. What was the point of digging up the past like this? From a faint but persistent memory, the arch-imperialist was, once again, centre stage, just as he'd been when he had moulded Southern Africa to his will.

The crude yellow mask someone had painted across Rhodes' eyes gave him the look of a blindfolded reveller from some strange carnival, a feeling reinforced by the crowds, dancing and chanting around the silent figure.

The mood of the students was a blend of protest and party-going that made it hard to know if they were furious or having fun, or in rehearsal for a piece of theatre. Cape Town University is slotted into the slopes of Table Mountain, on a series of terraces that made natural stages. What was playing out was an epic spectacle with a cast of hundreds. Some students commanded the stage, while others, in orderly rows in stone seats, played the part of the audience.

But there was no script, no director and the actors in this public act of exorcism had to improvise; baying, whistling and covering the face of the masked man with plastic bags, and slapping him repeatedly. All of them would have known that this

Cecil Rhodes' statue being removed from University of Cape Town

lump of bronze felt no pain, but they suspended their disbelief and played their parts as priests of the tribe, solemnly punishing the transgressor.

One of the students had a plastic bucket that contained, I soon realized, human excrement, and with this he slowly and solemnly laved the statue. It was provocative, it was even shocking, a man with a plastic bucket of shit publicly assaulting a hated idol. But if he meant to be deeply disrespectful, there was a problem because sacrilege was easier said than done. To be really effectively profane, to blaspheme on a Baudelairean level, you needed to know, and to take seriously, the religious beliefs of your enemy. I had the feeling that there were very few in the watching crowd who understood the role of the bucket-bearer.

What I'd been witnessing then was not a morality play or even a ceremony of exorcism; it had really been a festival of ignorance. Because very few in the crowd had the first idea what was going on even though the drama of it all made compelling viewing. The audience was split anyway, divided by that familiar spectre that bedevils South Africa, and it was not Rhodes, it was race. Because race, in the new democratic South Africa, far from being relegated to the past, was now more ubiquitous than it had been in the old days of apartheid, even if the word made people uncomfortable and which, until very recently, few mentioned without having an attack of the vapours. Race was never spoken about, nor was tribe, nor colour, nor identity. Such things were not to be mentioned and our old familiar angst had been replaced, rather suitably, by a new amnesia. In fact, the obsession with race and all that went with it was one of the very few things that in the new South Africa had not changed at all.

When the flimsy plastic noose was produced, and looped around Rhodes' neck, it seemed excommunication was to be followed by execution. It made me think of medieval punishments: of the village stocks, the pillory, the gibbet at the crossroads, or public executions in Iran, where hanged men dangled from construction cranes and crowds looked on. As the crane hoisted Rhodes slowly into the sky, the audience raised their phones or held up opened iPads, like prayer books, in front of their faces, and photographed, firstly, the masked and dangling man, then each other and then themselves.

2

I remembered an assault on the statue of Rhodes that had taken place some years earlier. An anonymous scribbler, searching for words to sum up what made the arch-imperialist so detestable to so many in Africa, and so admired by others, had scrawled on the plinth: 'Fuck you and your empire of dreams'. I liked the 'empire of dreams' bit. In a land where words had been corrupted and emptied of meaning by the linguistic vandals of the former regime, any lyrical lift was welcome. And 'empire of dreams' was apt because it caught the vast, mad vision of Rhodes. It was also rather forlorn because no one had less use for poetry than the great empire-builder. His prodigious ambition might be summed up in another four-letter word, better fitting than the obscenity the scribbler had chosen: that word was 'more'. And had Rhodes been asked, 'More of what?' I think he would have replied, simply, 'Of everything.'

That was another notable thing about the crowd. The White students were relatively few, unsure and timorous, while Black students were more numerous and more confident. They made up the centre of gravity with Whites clustered around them like iron filings on a magnet. As Rhodes was winched into the air and hung massively overhead, a mix of demonstrators, Black and White, climbed onto the plinth but Black students made the running;

11

they literally called the tune and, not only did their anger seem real, they seemed to know what they were angry about.

Such anger was never really accessible if you grew up White in South Africa, spoke English and lived anywhere near the diamond fields of Kimberley or the gold mines of Johannesburg. To English-speakers and people of Anglo-Saxon stock, what Rhodes did and what he stood for was exceptional but never scandalous. It was his amplitude that you felt, even if you were hardly aware of the man. Rhodes was not just there, he was *everywhere*. His ways and values we took in with our mother's milk, without a second thought. Rhodes was ingrained in us, a way of seeing things, a point of view; he was the mirror we looked into and saw ourselves.

Rhodes was held to be the apotheosis of British acumen and ability, whether you knew much about him or not. After all, he owned and ran the mines and the mines made the country what it was, in the view of its Anglo-Saxon settlers. Rhodes was the weather, an all-encompassing background hum, rather like the hiss of cosmic radiation left over from the Big Bang; his presence persisted and filled the settler universe where English was spoken. Rhodes' mark might be detected in the names, customs and thought-patterns in colleges, mining houses, sports teams, scholarships and 'founders' days in English-speaking schools across the country. It was Rhodes the indefatigable entrepreneur whom his English admirers celebrated, the sportsman, diamond magnate, jolly good fellow. In my family, living as we did in Johannesburg, 'on the Reef', everyone worked, in one way or another, 'on the mines'. Rhodes was revered as a man who 'made a mint', sent clever boys to Oxford on scholarships, and elevated sport into a religious obsession.

Although Rhodes never married and had no children, he had myriad heirs and most White English-speakers accepted as

natural and unexceptional the fact that we were they. This famil-
ial connection was to be hastily repudiated when, very recently,
Rhodes was found to be a monster – but denial and amnesia
have been traditional refuges for English South Africans. For
a long time Rhodes, the irrepressible racist, was glossed over. I
don't think I ever heard anyone ever mention that side of him. To
understand why this was so one needs only to follow the money.

Freshly arrived in South Africa, in 1870, just seventeen, this parson's son from Hertfordshire, with weak lungs and little money,
made his first fortune as a fruit farmer. He moved to Kimberley
and its diamond fields and made much more money. But it was
when Rhodes contemplated the reefs of gold buried deep beneath
the Transvaal veld that he saw such treasure it made even his
head spin. And he knew it all belonged, by divine ordination, to
the Empire and to himself – not always in that order – and he
made it so. By the end of his life, Rhodes had infused with his
presence and power huge tracts of sub-Saharan Africa, from the
Cape of Good Hope to Lake Victoria.

'What have you been doing since I last saw you?' Queen Victoria
is said to have asked Rhodes on one of his trips to London.

'I have added two Provinces to your Majesty's Dominions,'
came the reply.

And then, no doubt, he headed off to add several more.

But to Black students on the campus in Cape Town, Rhodes was
beyond the pale. Rhodes may have been inspired, and greatly
enriched, by Africa but he had no time for Africans. Disturbing
signs of his lifelong distaste came as early as 1890 when, as Premier of the Cape Province, he backed what became known as the
'Strop Bill', or the 'Master and Servant Act', which gave White

employers the right to whip their servants, as and when they chose, and which liberal critics dubbed his 'Every Man Wallop His Own Nigger Bill'. It was an inducement to assault so blatant it shocked even some Boers, never shy about walloping their workers, who felt that this time Rhodes might have gone a little too far.

But going too far was Rhodes' way. He was to show himself an exuberant racist, even by the standards of the times, backing laws forbidding Africans to move freely, restricting what land they might own, regarding them as not quite human. Rhodes laid the foundation of apartheid, and his messianic belief in White superiority was built on by successive regimes, well into the late twentieth century.

Law-making brutalities aside, Rhodes personified what was most insufferable in the colonial adventurer and a trait that went beyond conquest or greed or cruelty. It nested in the effortless assumption of exclusive power, guaranteed by guns, founded on money and backed by God. Rhodes was not the first settler to exhibit this dementia but he took it to a new level. In the history of European settlement in Africa, nothing stands out so clearly as this characteristic insanity.

Settlers, vagabonds, adventurers, explorers, freebooters, soldiers, missionaries and remittance men arrived on a continent that already had names, peoples and realities of its own but this seems never to have occurred to the new arrivals. They assumed that Africa was whatever they wished it to be. It provided limitless sunshine, loads of servants, endless sport; a world to be made up as one went along, where you might be a farmer, a fortune seeker, a fool or a hero, sometimes all of them, all the time. Where you might make a fortune or, better still, Africa somehow owed it to you to make your fortune for you. This *folie de grandeur* was instant and incurable. Settlers from Europe – Portuguese or

14

French or Dutch or British – all caught the fever; they had no sooner stepped ashore than they took leave of their senses. The Africans they encountered, when their presence was registered at all, were, at best, children to be helped or scolded, or slaves or fairly interesting savages to be saved or civilized or shot.

Rhodes was merely the most alarming example of the condition. It was palpable in his conviction that the English 'race' had a divine mission to uplift and humanize those it conquered and in his belief that missionary virtue would, and should, turn a profit. Pax Britannica was at its most benevolent when it was at its most bankable. Money and morals were so entwined it was hard to tell them apart and Rhodes summed up his winning imperial formula precisely: 'Philanthropy plus five per cent'.

It took an Irishman, Frank Harris, to point out the fatuity of this sort of thinking. After a meeting with Rhodes, who told him that Englishmen had replaced Jews as God's chosen people, Harris remarked that when God singled out the Jews as His favourites, He plumped for an attractive, intelligent people. If the English were now the preferred tribe it could only mean the deity was in His dotage.

So far, so bad. But the trouble with hate-figures arises when detractors claim exclusive rights and insist that their special villain beats all others. Black Africans certainly had no reason to love Rhodes and he also had plenty of enemies among his colleagues, compatriots and fellow magnates. But it was the Boers who had as much cause as anyone to detest the man and what he wanted – war. For Rhodes the only barrier between him and the treasures of the Transvaal was the stubborn, absurd figure of Paul Kruger and his deeply backward Boers. It followed therefore that if getting rid of Kruger and his tiresome republic required a war, then Rhodes would arrange one. He had done so before, when he destroyed Lobengula and his Ndebele Kingdom, which had stood between him and the goldfields of Bulawayo, and now he was ready to do it again.

The Boer War began rather badly and might very well have failed, but in the end Rhodes got what he wanted. Kruger was driven into exile, and the goldfields of the Transvaal became the property of the Crown, and the mining tycoons, or 'Randlords', of Johannesburg, and financiers in the City of London. The Boers loathed Rhodes, and saw him as the architect of the war, with its burnt farmsteads, extinguished republics and concentration camps where women and children died in great numbers. Paul Kruger summed up, in his memoirs from exile in distant Switzerland, what many of his followers felt and, for that matter, what many of the Black protesters at Cape Town University, demanding his hated statue must fall, would have echoed. Kruger was unsparing: 'Rhodes was Capital incarnate. No matter how base, no matter how contemptible, be it lying, bribery or treachery, all and every means were welcome to him.'

3

Watching the concluding ceremonies of the fall of Rhodes on campus in Cape Town, I got the feeling that the more you knew about Rhodes and what he got up to, the milder Kruger's judgement sounded. I also thought: and so what? Was there to be an open competition to decide who hated Rhodes more – and was first prize to be the right to topple his effigy? Rhodes was part and parcel of what made us what we are and he cannot be got rid of. And besides, Africa, from Cape to Cairo, then and now, has been littered with rulers and potentates who were killers, robbers and psychopaths. Airbrushing them out of history would be a very long job.

Again: the questions returned and perplexed – why Rhodes and why now? The sight of a demonstrator reaching into a bucket to pile more shit on the masked statue was strangely moving in its futility, and the excitement of those who lashed the heavy bronze figure, impressive in its suggestion that here was a real devil to exorcise, did not seem very convincing. The whole thing had been somehow very sad, soaked in a kind of helpless hysteria. The spectators were continuing to drift away, their fading attention further eroded by now having to choose between the cheerleaders dancing and whooping on the empty plinth, and the shit-stirrer assaulting the statue.

That was when I saw him or someone who looked like him. He waved to me. His palm was open to the sky in a kind of semi-salute, just as he'd done long ago. Even though he was quite some way off and I had to shake my head to clear it, I had a good idea who he was because it wasn't the first time he'd made one of his visitations.

It was Georgie, or someone who looked like him, though so many years had gone by since I'd seen him. In those long-ago days Georgie never seemed to wear much but this time he was dressed in a tan sports coat and dark trousers and there may have been a touch of irony to his open-handed salute, as if he was amused to find me in this crowd of noisy kids, all of them a lot younger than either of us. He was on the far side of the crowd, much older now of course, a little stooped, but that was to be expected – he had always been a tall fellow.

I was a child, it was wartime and my father had been killed in North Africa. My mother and I moved back into my grandfather's Johannesburg house, and because my mother went back to work, I was left with teenage Georgie for company. I think he must have done lots of other work around the house – cooking, gardening, cleaning – but he was also my friend, my ally and my substitute nanny. Each afternoon, he'd hoist me on to his shoulders, a small White boy in a sailor suit, and we'd head down to the nearby park and its playground with four swings and a well-used slide. Rather than pass the house nearby where there lived a man, said Georgie, named Dr Verwoerd, he would cross over the road.

When I asked Georgie why we did this, he waved his hand, palm open, fingers wide, more a waggle than a wave, as if brushing off a bad dream, and said simply, 'Bad *muti*.' Loading the word, which might mean medicine or witchcraft, or both. It was years before I understood that he was referring not to dodgy medicine but to a dangerous man.

Hendrik Verwoerd and I seem to have kept pace for a lot of my life. There has been a revisionist idea around of late that perhaps he was not as bad as he was painted, this man who formalized iron-bound, racial separation for all, from conception to cremation. Anyone who says this was not around at the time of his ascendance or was not paying attention. Georgie was right about the Doctor, as he was about much else. He had been not only my friendly guide, he had helped to counter my ignorance, which, in the way of small White boys, was abundant and fiercely protected. The fashion in which many South Africans moved through much of the twentieth century required that as many people as possible knew as little as possible for as long as possible. Cruelty blended with muscular stupidity formed the policy many Whites wholeheartedly supported or in which most were enthusiastically complicit. But its foundation was always ignorance, proudly encouraged. It was a land where what was on offer was never logic or truth or consistency, values to which for sentimental reasons I attached enormous importance, but rather competing versions of what most grown-ups always insisted was 'the real thing'.

Georgie, I imagined, had been sent to show me that there was nothing real about the 'real' thing. I also assumed that Georgie held the same sort of place in the household inventory as, say, the wheelbarrow, or the garden hose. He was simply part and parcel of the domestic equipment, a fixed feature, but never entirely a figure in the landscape, though he was always a familiar and much-loved part of the scene. He had been my constant guide from my earliest years and I imagined him as having always been there. When, as a Catholic child, I was taught to say my

Catechism and learnt that God had no beginning and no end and would be there, for ever and ever, Amen, I thought how very like Georgie He was, even if God lived in heaven and Georgie in a simple room behind our garage.

Georgie came with the house and his only function, as far as I was concerned, was to be there for me. He was faithful, rather like my black spaniel, Rex, but no more important. The only difference between Georgie and Rex was that Rex was covered in silky fur and Georgie seemed to be mostly naked. His long bare legs began at his naked feet and seemed to climb forever up into his floppy white shorts, over which he wore a white linen tunic, cut square at the neck, and edged with blood-red trim, framing his bare, smooth chest.

For my part, I was covered from head to toe, most often in a white sailor suit, a white hat, white socks and brown sandals. There was nothing about me that was bare. Our different costumes signalled the very different roles we were assigned in the great stage-show of our lives but they also revealed who we believed ourselves to be in 'real' life. We were actors, but we were always playing ourselves. For my part, I was rehearsing the role of little White master – soon to be majestic. Georgie's costume told you that he played the general factotum, who might seem rather large or tall to me but was so tiny in the scheme of things that you had to look very hard to notice him at all. I was the Principal Boy, a role of supreme value, while Georgie played any number of walk-on parts: dish-washer, kitchen boy, odd-job man, messenger, gardener – often all at once. Georgie's repertoire was much larger than mine and so were his language skills; he would speak three languages when I was still learning my first. But my words counted for something, they were law, and it went without saying that people like Georgie had nothing to say. He was able to speak only when spoken to but even then, no one was ready to listen to anything he said.

The crane lifted Rhodes into the sky and left him swinging. Some kids clambered onto the empty plinth and began dancing. They might have been DJs in a nightclub and the crowd relaxed; the dance indicated that the serious business was over, the scapegoat had been dispatched and the partying could begin.

The crane slowly lowered Rhodes onto a flatbed truck and someone solemnly looped a strip of plastic tape around his neck and knotted it. The dancers on the plinth stepped up the beat, the noose tightened, the crowds cheered, and took pictures as the truck slowly moved off, surrounded by a gauntlet of young men still belabouring the silent figure. The tension evaporated, tragedy turned to pantomime and all that was left to do was to boo the villain from the stage and everyone could go home.

The man I thought might have been Georgie turned now and began walking up the hill that led, I knew, to a second monument to Rhodes, much higher up the mountain. The crowd between us was too large for me to cross to him and I watched him go, telling myself I had probably been wrong anyway.

The truck carrying the statue, streaked with shit and wearing the plastic noose, trundled away to some retirement home for redundant idols. What now descended on the crowd seemed a kind of iconoclast's remorse. The show was over but the job was not complete. Rhodes had served as sacrificial symbol, quite literally a whipping boy, and that would have to do, at least until his attackers were able to go after the real thing. Toppling an effigy did not give quite the same explosive release as real revolution.

As the crowd drifted away, I asked the young man beside me

what it was the students wanted, and his answer was very direct.

'For guys like you to get out of the way.'

His companion was a girl whose placard warned: 'You ain't seen nothing yet!'

She was more specific in her answer.

'What you can do is give us our land back.'

I had trouble working out what the man meant. Who exactly were 'guys' like me and how were we to get out of the way? Was I to broadcast this demand to other 'guys'? The words of his companion were no less vague, if more menacing. Who were the 'us' who wanted 'our' land back? I registered her aggression but the demand was woolly. It reminded me of Queen Victoria's objection that her Prime Minister addressed her as if she was a public meeting. I had been addressed as if I was an occupying army.

I walked back down the main campus as sky-blue student shuttle buses rumbled by. These were known as 'Jammie Shuttles', and the imposing pile that I walked by was Jameson Hall, whose neo-classical bulk quite dominated the campus. It was named for Leander Starr Jameson, Rhodes' lifelong friend and dearest disciple. Much of the architecture of the university was a testament to the values and beliefs of men who thought as he did. Jameson always knew best what it was his chief required and tried to get the Boer War off to an early start by leading a raiding party against Kruger's Transvaal Republic, only to fail spectacularly. He was captured by the Boers and he was lucky that they didn't shoot him as they would have been quite entitled to have done.

The fiasco of Jameson's Raid destroyed Rhodes' political fortunes and he resigned as Premier of the Cape Province. But Rhodes soon got the war he wanted and the republics of the Transvaal and the Free State were destroyed. Paul Kruger was driven into exile in Switzerland and the gold of the Transvaal was open to Rhodes and his allies on the Rand, and in London. The campus had been purged of Rhodes but the faithful Jameson was still there, monumental in the architecture and mobile in the blue buses.

Rhodes had fallen; apparently the show was over, but triumph was tinged with anti-climax. The crowd drifted away amid talk of revolution, decolonization, free education and the rage to come. Discarded posters spoke darkly of blood and war. I heard talk of heading off for a few beers; 'Peroni' was the brand, the 'Water-front' the venue. Off they went: Black warriors and White fellow travellers, revolution in their hearts, phones in hand, American chic branded on T-shirts, trainers and baseball caps. Some on foot, some in German, French or Italian cars, heading to the giant shopping mall in the old Cape Town harbour, for a cold beer, after the Fall.

4

I left South Africa in the mid-seventies and settled in London, without expecting to return home. My poems had been prohibited by the ever-busy censors and prospects for political change were bleak. The Nationalist government, preaching racial superiority for Whites and tribal reserves for Blacks, seemed absurd yet unassailable, something even its opponents in exile and in the armed struggle admitted, at least when they were in their cups. Apartheid had locked us into the prisons of our skins and seemed set to last and even to prosper. Why was it, then, that the near-mystical belief of many Whites that they were destined to prevail seemed nonsense? Not just doomed to fail but already doing so? The vaunted power of the apartheid state was for me a gigantic bluff – cruel, stupid and ugly, certainly, but a weakness, not a strength, a desperate attempt to reinforce the illusion that Whites were on a roll when they were actually on the skids.

I had no evidence for this, and my feelings ran counter to all the apparent realities of the time. Those in exile in the liberation movements talked a good war and any sign of dissent or doubt was called defeatism. They needed, as much as Whites at home, to portray the apartheid state as a mighty war-machine. The South African regime returned the compliment by talking up the capacities of the African National Congress and its allies, something they may have been grateful for, because in those years the ANC was a most ineffectual troop and the South African forces and intelligence services were formidable. To Whites back in South Africa, a war between races felt remote, and the ANC a distant threat. Even so, like their adversaries abroad, they needed shows of fortitude and invincibility. Their need to pretend was not just a pose, it was destiny. But even then, what gnawed at the foundations of their being was a growing awareness not so much of defeat but of redundancy and it stared out at them every time they looked in the mirror. After all, the rampant White Afrikaner nationalists who ran the show from the mid-twentieth century reduced White English-speakers to a helpless, if noisy, minority, and however much they may have hated and opposed Afrikaner supremacy, they were just as hooked on the racial privileges it engineered for Whites.

Isolation intensified delusion. South Africans lived not just in another country but in a separate universe where extraterrestrial rules operated. The country and its rulers believed in their own rhetoric. Hubris mixed with ignorance, spiced with exceptionalism, made a heady brew and South Africans swallowed the stuff eagerly. The absurdities about race that White nationalists endorsed for half a century have their present-day counterparts. There are angry Black nationalists who imagine a world where Newton's law of universal gravitation is proven to be a ruse, put about by White racists. As local wits like to say – in the new South Africa, things all fall 'up'.

It was to portray the cruel absurdities that passed for 'real' life that I wrote a novel called *A Separate Development*. I told the story of a boy who did not know to which of the official racial groups he belonged and it was promptly banned by our watchful censors. A mutual friend in London mentioned that there had been interest in the book among members of the ANC, and took me to meet its exiled president, Oliver Tambo.

As it happened, Tambo lived in north London, in Muswell Hill, an easy walk from my home in Highgate. I did not expect a happy meeting. The eighties were bleak years for those who dreamt of a freer South Africa. Tambo headed a fractious, often dispirited, largely ineffective liberation movement and no one cared very much for writers and writing. But I was warmly received by Tambo, a gentle, owlish man, who looked like a rather benign geography teacher. We talked about musicians we liked, about Menuhin and Satchmo, and he told me how he'd loved the jazz he'd heard when he and Nelson Mandela were students at the University of Fort Hare, in the Eastern Cape. He was deeply affected by memories of his home in the Pondoland village of Nkantolo and spoke of it as a lost paradise. He recalled hearing the blues played in Sophiatown, the township of Johannesburg so hated by our grim governors for its free-wheeling, mixed-race manners that they razed it to the ground. He said he had heard my novel had been banned for ridiculing those who elevated racialism into the national religion. He took it to be an assault and was a little surprised when I called it a comedy.

'A comedy about a tragedy?' Tambo said. 'A boy of no known race. Unclassifiable? No wonder they banned the book.'

I said I imagined it had been suppressed because the White regime was often called wicked, but never absurd. Dedicated racists saw nothing funny about apartheid.

That was not surprising, said Tambo. He touched again on the neither/nor race of the boy in my novel and said how terrible it was to stake your life on your skin colour. When freedom came,

South Africa would belong to all who lived there. That was what we all wanted, was it not?

I knew this to be official policy of the ANC. Tambo was its leader and I did not doubt he believed what he said. But I knew that even he found it hard to placate Black members who resented the roles played by their White colleagues. Tambo had to play referee. What would happen when a Black majority took over at home?

Tambo looked at me through his large spectacles. Did I know what a café de move-on was?

As it happened, on one of my childhood trips to the park, as I rode on Georgie's shoulders, we passed a rickety wooden cart on metal wheels, with a hatch where Black passers-by were buying soft drinks. When we went by the next day the cart was gone and I asked why.

Georgie shrugged. 'That's a café de move-on… the police came, so it moved.'

I wanted to know why.

Georgie shrugged again. 'That's its job, moving on…'

'It made me sad,' I recalled to Tambo.

Tambo agreed it was sad, always chasing the café de move-on. 'We were the ones they were moving on.'

He wanted a country where no one was pushed out. Where no one ever felt 'the move-on blues'.

'Never?' I asked.

'Never,' said Tambo.

Again, the question returned to plague me: why Rhodes and why now? What good did it do to have him assaulted, smeared with excrement, pulled from his plinth, and hanged by the neck? Why not let sleeping demons lie? Why dig him up, parade his remains through the streets, the way the Inquisition did to heretics they felt had not been punished enough? Why bring him back?

Then again, maybe we needed him back – to wake us up. A great amnesia set in in the mid-nineties, after the settlement (some would say stitch-up) between the White nationalists who ran South Africa then and the Black nationalists who run it now. A fever of self-congratulation took hold and a miracle was announced – a new country was born, with no sweat, and without regret, and Whites were off the hook. They handed government to the guys who once did their gardens. Lulled by assurances given by Nelson Mandela and the promise Oliver Tambo had repeated to me, that South Africa belonged to all who lived in it regardless of race, creed or colour, and fortified by what is constantly dubbed the 'finest constitution' in the world, all was to be peace and harmony and happy forgetfulness for ever after. Watching the fall of Cecil Rhodes, I recalled what Oliver Tambo had said, some thirty years before, about the end of race and colour. Recent polls I had seen soon after the fall of Rhodes reported that, but for the animosity of a tiny minority, Blacks and Whites were getting along fine. But it would have been odd if the polls had reported anything else. This was a long-standing illusion we had always held dear. Then again, as recent elections in Britain and America had shown, conflicted voters sometimes lied to pollsters. And South Africans have always had a fondness for lying about race.

But the guys with the plastic noose, like the dancers on the empty plinth waving goodbye to Cecil Rhodes, saw things differently. It was blues time at the café de move-on, all over again. But this time around, it was Whites who would be moving. And if the message wasn't coming through loud and clear, then they were happy to turn up the volume.

5

As the statue was trucked away, an air of regret settled on some in the crowd. Rhodes had been given a good beating and it made his attackers feel better for a while. But sticks and belts do little harm to bronze and tilting at effigies can be frustrating. The man with a bucket of shit who smeared the statue merely added to the disconnection between human fury and bronze impassivity. The mood was more anti-climax than Armageddon. I could see why statues might lend themselves to violent assault. The removal of a hated monument relieved feelings of anger and impotence. You could disfigure an effigy, dress it in some mocking costume, daub it with mud or blood, lop off its ears, hack off a leg, smash it to bits or melt it down.

But somehow it left the iconoclasts frustrated, and wanting more. A similar dissatisfaction had been noted among those who vandalized Canterbury Cathedral, back in 1642. The iconoclasts, demanding that Rome itself must fall, trashed sacred images, tapestries and the tabernacle, then concluded by opening fire on the statue of Christ. Witnesses to the events noted that the image-smashers had to settle for less than they wished; pulverizing hated symbols of papal tyranny, yet their true targets remained out of reach.

But it wasn't really about Rhodes. Everyone knew at whom the attack had been aimed and it wasn't long before someone said so out loud. This turned out to be an arts official in the province of Gauteng and he may have been unaware of the full meaning of his words. After all, the department he worked for was responsible for 'Sport, Arts, Culture and Recreation', a windy title that suggested little interest in the meaning of words.

The government functionary announced on his Facebook page: 'I want to cleanse this country of all White people... we must act as Hitler did to the Jews...'

He was forced by his embarrassed employers to retract his call for ethnic cleansing but he left little doubt that he meant what he said. He was one of a number of angry Black nationalists who wanted to see the end of all Whites in Southern Africa, by whatever means would prove final.

After the fall of Rhodes, the calls grew louder and more frequent. In some ways this was not new. There had been for centuries the dream, among some Black nationalists, and the nightmare among their pale-skinned compatriots, that one day Whites would be 'driven into the sea'. What was most interesting about these sentiments was not the hatred they embodied but who was chosen as a role-model. When you wished to remove or liquidate an entire ethnic group, why reach for Hitler? Particularly if you were an anti-colonialist, dead set against adopting European models in, say, agriculture, why then, when it comes to annihilation, vote for a European despot? Why not, for example, look to Idi Amin, who killed lots of his own people and expelled from Uganda all the Asians who had lived there for generations? Or suggest doing to Whites what Stalin did to Kulaks, or Pol Pot to anyone he considered an enemy of the people?

But Hitler remains the preferred example, as the great executioner, or great organizer, or great model when solutions that prove final must be found. What makes it stranger still is that a fondness for Hitler among the more extreme Black nationalists in the country today, who call for an end to Whites, is an echo of the same admiration for Hitler once found among White nationalists who ran South Africa, and dreamt of an end to Blacks. Today these Black and White Hitlerites become brothers under the skin.

The functionary's demand caused a degree of shock and outrage as predictable as the swiftness with which his words were soon swept aside. It was suggested that their author hadn't really meant it, that he had exaggerated and was not to be taken seriously or literally. But it certainly led to confusion because there were, on the one hand, noose-brandishing removalists who declared Rhodes to have been as bad as Hitler – and now, on the other hand, it seemed there were also those who wanted to *be* Hitler.

To add to the confusion, anyone talking to people, as I had been doing, would have found a third, far larger, group of South Africans, Black and White, who were not disposed either to hatred or to Hitler. Who had watched, with blank incomprehension, the angry scenes playing out on television and took the view that these young zealots, in a frenzy of religious fever, must belong to some new cult and they did not speak for the country.

The more public statues I saw, as I travelled the country, the odder they began to look. You could almost say that the making of monumental images was a confession of how hard people tried to cover their embarrassment. Why did we do it? A desire to preserve memory, or as a form of frozen time, or a wish for immortality, deserved or decreed, or simply from hubris, the ambition of those who rule to make their power concrete? Or because we amounted, in the end, to less than we could bear to contemplate, and made memorials in stone or bronze, hoping these showed us in a better light? They may begin as reminders but they finish as reproaches. Brought face to face with our out-moded, over-valued gigantic selves, our long-past enthusiasms cast in stone, we shudder and hide the evidence. In South Africa, when Whites called the shots they got to build the monuments. When the old order ended and White rule dissolved, many of those memorials were lost in the landscape, or shorn of meaning.

An idol that has had its day is more than redundant, it is embarrassing and there is relief when it is carted away. But where to hide it? Fallen statues, effigies in retirement say so much. They may have begun as heroes and ended as villains but they stir sympathy for that bearded dreamer, that wild-eyed Amazon, that noble tractor driver. However awful the originals may have been in life, they seem lost and sad when put out to grass. I had seen for myself, in Moscow, East Berlin and Vietnam, the fall of the Communist system, and the demigods who went down with it. Charles Péguy's idea that what begins in mysticism ends in politics is apt, but in police states it may also work the other way around. I had visited the tomb of Lenin where he lies in Red Square, looking like a prosperous undertaker, and I had seen the embalmed body of Ho Chi Min, preserved in Hanoi, a wispy figure, like a blanched prawn, and I had visited the miraculously preserved bodies of saints. I had seen a park in Budapest, where luminaries of Communism, gigantic figures cast in stone and bronze, had been put out to grass. There were heads of Lenin and Stalin, in multiple versions, alongside soldiers, party bosses, mothers and daughters of the revolution, once-revered Soviet saints who had once commanded city centres and town squares, hulking ex-heroes banished now to a nondescript suburb on a hillside above the city.

There was something special about this collection in Budapest. Many of the figures, before they had achieved this stony divinity,

Memento Park, Budapest

had been humdrum functionaries, bad poets, aspirant priests, desk-bound pedagogues, house painters – then came elevation, deification, exaltation and their massive effigies were reproduced across entire countries as signals to the inhabitants that gods had come among them. Once they had been known to their grateful and suitably terrified people as 'Dear Leader', 'Mother of the Nation', 'Number One Peasant', 'Great Helmsman'. And now here they were, in Memento Park, across the way from a back garden where washing flapped in the breeze.

Much South African history has been bogus but it helped to be reminded how we were deceived and how description sometimes encouraged deception. History and memory were weapons to be manipulated in a war of possession, where monuments, statues, dams, universities, airports, streets, mountains and rivers were named not for the convenience of cartographers, but because that was how you took hostage people and places, as well as ideas and histories. Those who admired Rhodes, and erected monuments and named streets and clubs and towns after him, were saying something about themselves. So were those who happily saw him off, with a plastic noose around his neck, to the wrecker's yard.

If reliable old heroes were now the new villains, could one redress past injustice by airbrushing such figures from the record? If you succeeded in deposing an effigy of Rhodes, as the demonstrators on the campus with their sticks and hangman's noose had done, how did you dispel his influence? You might forget Rhodes, but his ghost might not forget you.

There was no putting the genie back in the bottle. The fall of Rhodes and calls for 'cleansing' had worrying echoes. Whites were put in mind of another place not far away: once called Rhodesia. A country that Rhodes had, quite literally, owned and had later been transformed into a new country called Zimbabwe. Even the name itself had become shorthand for removal and dispossession of Whites.

Back in the nineties, before White farmers had their lands confiscated and were chased into exile, I travelled a good deal in Zimbabwe. It was a strange experience, meeting and talking to people who seemed to be in a trance, existing dreamily in what felt like a land of perpetual afternoon, filled with shopping, golf and sunshine. I was reminded of the lotus eaters in Tennyson's poem, sleepwalking towards disaster, unaware of who or where they were, or what their Black compatriots really thought of them, and deeply, and almost suicidally, uninterested in any such concerns.

One ambitious young politician, later a minister in the Mugabe regime, was keen to tell me what he thought of those he referred to as 'our lot'. He was behind a push for what he called 'indigenization', an ugly word with an ugly meaning, as he was happy to explain. He proposed a programme for whittling down unwanted settlers, so as to reduce their numbers, and then to rid his country of those he saw as not only wicked, but useless.

'Our lot can barely cross the road,' he told me. 'If we must have Whites in Zimbabwe, at least send us some able ones.'

But if they would not leave voluntarily, I asked, what then?

His answer was a single word: 'Rwanda.'

The rhetoric was ugly, overblown and wearingly familiar – the sort of thing you heard when someone wished to make your flesh creep. Nonetheless, his star was rising in the ruling party, and he was in touch with a growing feeling that Whites in Zimbabwe had had it too good for too long.

When I wrote about our meeting for a Sunday paper back in London, White Zimbabweans wrote angry letters to the editor, insisting that theirs was a lucky little country where Blacks and Whites lived in harmony, and kindly Bob Mugabe could be relied upon to keep it that way.

The assault on Rhodes had been the opening shot in a war of words and images. Soon I was reading of other monuments being attacked across the country. And it did not stop with the identifiable enemies – everyone had their villains now. Nothing like it had ever happened before, despite regular upheavals in the political landscape. Previous regimes, no matter who it was that the monuments remembered, or offended, preferred to let statues stand. But the fall of Rhodes signalled that it was now open season because it soon became clear that this was a game anyone could play.

The new iconoclasm raised old and bitter questions that lay at the heart of the South African tragedy: who came first? Who stole most, or lost more? And whose country was it anyway? Which statues were being singled out, and why, and where was it happening? Who got to be memorialized, or toppled, and what happened when you declared some effigies, but not others, *simulacra non grata*? These were questions I hoped, if not to answer, then at least to ask. And that is what I set out to do, taking each memorial or effigy as a destination and finding that the map that this made would take me from one end of the country to the other, beginning in Cape Town and moving in a great circle through most of the provinces until I arrived back where I had begun.

Part 2

SALDANHA MAN

6

would not push the comparison too far, because South Africa is not Zimbabwe, at least not yet, although the parallels are troubling. What the fall of Rhodes revealed was that the hunt was on for someone to blame. President Jacob Zuma was the cause of noisy argument when he charged that 'the trouble' originated long before Rhodes. It all began when a Dutch official named Jan van Riebeeck arrived in the Cape in 1652, and began shooting the indigenous locals, starting wars and stealing land.

This was, at least, an attempt to put a starting date to the 'troubles', and carried some truth. But assigning blame to one ethnic group and running witch-hunts along racial lines has proved unhelpful, when not downright misleading, although it has been done for a long time, and by all sides. It worked by laying claim to historical or biological or cultural 'facts', and then proceeded to identify the enemy. The old apartheid regime did this all the time. It is voodoo ethnology because, in matters of race and ethnic background, no one had ever agreed about anything in South Africa and what passes for historical analysis is very often war by other means.

When the Dutchman Jan van Riebeeck was fingered by the president as the ur-villain, some Afrikaners, mostly White, objected to what they saw as a slur on their Dutch forebears in general and Afrikaners in particular. But there is another, larger, community of mixed-race or Coloured Afrikaners, and its members had no quarrel with this portrayal of a Dutch colonialist to whom they felt no loyalty. Once again, it was a statue that got it in the neck. The monument to Jan van Riebeeck that had stood unmolested for decades in the centre of Cape Town was daubed with paint and a banner hung around its neck, declaring: 'I stole your land. So what?'

The name, blame and shame game is an old and bad one. Names are altered, whenever convenient or desirable, to signal the state of power play and to indicate who is up or down. When

Jan van Riebeeck, Cape Town, April 2015

on top, you might do as you liked; but when down, you did as you were told. This depressing formula held sway from the first Dutch colonists to the British imperialists; and from the old White race-obsessed nationalists to their Black race-obsessed counterparts. When power was yours you named avenues, airports and police stations after your leaders, yourselves or your friends. Once power was lost, the winners took away your names and wrote you out of the history books.

The Dutch settlers did as they chose with the land and the people of the Cape and wrote their names on the maps they drew. The British, when they triumphed over the Dutch and then again over the Boers, awarded themselves with more new names than you could shake a stick at. There was East London, Port Elizabeth, Queenstown, Durban, King William's Town, several Victorias, the seaside resorts of Margate and Ramsgate, a race course at Milnerton, naval stations, military forts and a multitude of mountains. Not surprisingly, Cecil John Rhodes scored very high in the name game, with entire countries to his credit, the two Rhodesias, south and north; plus a university, a pretty town in the Eastern Cape, effigies galore, along with clubs, societies, scholarships, crescents, avenues and corporations. Paul Kruger, his great opponent, became a town, a game reserve larger than some countries, a cache of gold coins, as well as innumerable streets and squares all over the land. When the new apartheid regime of White Afrikaners came to power, besides erecting the Voortrekker Monument to glorify their forefathers, the name game took on a keen intensity as favourites of the *volk* were immortalized. New towns, like Verwoerdburg, were anointed, and police stations, airports, schools, colleges and suburbs flourished their new identities as evidence that the White nationalist Afrikaner, for so long kicked around, was now top dog.

An added pleasure for the victorious National Party and its apostles of apartheid who took power in 1948 was the abolition of people as well as places. They made townships vanish, as well as entire communities, if these were deemed too Black, or too British, or too 'mixed', or simply too interesting to be allowed to survive. Old scores were settled when 'Roberts Heights', which paid tribute to the British general who helped to win the Boer War, became 'Voortrekker Heights'. Up and down the country, towns, cities and hamlets were torn in two or three parts, and their residents forced into same-race ghettos, where streets, parks and suburbs were rebranded with the names of Voortrekkers, patriots and prime ministers. Out went Sophiatown, a nursery of artists, playground of Nelson Mandela and Oliver Tambo, home to more writers and musicians than the country ever again produced, to be reborn as a nondescript satellite suburb of Johannesburg, named Triomf ('Triumph').

But there were no innocent names and what you called others, or yourselves, came at a price. Apartheid made for linguistic paradox: less and less could be said out loud, yet more and more weight was attached to what words meant, or were deemed to mean, by the linguistic police. In the sixties, racial divisions were hardening like concrete. You had to watch what you said or wrote because words might get you banned from public places, or fired, or disqualified from your previous ethnic group and assigned to a new one. Words, indeed, could get you killed.

Zuma's desire to blame it on van Riebeeck was not only short-sighted, it was also sentimental revisionism and it vies with the story of van Riebeeck's tenure, still put about by some White nationalists. In their telling, once upon a time a gentle Dutchman planted a garden in the Cape in 1652, introduced Western civilization to Africa, where it prospered under White tutelage until the late twentieth century, when the heirs of van Riebeeck helped to usher in true democracy by handing over power to the present governors – which, sadly, the present governors have seriously messed up.

The contrary fable, alluded to by Zuma, and preferred by Black nationalists, is that Jan van Riebeeck, a capitalistic lackey of the Dutch East India Company, occupied the Cape in 1652, robbed indigenous Black people of every bit of the land and wealth he could get his hands on, and, to this day, his heirs refuse to hand it back. This view has growing currency and what Zuma did was to give the charge a historical context.

The Dutch burghers who accompanied van Riebeeck when he arrived in 1652 were presented by the propagandists of apartheid as puritan pilgrims who brought civilization to a benighted Africa. In fact they were freebooters, mountebanks, scroungers and slave-dealers who diddled their compatriots and regarded the native peoples of the Cape with fear and loathing. The Cape itself, not to put too fine a point on it, was small potatoes. The real prize lay in the East Indies. As soon as he could decently leave the Cape, Jan van Riebeeck headed east for what is now Malaysia, where the real loot awaited. Some time ago, I came across a portrait in oils of van Riebeeck, in the museum in Malacca, and the look on his face was one of signal content.

The charge levelled against van Riebeeck and his settlers – that their arrival in the Cape started all the 'trouble' – has substance. But to believe there was conscious purpose and rational aim in the minds of the first White colonists is too high a compliment. The instruction to van Riebeeck from his employers, the Dutch East India Company, was to grow vegetables to supply ships rounding the Cape. But he and his men inclined not to gardening but to smash and grab. The pattern was established and endures into the present day. The only consistent operating principle of those who colonized the Cape and, later, the country was that you helped yourself to just about anything that wasn't nailed down because it all belonged to you.

Later, the wandering Boers who trekked north wanted to get away from British rule, but also wished to keep their slaves and their independence. The idea that you measured your freedom in the number of slaves, servants or indentured labourers you possessed has blighted the country ever since. The Trek-Boers took whatever territory they managed to wrestle from the people they found there, resisting fiercely any idea of developing the land or the people they imposed themselves on, took it for themselves, and saw it not as theft but as their God-given duty.

For the present rulers of South Africa, larceny has become a very delicate subject. The liberation movement of Oliver Tambo and Nelson Mandela has deteriorated, under Jacob Zuma and his cohorts, into such prodigious looters of state coffers that Rhodes and his successor business barons of White South Africa, certainly no slouches when it came to grand larceny, would be giddy with envy. The problem with Zuma's analysis of where the 'trouble' began was not that it went too far, but that it did not go far enough. If the question of who owns what is to have any chance of being honourably decided, you must go back to the San.

When van Riebeeck and his men arrived in the Cape, they took whatever land they wished and, as settlement became more established, Whites pushed ever further into the interior. What is now called the Western Cape, the Karoo and the Kalahari was an enormous expanse, covering half the surface area of the country. White settlers, first Dutch, then Boer and then British, appropriated land where they liked, and they took it from San hunter-gatherers, who had lived in the Cape for well over one hundred thousand years, and from the Khoi, or 'Khoekhoe', herders, whose arrival in the Cape dates back some two thousand years. It was these indigenous KhoiSan, once called Bushmen and Hottentots, who were dispossessed, dispersed and destroyed by the colonists.

Among the surviving descendants of the KhoiSan there is still heated disagreement over the right name to give them since they resent, and resist, being called 'Black'. What is beyond doubt is that the arrival of White settlers in the Cape was a catastrophe for indigenous people. But it was also the case that the San fared little better at the hands of Blacks, in other parts of the Cape and in other parts of South Africa.

'Give us back all our land,' said the young man to me, as we watched the fall of Rhodes. But angry abstractions raise more questions than answers.

I wanted to ask: 'How much is "all"? Who is or is not "Black"? Whose land was it anyway?'

Once upon a time the Cape was home to San hunters with their bows and arrows, and to Khoi herders with their fat-tailed sheep. Then came the men in ships and disaster came too. It is not impossible that the San may have had some inkling of what danger these billowing apparitions off the Cape west coast might have presaged. There are rock paintings that show Portuguese and Dutch sailing ships, often in detail. It is possible word had begun to spread because in what is now called Porterville, a long way from the sea, a KhoiSan artist painted on a cave wall a three-masted ship under sail.

Among the first Whites to set foot in this part of Africa was the Portuguese explorer Vasco da Gama, on his maiden voyage from Europe to India. On 7 November 1497, he sailed into the bay on the northern edge of this peninsula, to which he gave the name of St Helena. On the beach he was confronted by a group of the indigenous people who might have been either San or Khoi-Khoi. Whoever they were, they did not like what they saw and speared da Gama in the thigh. Da Gama, once he'd regained the safety of his vessel, retaliated with crossbow fire. It was not the first recorded clash with the original people of the Cape. A few years earlier, in 1488, Bartolomeu Dias rounded the Cape and stepped ashore in Mossel Bay, watched by a band of Khoi, one of whom heaved a rock at the new arrivals and Diaz sent a bolt from his crossbow through the man. There began very early a series of fierce wars of resistance that lasted decades as the KhoiSan battled, and failed, to repel waves of pale invaders.

The San and the Khoi of the Cape were decimated by European settlers but if you tried to return their land you would have a hard time of it. They have, almost entirely, moved on and left no forwarding addresses. The San or Bushmen's haunting memorial is their palpable absence, the gaping hole left in the landscape by those who were once at home here. It was inevitable that those who claim to be related to the former landowners, their few distant surviving relatives, should lodge their own claims for compensation. One group, calling itself the KhoiSan Revolution Party, asks for not just a homeland but the whole damn lot. The KhoiSan alone, they argue, have the provenance, and the evidence, to prove that they, and not Blacks or Whites, were the rightful proprietors of what is now South Africa. Proof of ownership was registered in thousands of rock paintings across the country, which, with a nice touch of legalese, the claimants call their 'title deeds' to the land.

But of course they lost. The operating rule of those who have always run the show has been brutal: first smash and then grab – and if you don't do it first, it will be done to you. The forced removals of people and communities, whether by military or bureaucratic means going all the way back to the KhoiSan, has been a most South African phenomenon from the start. Violence was the way, woven into the fabric of power – in everything from government to grammar. The ghostly silence of the KhoiSan of the Cape, the spectral inhabitants of a vast territory colonial map-makers called 'Bushmanland', is a bleak reminder of the fate of those who did not know the rules.

The ghosts are there still. Sometimes, in the people I've met in the Karoo, the family face looks out. Signs of their presence are everywhere if you walk the countryside. The San of the Cape, so fugitive that few even agree on what to call them, left behind tell-tale clues and reproaches: pottery, spear points, ostrich-shell jewellery, as well as the finest treasury of original art ever created in South Africa, thousands of rock paintings that speak of a fallen people. Besides leaving behind a void in the landscape, I some-times hope they have left us the chance of acquiring a conscience.

But even going back to the San does not get to the bottom of things. Why stop there? These hunter-gatherers inhabited Southern Africa for millennia, but long before the San became identifiable human figures in the landscape, there were even older, more shadowy, others. There is tantalizing evidence that the first hominins evolved in the Cape, and grouped in sparse communities along the shoreline. Dutch settlers gave a name of 'Strandlopers', beachcombers, to roving bands of foragers they met when they first arrived in the Cape. These people descended from very much older, human-like predecessors who had been around since the Stone Age and left behind middens of discarded shellfish and fossilized footprints that date back over a hundred thousand years. And what of earlier hominids, possibly Neander-thals, who once lived on the Cape west coast, near what is now Saldanha Bay? Should one not spare them a thought? Would not they too have claimed the land as very much their own?

7

B ack in the very early sixties, I did time in Saldanha Bay, which is a couple of hours' drive north-west of Cape Town. It is not far from the place where, back in 1497, an angry Bushman stuck his spear into Vasco da Gama. In 1960, compulsory military service had been introduced and all young White male South Africans had to do a year's training in one of the three services. I was drafted into the Navy and posted to the Gymnasium in Saldanha Bay as an able seaman.

Saldanha seems, at first, an inconsequential seaside settlement. A bay, a large lagoon, beaches popular with windsurfers, a sprawl of suburbs where those seeking a quieter, safer life have congregated. Saldanha taught me that just because a place has little to show does not mean it has nothing to tell you. Dig deeper and you learn a lot in Saldanha about how we got to be the way we are and how little we have changed. These days the western coast of the Cape, running north to Namibia, is celebrated for whales, waves and seasonal wild flowers. Driving back to see it half a century later, it strikes me that the naval Gymnasium looks much the same as it did when I spent my year there. It also seems clear that the conflict that haunts this country has its roots in words, in what we call each other, in the names we give to people and places, and in the violence used to make those claims stick.

South African history is difficult to explore as a chronicle of past events because it is more like analysing a crime scene; often a rather nasty homicide or an exuberant massacre. There are cover-ups, frightened witnesses, tainted evidence, and testimonies are riddled with subterfuge and deception.

Even the name of Saldanha, seemingly resonant and historically interesting, was a salvage job, a hand-me-down second-hand name borrowed from somewhere else, a name once given to a place now called Cape Town. The seventeenth-century Dutch colonists wanted to remember Antonio de Saldanha, the Portuguese mariner who first anchored in the Cape in 1503, and they gave to the bay, under the flat-topped mountain, the name Saldanha. When the British displaced the Dutch in the struggle for Africa, they changed the name to Cape Town, and Saldanha was recycled and applied to a harbour far up the west coast. It was once on the verge of becoming really important. In the Second World War, after Great Britain lost Singapore and Malaysia, an anxious Admiralty considered transferring the entire Grand Fleet to Saldanha Bay, with its reliable deep-sea harbour.

Saldanha Bay, desolate and downwind from a whaling factory, seemed a drear and harsh place to young conscripts, many from land-locked up-country cities like Johannesburg, a thousand miles away. On our first day, still in civvy dress, we were marched to the windy beach, blinking back tears because the stench from the nearby whaling factory made our eyes water. We stood on the shingle, confronted by the icy greasy-green Atlantic, where frozen penguins floated toes-up among garlands of rubbery kelp. It was here that we novice sailors were to be taught the crafts of war, to march, to sail, and to kill, in readiness for the confrontation to come.

In the next months we were drilled, indoctrinated and taught to shoot or bayonet the enemy. As time went by we began to realize that the enemy was a spectre, but then so was the Navy itself. South Africans were not a seafaring people. We were preparing to hunt Russian submarines, detect Communists, confront massing squadrons of the Black enemy, but increasingly it dawned on us that we were chasing shadows. We were also hopeless mariners but then it was never likely that any serious attack would come from the sea. However, we were required to go through the motions of believing it would do so and, even more fatuously, that we would be ready.

I was one of the few to go to sea, first on a mine-sweeper, sailing from Simonstown. The little crafts bobbed about like corks on the Atlantic swell, as we scurried around pretending to search for fictional mines. Next, I served aboard the *Good Hope*, one of the elderly frigates, a cast-off from the Royal Navy. We would set sail uncertainly into the Atlantic, reeking of diesel, to play lonely war-games. All we ever found were Japanese trawlers, illegally fishing in our territorial waters. Sometimes we gave half-hearted chase, but the Japanese ships, being new and nimble, quickly outran our old frigate, labouring in their wakes, her rivets popping.

Nonetheless, our adversaries were said to be everywhere and killing them was top of the agenda. We heard the chief petty officer warning us about Russians and Coloureds, each large on his list of enemies. The Russians were in submarines, gliding deep beneath the ocean and landing by night on remote beaches to suborn the natives. Coloured people were more subtle, the chief warned, because some of their women looked just like Whites. When we met one of these impostors on shore leave, how on earth were we to tell a 'real' girl from a 'fancy fake'? What you did, said the chief, was to examine the half-moon beneath the girl's fingernails. If the moons were pale, she passed muster.

If pale blue, she was to be shunned, and, if in doubt, 'ask to meet her mother'.

Our real enemy, we soon realized, was very much closer to home and our military training exploited a familiar South African trait: dressing up the past and calling it the future. The real conflict was not new, it was old; it did not lie ahead, it was here and now, and it was not really a fight against a shadowy Red menace or Black guerrillas. Instead, we were being readied to fight each other; this was really the Boer War all over again, pursued by other means.

The dead weight of routine lifted for brief and intriguing moments, sometimes for odd reasons. It happened when our chief petty officer, a determined man, decided to kill a fellow trainee whom we knew as 'Snake'. I don't recall his 'real' name because, to the forty young men in the long shed, lined with beds and steel lockers, that made up our dormitory, Snake *was* his real name. His collection of reptiles ranged from the harmless right up to deadly Cape cobras and puff adders. This ardent herpetologist liked to keep his pets in a sack, and deposited it overnight in the steel trunk, filled with the rags and brushes we used to polish the wooden dormitory floor. When annoyed, Snake retrieved his sack and walked through the dormitory after lights out, dropping these creatures on the floor, making us scramble up onto our beds and lockers, begging him to put his friends back in the sack.

When the chief decided to kill him we were all rather relieved. We knew nothing about the chief's motives but a murder might mean a change in routine and that was promising.

'What is your name?' the chief asked him.

Snake looked at him and said, 'Snake.'

'Dead men need no names,' said the chief.

Snake was 'English', in the very loose use of the term, meaning he was not Afrikaans. He may have been Syrian or Lebanese or

Irish or Jewish, because any of these identities made him English enough. The cause of the war was that one day, not realizing the chief was nearby, one of us referred to him as 'a bloody Dutchman'. I don't remember who used the phrase but it was Snake who got the blame.

The chief petty officer was proudly Afrikaans. On the face of it, 'Dutchman' might not seem a significant insult. After all, many Afrikaners came of Dutch stock, or descended from immigrants from the Low Countries. But to Afrikaners the term had always been the worst of insults, along with epithets like 'cheese-head' and 'hairy-back'. The chief, now bitterly angry, reached into his rich store of expletives and called Snake a '*fokken soutpiel*' (Salty-Cock). This striking insult depicted male English-speakers as so helplessly torn between England and Africa, and compelled to criss-cross the Atlantic so often, that their penises turned to salt.

All effective insults were, at root, racial or tribal or both. In this case, it was part and parcel of the mutual detestation that existed between Boer and Briton in the Boer War, and still hit home, long afterwards. The chief let it be known he was proud to be a 'bloody Dutchman', adding that the accursed British had only won the war by locking up Boer women and children in concentration camps run by '*fokken soutpiele*'.

The chief told Snake he was going to teach him 'military discipline'. His plan was to kill Snake by exercising him to death. Each day, after our patrol had jogged several miles in blazing sunshine to the shooting range, he would order Snake to run to the top of a distant hill, wearing full kit, carrying his heavy rifle. The rest of our squad watched, with diminishing concern, as Snake vanished into the heat haze. We tried not to hope Snake would not come back. Our reasoning was as brutal as the chief's assassination plan. Snake might collapse – but then we would win a welcome break. It might even bring a day off for the funeral. We began to want it, even more deeply, perhaps, than the chief did. We marched, we went on manoeuvres, we learnt to use rifles and machine guns, but mostly we waited to see if the chief would manage to kill Snake.

We looked on the chief's murder campaign with interest but without much hope. Cynicism struck early. The imminent war, for which we were being prepared, the enemy we were warned about and the country that we were urged to defend, the ranks and titles and uniforms of those in the Gymnasium, all seemed less and less real and, increasingly, a gigantic seaside farce. But murder was another matter. We watched Snake running up and down the hill, trying not to get our hopes up. Waiting for him to go down for good.

He never did. Snake was tough and the reason he gave for surviving was simple: 'I hate him more than he hates me.' He collapsed a few times with heat stroke, and we appreciated the break while a truck was summoned to ferry him back to base. We felt, if we were honest, a faint disappointment. Snake had let us down. We felt as well some small guilt, but it did not last. If we had learnt anything about ourselves, it was that we would cheerfully sacrifice a comrade in exchange for an hour or two in the shade.

At our passing-out parade, the commander of the base quoted from a poem by Sir Walter Scott:

> Breathes there the man with soul so dead,
> Who never to himself hath said:
> This is my own, my native land!

He said he knew that deep in our hearts we all felt the same way. We were patriots, he said.

We felt ourselves to be nothing of the sort. No one used the word 'soul'; and the 'land' never felt 'our own' because many others shared it, or had competing claims. 'Land' suggested a contiguous area but our country was split into balkanized tribal chunks called Bantustans. Above all, we were not 'native'. That sort of talk could get you arrested. The term was only ever used to describe, in a fairly polite way, a Black African. As for the patriotism of Scott's lines, it made everyone very embarrassed.

When our year came to an end, Snake donated his collection of reptiles to the Gymnasium and a snake-pit was built to house them. It was here, some years later, that the chief petty officer, after a few drinks, went to take a look at the snakes, got too close or too careless, and was fatally bitten. It was a minor replay of the Boer War and victory went, once again, to the 'Salty Penises'.

The nearby West Coast Fossil Park preserves relics of life in Saldanha, five million and more years ago, when bears and short-necked giraffes and sabre-toothed tigers ruled the roost. It also houses a memorial, not in stone or bronze but in bone, of very early human habitation. What interested me most about this particular fossil was the way it linked the most ancient South Africans to their contemporary cousins.

The fossil is a heavy-browed skull, reassembled from frag-ments of a hominin cranium, discovered in 1953 on a farm called Elandsfontein. It has been dated to somewhere on the further side of a hundred thousand years, but may be much older. Stone Age tools have also been found in the area and the names of materials used to make them have a music of their own: creamy silcrete, hornstone quartz, feldspar, porphyry and lydianite.

This skull belonged to an individual who came to be known

as Saldanha Man. There is evidence suggesting he was a Neanderthal, but to whichever branch of hominins he belonged, he was one of our family. And here, once again, Rhodes makes an entrance and reminds me that it will be far harder to expunge his ghostly presence than to topple his effigies because he haunts not just the present but prehistory as well. Saldanha Man, it seems, was closely related to another ancient hominin, once known as Rhodesian Man, or *Homo rhodiensis*. His skull was discovered in 1921, in what was then Northern Rhodesia, now Zambia, and Rhodesian Man has undergone an obligatory name change and is today called Broken Hill Man, after the copper mine where the fossil was found.

There is no end to the complication of names. Even the identity of the cranium in the glass case of the West Coast Fossil Park has changed over time. Saldanha Man was once called Hopefield Man, after the little town where his cranium was found.

What makes him very alarmingly up-to-date is how he died. The clue is there in the fractures to the skull. Some palaeontologists speculate that he died from a sharp blow to the head. If Saldanha Man was deliberately done to death, then he was probably killed by one of his own, perhaps some earlier version of our angry chief petty officer. It makes him, more than ever, one of us. Life in Saldanha, and in South Africa, then as now, was often violent. Saldanha Man is remembered in the Fossil Park and he has a special place. But in South Africa over fifty murders happen each day and the violent death of some modern Saldanha Man might rate a paragraph in the local paper, if he made the news at all.

As I prepared to leave Saldanha, I waited to fill up at the local petrol station and a small saloon pulled in beside me, driven by a middle-aged White man. He rolled down his window and sat staring ahead, his keys in the hand he held out of the window. A Black attendant took the keys, opened the petrol cap, filled the tank, cleaned the windscreen, handed back the keys and took the proffered notes held out to him. Not a word, not a glance, not an acknowledgement by the driver, or the attendant, hinted that either was aware that another human being was beside him. When the attendant handed back the keys, the hunched and silent driver closed his window and drove off, the embodiment of three centuries of White power, prestige and profound separation. These were not just closed-off people but entirely different worlds, rather like those universes that physicists speculate might exist, unseen to us, right beside our own, each sealed off from its neighbour, so that we will never be aware of the world next door.

The coastal countryside around Saldanha was empty but for two ostriches, high-stepping like chorus girls in perfect time. In a shallow pan, flamingos perched like pink flags. I drove to Hopefield, where the intriguing skull of Saldanha Man was found. The tall, shapely Dutch Reformed church loomed over the little town as if everything else was beneath its attention, and the noticeboard advised: 'Save Our Planet – it's the only one where you find chocolate…'

Saving was very much needed; especially of our past. There was a remoteness and an eerie quietness as I drove on into the Karoo. But the silence was noisy with news of all that had gone missing.

Part 3

THE KIMBERLEY LINE

8

You may trace the history of South Africa in dates, land claims, name changes or skull fractures. Another way is to follow the money; where it was to be made, action followed. The most graphic illustration is the railway line that leads north-west from Cape Town to the Kimberley diamond fields. It was known as the Kimberley line and it fattened the wallets and increased the power of those who shaped the country. It was all about money and munitions, and to Rhodes and those who followed his lead, the two went hand in hand.

I was heading for a town on the Kimberley line called Matjiesfontein, one of the most improbable places in the country. To get there from Saldanha meant a drive of several hours, due east, and it would take me through the heart of the Karoo, an immense dry land that, long after its original inhabitants had vanished, the maps still identified as Bushmanland.

The name 'Karoo' is deceptive, unsatisfactory and little understood. It refers to the swathe of semi-desert stretching across the midriff of the country. Scant rainfall, harsh winters and searing summers make life hard-going, even for sheep and those who raise them. The Karoo has never offered much to exploit or steal. It has always been stone country, a place of tumbleweed, derelict farms, neglected graveyards, iron wind pumps, jagged aloes and, when there is rain, a brief, vivid flowering of desert ephemerals. The little Karoo towns impress not by their size or vigour but by daring to be there at all, pretending to an importance they do not possess.

'Karoo' might be a San word, from the Bushmen who lived here; then again, it might not. To some the name means heat, cold, boredom and emptiness as far as the eye can see, parched plains and stony mountains, a great deal of nothing very much, under an immense sky. To others it is a magical world where the eye is free to see whatever it likes. Because no one has known what to do with it, not too much damage has been done. Its salvation, at least until now, has been its extreme worthlessness. I'd lived in distant parts of the Karoo and returning was always like coming home.

The drive through the Karoo took around four hours and when I reached Touws River on the Kimberley line, one rail stop from Matjiesfontein, I found myself blocked by demonstrators who surrounded my car. Some were burning tyres on the road and waving placards, demanding clean water, better roads and electric power. This was what is known as a 'service delivery protest', a portentous phrase for a minor riot. It has been a feature of polysyllabic political promises that, as the syllable count multiplied, so the meaning drained away. Many people in townships and informal settlements were angry about the lack of water, sanitation and electricity and took to the streets, in one part of the country or another, two or three times a week.

The temperature of the crowd was uncertain, hard to gauge – would the protestors wave me on my way, or stone my car? Good humour won out over anger – and to ironic cheers I drove through thick clouds of smoke from blazing tractor tyres. As I looked back, I saw police reinforcements arriving and I knew that the protestors would be dispersed before long with tear gas

Service protests, like this, occur two or three times a week

and rubber bullets. There was a pattern to these things. Such disturbances are so common they barely rate a mention. A quarter of a century after Nelson Mandela walked free from jail, and a bright new world was promised, too many people find too little has changed. The anger is often aimed at government appointees who feather their own nests, enrich family members and colleagues but fail their voters. Predatory looting of state resources has become endemic.

There are those who claim such corruption is something peculiar to the present government. But political placement of a favoured few, what is now called 'cadre deployment', is as old as the hills in South Africa. Everyone from van Riebeeck to Rhodes and Paul Kruger would have recognized its contemporary version: it has been adopted by successive regimes of every stripe and colour as the tried and tested way of dunning the poor and plumping your purse. From the first White settlement in 1652, to the soccer World Cup of 2010, and beyond, politicians, bankers, construction companies, trade unions and mining houses peddled influence, rigged tenders, colluded, cornered the market where they could and embraced the cartel.

In the nineteenth century, Boer officials in the independent South African republic of Paul Kruger were mocked as dizzyingly corrupt. They made fortunes for themselves and their favourites from monopolies in dynamite and gunpowder, essential to the new gold mines of the Rand. The English Randlords, in their mansions in Johannesburg, and the gold diggers who streamed to the Rand from every corner of the Empire to this new great mining town with its bars, brothels and boarding houses (or 'Devil's Town', as Kruger dubbed what he regarded as this swarming money-grubbing maelstrom) were hardly any better. The whole point about Jo'burg was to get rich fast. The novelist Olive Schreiner, most trenchant of observers, called it 'a great, fiendish, hell of a city which for glitter and gold and wickedness, carriages and palaces and brothels and gambling halls, beat creation'. Schreiner's portrait was a restrained depiction of my home town. The pattern, however, had been in place far earlier; Jo'burg 'goldbugs' and Randlords simply put it on an industrial footing.

When White Afrikaner nationalists took power in the mid-twentieth century, they adapted quickly to the model, greasing palms, buying allies with tenders, jobs and under-the-table deals. If this left those who lacked property, power, influential friends or family connections, impoverished and angry... well, then, whatever were the poor there for? In the age of apartheid, the regime had a way of dealing with the angry poor – displacement. The regime declared the poor independent and banished them to distant tribal reserves, called 'Homelands', where the 'land' was horribly eroded and 'home' a cruel joke.

In South Africa these old patterns constantly repeat; the first time as brutality, then as hypocrisy. The new rulers no longer exile the poor to distant tribal 'Homelands'; instead they permit them to crowd into shacks, on the edges of cities, with minimal access to water and electricity, and no jobs. At election time, ruling party bigwigs pay courtesy calls to these settlements, murmur consoling mantras like 'transformation' and 'National Democratic Revolution', hand out free T-shirts, then head back to the bright lights. Political jamborees see leaders of the ANC toasting their faithful, far-away voters in French champagne, and doing it in their name.

I left Touws River, following the national road that runs beside the Kimberley line. When diamonds were discovered in 1871, the Prime Minister of the Cape, John Molteno, decided that the port of Cape Town needed fast, reliable access to the interior. What had been seen by the colonial government as miles of desolate veld, empty of all but rebellious Trek-Boers, was now a fortune hunter's heaven. Molteno, it is said, took out ruler and pen and drew a line straight from Cape Town to Kimberley. His engineers protested that the proposed line would run slap-bang across rivers and through imposing mountains. But Molteno was unmoved – 'that is the way I want it to go', he said. And so it did. Disdaining puny natural obstacles, the line arrived in Kimberley by 1885 and, not long afterwards, reached the goldfields of the Witwatersrand. The Kimberley line was the axis around which South African history, and Rhodes' fortunes, were to revolve. This was the railway he hoped would one day run from Cape to Cairo. But for the meantime Kimberley would do nicely.

The line was not built by the men whose fortunes it made. An early article of faith among European settlers in the Cape, Dutch and British, held that – as the old phrase went – 'a decent fellow doesn't work'. At the outset, rails were laid by imported English navvies but this proved expensive – they had to be fed and housed – and so they were increasingly replaced by cheaper Black labourers who were, and still are, the backbone of the country. The solitary, silent White driver who pulled in for petrol at the Saldanha service station and waited, while unseen flunkeys did whatever work was needed to get him back on the road, was the idle heir to a long tradition, so natural to generations of settlers, that to question it would have amounted to an act of lunacy or treachery or both.

The Kimberley line, then, was not just a railway; it summed up, in steel, the settler dream; it was the mantra at the heart of European settlement as well as its measure of success. Rhodes made the model, and it holds to this day: if it grows, chop it down and sell it; if it's buried, dig it up and sell it; monopolize, rig prices and, with bribes and surrogates, make the state your own; prefer cartels not competition. From banks to bakers to builders, from mines to football arenas, to accountants and public relations outfits and newspapers, connivance with useful politicians, masquerading as daring entrepreneurship, has been the way. The model involved the capture of state resources and the allocation of assets to party officials, family and friends. Where possible you made the regime complicit – better still, you *became* the regime.

9

F ew places better sum up settler dreams than Matjiesfontein. It is a complete confection, artificial right down to its cricket pitch. Only its name is genuine and stands as an epitaph to something real, original and authentically African – and being real, it perished. The town began as a settlement of indigenous Khoi people beside a river, in the hot, parched plains of the Karoo. It metamorphosed into the very model of a bucolic English village and modern visitors find it charmingly quaint.

Travellers in the bone-dry Karoo often added the word 'fountain' (it might be a spring or a muddy pool) to some vital water source, and defined it by the game they found there, elephant, lion, buffalo or hippo, or by some feature of the place. Matjiesfontein took its name from the mats the Khoi people who lived there wove from reeds growing in the shallow waters of the Baviaans River. These they draped over hooped staves to create light, portable shelters.

The Khoi were pushed out by White Trek-Boers, who were ousted in turn by mixed-race settlers known as the Griqua, or Basters, who were then supplanted by the British when they annexed the Cape. The real story of Cape settlement is encapsulated in the history of Matjiesfontein, with the arrival of each stronger, better-armed group, removing those who once lived there. Perhaps that is why it is rare for South Africans to have a true sense of a local habitation. Almost everywhere was once home to others, so many spaces are contested, either by the living or by the ghosts of former inhabitants.

But its original name survived; it was never rebaptized in the name of the monarch, or some far-away imperial official. In every other way it was 'transformed' – an overused contemporary canting word, meaning to take something by the scruff of the neck and force it to be something else. On a much larger scale, something similar could be said to have happened to South Africa.

When I arrived in Matjiesfontein, the old red London bus was waiting for passengers outside the pub, the Laird's Arms. The 'Laird' had been the owner and sole proprietor of the village, the man who created the town in 1884 – to use the Disney word, he *imagineered* it. James Logan was a penniless young Scot, from a family of railway workers, who left home very young, possibly one step ahead of the law, and sailed for Australia. He may have been shipwrecked off the Cape coast or he may have deserted, but he got himself to Cape Town and worked there for a while as a porter on the new Cape railways. Logan was to create at Matjiesfontein a miniature English village, his private fiefdom, and proclaimed himself 'Laird' of all he surveyed. The one-time KhoiSan camp was reinvented as a European folly.

Logan was quick to spot the riches the new railways offered – especially if you had the monopoly to supply every train that passed your station on the Kimberley line. Logan knew that the trains from Cape Town, heading north towards Kimberley, carried passengers who would want feeding. As a railwayman he understood steam locomotives needed water. A consumptive, Logan also saw in Matjiesfontein, with its clear dry Karoo air,

Matjiesfontein station

a niche market where fellow sufferers might recuperate. Logan's Matjiesfontein began as a couple of iron sheds beside the rail line, baking in the Karoo sunshine. He founded the first health spa in the country; he sold mineral water, as well as beds and breakfasts; above all, he sold 'England'. Everything he touched he turned to cash.

It seems appropriate that Logan happened to be a professional magician and belonged to the Magic Circle. But his greatest trick was to change what was regarded as a Hottentot hamlet into an English village, where Rhodes and many visiting imperial grandees felt at home. Though a Scot himself, the brand he sold and celebrated was British imperial pride. Matjiesfontein was a monument to the brass nerve of the man who created it. He imported English craftsmen and, on the arid plains of this vast half-desert, he built a model English village with pretty cottages, a Masonic hotel, a colonial country house with fountain, fruit trees, fish pools, the first flush toilets in Africa, running water and electric light, a cricket oval, post office, court house and the Laird's Arms. Logan understood what the colonists wanted and missed when they landed in Africa. He flattered their conquistador spirits while at the same time soothing their homesickness. His village was quintessential Cotswolds, recreated on the baking plains of Camdeboo.

Matjiesfontein was perfectly pitched to appeal to Rhodes. Few places better encapsulated the blend of barefaced cheek, chicanery and sentimentality at the heart of colonial rule. Matjiesfontein was comfortable, the dry desert air favoured Rhodes' weak lungs, it was like home and, above all, it was English. It made but did not flaunt its money. But then money in itself was never of first importance to Rhodes – it was his 'empire of dreams' that drove and enticed him; his cosmic ambition was truly Faustian – he longed to fashion new worlds in his image and for that a powerful magic was needed. Matjiesfontein passed the acid test of great illusions: it was good enough to fool not only its customers but even its creator. But it was Logan, consummate con man, whom Rhodes so admired. Energetic, patriotic and ambitious, he seemed the very model of the new South African superman and the only other person Rhodes declared to be in the same league as himself.

Cecil Rhodes and Jimmy Logan had a lot in common. Rhodes was the sickly son (there were eight other boys) of an almost penniless parson. Logan, too, was consumptive, a boy from a working family who made himself into a millionaire. Logan was also a fervent imperialist, hiding several Jameson Raiders down in his cellars when they were in flight from the authorities, and he billeted thousands of British soldiers on his property when the Boer War broke out. He even raised his own small squadron of soldiers and eventually became an MP in the Cape government.

But strip away the show-biz and imperial enthusiasms Logan shared with Rhodes, and you get down to those that really counted: exuberant corruption and a lively disdain for moral scruple. This was how it worked for Logan. A friend and fellow Scot, James Sivewright, was in charge of land, transport and the railways in the Cape government, led by Cecil Rhodes. It was Sivewright who handed Logan a monopoly on all catering concessions along the length of the Kimberley line and, with it, a fortune in the making. When the news at last got out, scandal followed and severely damaged Rhodes' political reputation. But the pattern survived and endured: politics and big business were locked together like mating snakes.

I walked from the Laird's Arms to the cricket pitch, now really just a dusty bit of veld. Logan was a strong supporter of the game. In his eyes it conferred social status and aligned the Cape Colony more closely to the Empire. But he took a broader view than Rhodes and believed that you picked your best players, especially if you were to face the English team in the first test match ever between South Africa and England.

Logan might even have backed the selection of a cricketer named Krom Hendricks, one of the most talented fast bowlers ever to emerge in South Africa and a natural choice for the 1894 tour of England. The English players confessed to being nervous about facing this speed merchant but he was never selected. It would be 'impolitic', Rhodes ruled, to have him in the team and, as Premier of the Cape, Rhodes spoke for White propriety. Hendricks was of mixed race, a Cape Malay, and to include him in the South African team on a tour of England would offend the hosts. In a tone that would ring down the years, and makes me wonder if Rhodes ever really knew the difference between Africa and Australia, the selection of Hendricks was blocked because Rhodes feared the bowler 'would have been likely to start flinging boomerangs in the luncheon interval'.

The *Star* newspaper in Johannesburg, a paper of uncertain liberal principles, backed this decision. Hendricks might be the best man for the job, wrote the editor, but he was the wrong colour. If the South Africans lost to England, as a result of leaving him out of the team, then they should face up to it and 'take their licking like White men'. Hendricks was never selected for the national team and, from then on, sports administrators were almost always either apologists or ambassadors for apartheid. They were, if anything, even more abject in their surrender to the racial fatuities of the time than those who ran business and industry. It was to be another century before players other than Whites were permitted to represent their country.

Matjiesfontein is still a very good show. Someone who seems to have imbibed the theatrical spirit of the Laird of Matjiesfontein is 'Johnny', a splendid figure of many roles: fairground barker, impresario, showman, raconteur, ghost-buster, pianist, guide, satirist and maître d' of the Lord Milner Hotel. Decked out in bowler hat and waistcoat, playing with great vivacity on his bugle, Johnny has for many years welcomed visitors to Matjiesfontein, and waved his charges aboard the ancient London double-decker bus, with its fading advert for Beefeater Gin. As the bus swayed and hiccupped around the village and trundled past a pair of vintage petrol pumps, he gave an irreverent commentary over the loudspeaker.

'Look at those empty pumps. Dry as a bone – that's what Mugabe did for Zimbabwe. And if we don't see him off soon, it's what Jacob Zuma will do for us…'

As we passed the dusty, grassless cricket field, he pointed to the old slave cottages where he was born, and where his mother, who worked in the Lord Milner Hotel for half a century, raised her children. Johnny announced cheerfully that he was a 'cappuccino' and raised his trouser leg to show what he called 'the tide mark', a line where White met Brown. 'I'm bi-tonal, you see.' It was a very South African joke and puzzled the Japanese tourists.

The trains to and from Cape Town still stop at Matjiesfontein and passengers admire the quaint hamlet, a little faded, but as odd as ever, under the high blue Karoo sky. Johnny reminded me that Olive Schreiner had kept a cottage here and how, to begin with, she had been a passionate admirer of Rhodes, and quite possibly in love with him. She met him first in Matjiesfontein and was dazzled by a figure who seemed to rank with her other heroes, Havelock Ellis and Karl Marx.

Her disenchantment began when Rhodes backed the 'Strop Bill', the law giving Whites the right to beat their labourers as often and as brutally as they liked. She was scandalized again when details emerged of the concessions granted to Logan by Sivewright, Rhodes' Minister of Railways, and the impunity of those who courted the Premier. It was also in Matjiesfontein that she saw through Rhodes' subterfuge. He was no visionary reformer but a ruthless mountebank and ardent racialist.

She recounted in her notebook how she had watched Rhodes greeting Sivewright, newly arrived on Matjiesfontein station, with a warm handshake. That was the end for her. 'I turned on my heel, and went to my house.'

Schreiner, ever after, was his most potent and unrelenting

foe: 'We fight Rhodes because he means so much of oppression, injustice, and moral degradation to South Africa; – but if he passed away tomorrow there still remains the terrible fact that something in our society has formed the matrix which he has fed, nourished, and built up such a man.' When he died in 1902, she saw him as 'a great might-have-been'. Her judgement of Rhodes was a very long way from the scenes on the campus of the University of Cape Town, the mock-execution and quasi-religious ritual of defilement, the plastic noose, the layers of excrement followed by the catharsis when some of the congregation headed down to the Waterfront for a couple of Italian beers. Schreiner's verdict was more interesting and more lethal.

10

From Matjiesfontein the road leads northwards to Kimberley, indeed insists you go in that direction. The perceived advantage, in the minds of the British colonial officials who made this happen, was mercantile: to move gemstones and goods swiftly between Cape Town and the Kimberley diamond fields and, a little later, the Johannesburg gold mines. The other benefit was military and, this being South Africa, the two motives were soon so tightly intertwined no one knew the difference.

But to get some idea of what happened to Kimberley, before and after Rhodes became its king of diamonds, it's useful not to go where the important roads insist on taking you. I preferred to head in the opposite direction, to a town where I lived, and where nothing at all appeared to happen. But then, in South Africa, the apparent absence of anything of note in some village or hamlet is an invitation to look more deeply. What is to be found in forgotten places sometimes beats the hype and hypocrisy of more flamboyant cities. I think that is because, in forgotten places, far from centres of power, people don't feel the need to tamper with the evidence or intimidate witnesses.

The road and rail line to Kimberley passes a little settlement called Leeu-Gamka. This tiny rail-siding stands at a point where two rivers meet, and the two halves of its unusual name, 'Leeu' and 'Gamka', both mean 'lion'. *Leeu* is the word in Afrikaans, and *Gamka* in the language of the /Xam Bushmen, the particular branch of the San family, who once flourished in the Northern Cape. In Leeu-Gamka there are no lions, and passing the nearby Bushman's River is to remember that there are no Bushmen. Time has also whittled away at the mountains, brutally reducing them to rubble, scattered boulders of what were hills brought down over the aeons, quite literally, to rock bottom. The language of the Boers, however, and those the Boers gave rise to, the Afrikaners, has survived and prospered. But the /Xam Bushmen are gone and no speakers of their language survive. Leeu-Gamka is an intriguing name to give a hamlet but like many labels that purport to tell you something about the country, and lie as they do so, the name is a later revision. To begin with, this settlement was first called Fraserburg Road, almost as if this tiny blip, on the railway line to Kimberley, hoped to claim kinship with some larger, more important, destination.

As it happens, Fraserburg was never important. I lived there for a good while and it lies over the hills and far away and it is self-effacing to the point of invisibility. True, it is bigger than Leeu-Gamka – but then just about anywhere is bigger than little Leeu-Gamka, which at least can claim connections, being on the Kimberley line and Kimberley was a real destination. Fraserburg has never seen a train, has no connections and not even its friends would call it a destination. It is a remote sheep-farming town in the high and lunar Karoo and, like several settler towns, took its name from a Calvinist Scotch pastor who ministered to far-flung Boer farmers. But it has things to say about who we are and how we got to be that way.

The 'real' Fraserburg road leads sharply away from Leeu-Gamka, heading west, and climbs to the high ground of the Great

Karoo. The expanses of sandy, stony escarpment are remains of the vast shallow inland sea that the Karoo once was. An hour passed and I saw no traffic. An immensity of veld speckled and freckled with rocks. The only living beings were wide-eyed meerkats, scanning the terrain, and patrolling monkeys. Now and then I passed a deserted farm, tumbling dry-stone walls of sheep pens or *kraals*, an abandoned graveyard with its carefully closed gate. Heavy rain had fallen a week earlier – a rare event in a desperately dry land. Great sheets of water lay naked beside the road, almost shamelessly sunning themselves. A signboard tacked to a roadside fence insisted I had passed a place called 'Good Luck', though there was no other sign of the place. But I got my bearings when I spotted a *koppie* where a farmer once had himself buried on its stony brow, from which vantage point he kept an eye on two daughters whom he did not trust to look after the farm. After a couple of hours, Fraserburg at last showed itself, a distant smudge on the immense plain.

Back in the early nineties I lived for a time in Fraserburg and came back for long visits over the years. Like many Karoo *dorps*, Fraserburg hid amid the enormous, energizing emptiness of the Karoo, where the eye travelled forever down roads that ran straight as arrows, towards the horizon. Where nothing much moved in the heat, except sometimes a sheep or two, or in the corner of an immense stony field an old and rusty wind pump clanked and grumbled, whirling tumbleweeds, kicked by the wind, scooted across the iron-hard ground, hit a fence, snagged on the barbed wire and stuck. After this unusual burst of energy, the desert lay back, as if exhausted. Nowhere did less happen and yet nowhere did the past press more heavily or disturb me so much.

Among the few public memorials in Fraserburg, and it has a dutiful look, is a stone wagon wheel set on a plinth, a monument to the Voortrekkers. But it is another secret monument that I always come back to see. It is in Rossouw Street, a nondescript thoroughfare, and halfway along its length is what looks like a kink, a sudden bend, in the road. What it does is make you change direction as you drive down Rossouw Street, and leads you firmly into Voortrekker Street, which many decades ago replaced Rossouw as the main road through town. There were reasons for this. Rossouw Street, in the nineteenth and early twentieth centuries, was lined with shops and trading posts, and its traders catered for traffic heading into Fraserburg from neighbouring settlements like Loxton, Carnarvon and Sutherland. The shop-owners and traders were the thriving Jewish community of Fraserburg. But in the thirties nationalist bile was rising and, with it, an ugly, familiar anti-Semitism took hold. The Afrikaner traders of Fraserburg decided that their Jews were too rich, too dominant and must be moved. The method chosen for what might be called a municipal pogrom was simple. Rossouw Street was given an awkward but persuasive sharp turn to the right, obliging traffic heading into town to now travel one block further south, and to be decanted into Voortrekker Street, where Afrikaner shopkeepers set up their stores. The results were as desired. Business in *judenfrei* Rossouw Street dried up. Over the next few years, the Jews of Fraserburg left town and never returned. This exercise was to be scaled up after the Second World War into the state-sponsored ethnic cleansing we call apartheid. That kink in the road remembers, in its mean-minded and self-defeating stupidity, the removal and obliteration of a flourishing community. It was among the first of very many similar removals of Blacks, Coloureds and Asians from every single town in the country.

There never has been any formal marker or reminder of the manoeuvre in Rossouw Street. Few ask today what had happened to the Jews of Fraserburg or notice that sharp bend in the road. But we all have our own memorials and I retrace the route each time I go back to the town. It reminds me how unremarkable they once seemed, the customs of White settlement, the obsessions with race, religion and skin colour; views regarded as utterly normal, carried out everywhere but which are now little admitted and seldom discussed. Because whatever route you take or line you follow in trying to understand how we got to be where we are, there is always, somewhere, sooner or later, a kink in the road.

When I lived in Fraserburg in the early nineties, it was pale and portly Abraham who ran the Central Hotel, 'round as the moon and twice as White', the locals said of him. His assistant manager was a skinny fellow we called 'Rick the Stick'. These two were among the first of what was to become the retreat of Whites to small, out-of-the-way country towns and villages. Abraham and Rick, urbanites from opposite ends of the country, washed up in Fraserburg and now presided in tandem over the hotel where the bar, that is to say the White bar, hosted hard-drinking sheep farmers who had been known to assault each other wielding frozen legs of lamb as clubs, and the second, or Coloured bar, served farm labourers.

An air of make-believe, characteristic of South African life, hovered over the pair. Many Whites in the mid-nineties were celebrating the Mandela accession, declaring their belief in racial peace forever and business as usual. But Abraham and Rick were not buying it. Abraham told me they had escaped from the real world, and that the self-congratulation of the city elites was a mistake. He had taken refuge in this out-of-the-way *dorp*, where history would never find them because, said Abraham, nothing ever happened in Fraserburg.

As he explained it: 'I semi-grated to safety.'

It was a term I heard often in later years, but he was among the first to make it his own.

A few years later, when I was next in Fraserburg, Mandela had given way to the next president, Thabo Mbeki, race relations had soured, and alarm was setting in. Something seemed to be happening, even in Fraserburg. Worse still, things were changing.

'Now, we're stuffed,' was Rick's repeated view.

'Patience, Richard,' Abraham said, always the philosopher of the duo. 'We will just hunker down here until the storm has passed.'

'And if it doesn't pass?' Rick wanted to know.

'When we see them coming over the hill, we head south for Cape Town,' came the reply.

'Why not go now?' Rick asked.

'Because here we have a fall-back position, should the other side advance. Go to Cape Town now, and we've our backs to the sea. And the only move is out…'

I rented a small Victorian cottage on the edge of town. Its previous owner, known simply as 'Baby', my neighbour explained, had kept a servant. As a young child, this girl had been 'bought' from a family in the neighbouring mixed-race township. Like every town and village, once Fraserburg had been set aside for Whites only, a mirror-image settlement, dusty, forlorn and poor, where non-Whites were obliged to live, was built some distance away.

It wasn't unheard of for indentured or, as they were known locally, 'booked-in' Coloured children to be 'bought' by White citizens of Fraserburg to work as live-in servants, and the tradition had survived in some communities into the fifties. Sometimes, a White employer might acquire a live-in child in exchange for no more than a cake of soap. Indenture of this sort was a kind of domesticated slavery. The little girl whom Baby had brought into her home was not allowed to leave the house, worked without payment and slept in the woodshed. When she was in her twenties, so the story went, she had run away. Her mistress demanded that the police find her and bring her back. The police had to explain to an indignant Baby that this was no longer their job and had not been since the slaves were emancipated. But because slavery and service were often so similar, and the line was so blurred, Baby had trouble accepting the change.

When the first freely elected administration took power in 1994, under Mandela, the Whites of Fraserburg did their best to adapt. Fundamental changes had taken place, and people knew this must have consequences. Those once regarded as servants and workers were now running the country. On the other hand, as time went on, change was minimal, even imperceptible, for which they thanked their lucky stars. Perhaps life might go on more or less as before? Maybe the burden of guilt Whites had carried for many decades was lifting from their shoulders – and they might be free to be themselves? But my neighbours in Fraserburg were uneasy and saw the apparent lack of change as a delusion. Life in the Karoo taught you to get things right or risk removal – and anything that looked too good to be true probably was too good to be true.

In the big cities it was different; euphoria reigned. The words 'miracle' and 'rainbow' were on many lips. The widely held, upbeat belief, around 1994, was that Whites and Blacks had come together, signed a deal to overlook the past. Those who had once played the apartheid game were scoring points for patriotism. Such a rush of enthusiasm at the arrival in power of a new Black nationalist ruling caste, in 1994, had not been seen since the rush of enthusiasm at the arrival of the new White nationalist ruling caste, back in 1948.

There was impatience in the big cities at the slow pace of change in remote *dorps* like Fraserburg. Political bigwigs arrived on flying visits and talked about 'mobilizing the structures', 'empowering the masses', 'consulting stakeholders' and 'levelling the playing fields'. On the newly proclaimed 'National Peace Day', I watched a group of police officers arrive in Fraserburg on a surprise visit to the Coloured township. They carried a couple of saplings in the back of their van and persuaded doubtful locals to dig holes and plant trees for peace in the thin, poor soil. Then they handed out free oranges and posed for photos. The township dwellers played along and assured the visitors that their descendants would one day relax in the shade of the peace trees. But no one was betting on it.

And yet there were stirrings. The Coloured people, stuck out in their township, talked of a time when they had lived alongside Whites in Fraserburg. When they had owned livestock and property, a time before the forced removals of mixed-race people tore apart the town and those on the wrong side of the colour bar were banished to 'the location', or township, well out of sight. A time before their houses were demolished, before their church was turned into a municipal garage, when the town was not given over to the new and ugly face-brick villas of White *Übermenschen* who paraded their superiority much as Roman garrisons lorded it over local tribes.

The awakening was summed up for me by a certain Mrs Steenkamp, who asked me quietly: 'Why don't the Whites give our houses back?' It was not a question that anyone could answer. People in the township recalled who had been buried in the original town cemetery, now long abandoned, with its shoebox babies' graves and monuments to soldiers who perished in White men's conflicts, in the Boer War and the First World War, thousands of miles away. They were beginning to recover from the lost decades when their homes and lives had been re-engineered by the White commanders of the town, and even their sense of themselves has been obliterated. But there was scant sign this recovered memory might endure. On the contrary, Fraserburg seemed to favour extinction.

It was during my first stay in town, years before, that the English teacher of the local school had asked me to talk to her students about writers and writing. She suggested I speak English because her students found it hard to speak the language themselves. They were native Afrikaans-speakers who disdained English, and she hoped I might boost interest in the detested tongue. I spent a lively hour with her class and, the next day, I received a note of thanks. 'It is not often,' the teacher wrote with careful politeness, 'my students meet an extinguished person…'

Fraserburg had always taken very long views, and you might say that extinction is its metier. It is best known for its collection of fossils and calcified footprints of creatures, much older even than the dinosaurs, that became extinct at the end of the Permian Age, some 250 million years ago, when this part of the Karoo was a great plain bounding an immense shallow sea. These pre-dinosaurian creatures were the stars of the town,

Rock painting of Bushmen hunting, Karoo

exactly the right mascot for the place, and they came in for more attention than the former inhabitants, the /Xam bushmen, whom the first White farmers of Fraserburg hunted to extinction.

Then again, extinction may not be all it seems. It was pink and portly Abraham, looming large behind the bar of the Central Hotel, who taught me that when I first came to Fraserburg.

'Take a hike and see for yourself. They were here in their hundreds, perhaps in their thousands,' he said, opening his arms wide as if to encompass ghostly multitudes. 'But that was once upon a time.'

I saw what he meant when walking in the veld. I found arrowheads, beads fashioned from ostrich shells, pierced, painted and fashioned into jewellery. I found rock shelters and overhangs in the hills, vantage points on rising ground that gave clear views of the plains. I found drawings and fire-blackened walls of old cooking sites. The veld that had looked so empty at first became crowded with relics. A scattering of arrowheads and ostrich-shell beads spoke more poignantly about a vanished people than any number of histories.

The Bushmen of what was once called Bushmanland, and the area around Fraserburg, were, for the most part, members of the /Xam. A people so complex and individual that European missionaries struggled to learn their language, and White farmers saw them as a form of pestilential wildlife. The solution, reached regretfully in some cases, eagerly in others, was to wipe them out. Over a couple of centuries that was what happened. But it took some time and effort, this annihilation, because these bands of indigenous nomads had the effrontery to fight back. The first Trek-Boers who moved into the Northern Cape at the end of the eighteenth century were fiercely resisted by the /Xam. There unfolded a series of unequal wars between advancing Whites, with their guns, and the /Xam, with their bows and poisoned arrows.

A venturesome Dutch pastor named Kicherer built a mission station in 1799 on the Zak River, not far from present-day Fraserburg. He named it, with notable optimism, 'Happy Prospect Fountain'. Some local Boers, as a last resort, backed Kicherer's mission. They had discovered that the Bushmen made formidable opponents and, however many were killed, the /Xam refused to surrender. Pastor Kicherer's flock were equally intransigent in spiritual matters and took little notice of his God, or of the good of their souls. Kicherer tried prayer, he tried punishment, he tried bribing the Bushmen of Happy Prospect Fountain with marijuana, brandy and tobacco. None of it worked. After four years of ceaseless but futile attempts to change them, he gave up and went home to the Netherlands. Robert Moffat, another missionary, whose daughter was to marry David Livingstone, sympathized with Kicherer's mission but he lamented that the Bushmen simply could not be helped: 'Harsh is the bushmen's lot, friendless, forsaken, an outcast from the world...' They were beyond salvation.

The Bushmen, for their part, apparently found the White invaders, or 'hat-men' as the /Xam referred to the interlopers, with their guns and their God, every bit as incomprehensible. Moffat was given a blunt answer when he asked a San hunter why he refused to visit Kicherer's mission station: 'I have been taught from my infancy to look upon "hat-men" (settlers) as robbers and murderers... Our friends and parents have been robbed of their cattle and they have been shot by the hat-wearers.'

In the 1860s the anthropologist George Stow collected

and preserved paintings from caves all over the country, and described best the consolidated assault on Bushmen, not just by the 'hat-wearers' but by fellow Africans. The war on Bushmen was one 'where all, however much they differed from one another, were against the bushmen'. Accounts of the period speak of repeated attacks on the /Xam by Boers from the Orange River area, Blacks from Schietfontein, Coloured and other White farmers from Namaqualand, as well as farmers from Fraserburg, all the way north to Hope Town. The aim of those who attacked Bushmen was clear, Stow concludes grimly: 'To exterminate, if possible, the last vestige of those who so resolutely opposed their unjustifiable usurpation. The struggle ended, as all such conflicts ever do, in the ultimate triumph of the strongest, while in its course little forbearance or mercy was shown on either side.'

The White incomers pushed deep into Bushmanland, shot the game upon which the San survived and drove them from their hunting grounds. They brought with them European diseases like smallpox against which the San had no resistance. If San children survived a raid by Boer shooting parties they could be sold into service on the farms. I can recall, as a child, my farmer uncles explaining how impossible it was to 'tame' a 'wild' Bushman but a child, captured young enough, might be moulded into human shape. The little servant girl whom Baby, the former owner of my cottage, 'bought' for a cake of soap was a victim of a tradition seen, by those who took part in it, not as slavery but as charity. It was hardly surprising that, by about 1910, the San Bushmen from the countryside around Fraserburg and beyond were gone forever.

But not quite forgotten. Certainly not in Fraserburg where I would sometimes catch glimpses of the people who once lived in and owned these Karoo lands. And this time was no exception.

My first glimpse of the spectral presence of the vanished ones was a small wooden cart, moving slowly down Voortrekker Street on very bald rubber tyres. The cart was being pulled by two small slow donkeys that plodded along the flat, straight, sandy roads that lead out of the town and into the great beyond. The cart drew level and the driver raised his whip in greeting. He stopped, we talked, he told me his name was Klaas, and he was heading 'out'.

Klaas was short, lithe and honey-coloured and when he took off his hat to wipe his brow he had dark curly peppercorn hair. But most moving of all for me was that out of his almond-shaped eyes stared his ancestors, the /Xam. Naturally, in Klaas' gene pool there had been admixtures along the way. But then nothing and no one in South Africa was solely one thing, or one race, despite the decades when this foolish pretence was enforced. Klaas' language today was Afrikaans, the White man's tongue and the patois of the Cape. He showed little surprise when I asked if I could ride along for a while, and so I perched in a tiny space at the back of the cart and we moved on towards the huge pale horizon.

Beside Klaas sat his wife, Klara, and piled on the cart was everything they owned: several pieces of corrugated iron, an old kettle, blankets, knives, a plastic telephone toy made by Fisher-Price, bottles of water, a catapult, fire-blackened tin cans and several buckets, roped to the sides of the cart. Sitting behind their father were Klaas and Klara's two children, Brand and Mina, plus two skinny dogs named Fire and Lightning, and a kitten known only as 'Cat'. The worn tyres on this small wooden cart were made by Firestone and his little girl's telephone toy was from Europe, and yet Klaas and his family and his cart were a more natural part of this place than any house-owner or farmer anywhere to be found in Fraserburg. His line stretched back thousands of years and his sense of himself in this landscape was easy and assured and yet, somehow, infinitely sad. Not that he felt like that… but I did.

Klaas had been working for a few days. 'We had sheep to shear,' he told me, 'the farmer gave us one, and some money for our work. Now we are on the road again.'

Klaas and his family were known by various names – they were 'cart people' or '*swervers*', simply 'wanderers'. That was when they were known by any names at all. For the most part, few in the Karoo towns notice them go by. Klaas and Klara may have piled their lives and their family on their cart, but they came and went like ghosts, which in some ways they were. Klaas and his family were nomads, itinerants of the Karoo, and they travelled the arrow-straight roads, camping by night whenever there was water to be found and kindling to make a fire. When he needed work, Klaas might fix fences for a few days, or find shearing work at one of the farms, or set traps for the jackals that take the sheep, but he and his family never stayed long. I asked him how he knew when it was time to move on.

Klaas shrugged. 'My spirit tells me. It's my blood. Time to go, it says.'

I travelled with him for as far as I dared, trying to calculate how much time I would need to walk back into Fraserburg before dark. The family stopped around three in the afternoon, beside one of the old dry-stone beehive houses that are to be found in the veld and where they planned to camp overnight. These corbel huts look a little like stone igloos and are typical of this part of the Karoo. Built in the nineteenth century, some served as dwellings for White farmers until well into the middle of the twentieth century. Klaas outspanned the donkeys. Klara brewed coffee in the old pot over a small fire of brushwood, blowing on the flames. Their son Brand took out his catapult and shot at roosting birds, and little Mina pulled the Fisher-Price phone to and fro across the ground and stopped, now and then, to pick up the receiver and make a call. Klara heated a flat-iron on the fire, spread a blanket on the ground, laid her dress on the blanket and slowly ironed it while Klaas fed his dogs. 'These are my wind-hounds,' he said, 'because they run like jackals.'

Tonight, to be camped beside a corbel hut, was a luxury. 'Five star,' said Klaas. He and Klara set up camp, using the corrugated iron as a windbreak and the plastic cans and cardboard as a roof. The children were to sleep in the shelter and Klaas and Klara would be happy in the stone-built house. Klara and the children foraged for more kindling. Winter nights in the Karoo were breathtakingly cold and a fire was essential.

'It's good but it's also dangerous,' said Klara, stoking the fire.

'For you?'

'For the children.' Klara called to the girl: 'Mina, show the man your burns.' Little Mina took off her jersey and I could see she had been badly scarred on both arms. 'She came too close to the fire', said her mother. 'It happens many times with the children here.'

I understood why this happened. The clothes the kids wore were mostly nylon or some artificial fibre, and if brought too close to the fire it exploded into flame.

I left Klaas and Klara beside their corbel hut and walked into town as the last light faded. In the dusk, Fraserburg seemed to have changed hardly at all since I was last there. I passed the little cottage where I lived twenty years earlier. The owner had offered it to me then for a few thousand Rand. Now the price was half a million. I reckoned there could only be one explanation for the leap in prices in a town once lost in the immensity of the Great Karoo and that was White Flight, or what Abraham called semi-gration.

I walked down Rossouw Street, with its pronounced rightward kink, and on past the hulk of what used to be the Central Hotel; silent, sunk in gloom and anonymous. Its only sign of life the slither and slap of the 'For Sale sign' on its facade when the wind got under it. No one would have known it once possessed two bars, and was famous for the wild horseplay the White farmers of Fraserburg favoured, for fights, feuds and boozy camaraderie, and was the centre of the only nightlife in town. Where, I wondered, had large and lunar Abraham or skinny Rick the Stick moved on to now? Cape Town, perhaps? The last stop on the semi-gration trail, where refugees ran out of road and hit the sea. The next day, I was to learn why the Central Hotel had been abandoned. Some years before, disgruntled customers, angry at being refused a drink after hours, returned in the small hours, pushed a Molotov cocktail through the letterbox, and fire gutted the hotel interior.

Abraham had another favourite phrase: 'I can trace my family back to the first settlers, the 1652-ers.' I didn't believe him. I doubted he could trace his family back more than a generation or two but I enjoyed his orotund pronouncements. It was a coded boast – by mentioning 1652, he was claiming kinship with the first White settler, Jan van Riebeeck, regarded by some in the old apartheid era as our very own Pilgrim Father. Tracing your family back to the first settlers was as close as you got to becoming South African aristocracy. But today, no one claimed kinship because van Riebeeck was a symbol of everything many Whites wish to forget. To associate yourself with van Riebeeck now was to be found guilty by association with the Dutch governor and his 'gangsters' who robbed the locals blind.

It needs to be repeated that those who lost land and life to the White settlers were the ancestors of the cart people, Klaas and Klara. There is still much to be learnt about the identity, genesis and gene pool of the KhoiSan but that they were the First People of Southern Africa seems beyond doubt. Indeed, there is evidence they are the line that leads to the origins of *Homo sapiens*, and that would make their ancestors the very first people of all. Recent research into the DNA genome of the KhoiSan, published in *Nature*, suggests that, around twenty-two thousand years ago, the KhoiSan comprised the principal human group on the planet.

The realization has been stirring among KhoiSan, together with descendants of the Koranna, a branch of KhoiSan living in the Cape when the first Dutch colonists arrived in 1652. This much-diminished minority struggles to be heard over the noisy Black /White arguments about who stole what from whom. The intractable ethnic enmities go on and on, but those who lost out to both Whites and Blacks are no longer silent.

'This is Khoi land,' insisted /Xam Koranna, a spokesman who takes his name from the Koranna people of Hangberg. At a meeting to discuss just who lost what and to whom, he asked: 'Why are we not Black enough to get back what is ours?'

He poured scorn on the notion that Blacks were the first victims. He mocked the dangerous and ultimately fruitless division of groups into 'Black' and 'White', a distinction that racists of the apartheid age held dear, and which has become more attractive than ever to those in thrall to racist fantasies. His caustic observations were all the more stinging, coming from one who belonged to a people whose home was in Southern Africa long before colour-coded beings emerged on the human stage.

/Xam Koranna was withering in his impatience: 'The government call themselves African people, but they don't know

92

the history of Africa. They are not African people. They are invaders – they are foreigners.'

The winds of change are blowing again and nobody can be quite sure when they will stop and who will be left standing when, or if, they do.

I walked the darkened streets of Fraserburg, under a jet-black pincushion sky so thick with stars they looked like brilliant foam. I passed the curious whitewashed structure known as the Pepper Pot, where the curfew bell hangs. Long ago, the town constable would ring it in the evenings as a signal for all Coloured people to leave town and Fraserburg was rendered, in the old phrase, 'White by night'. It is said that those whom the nightly curfew bell effaced have taken over control of the town, ever since the Mandela election of 1994, when voters handed power to the ruling African Nationalist Congress. But their control is unconvincing since the ANC is a shadow of itself and a long way from the move-ment Oliver Tambo once led. The 'hat-wearers' still occupied the houses in central Fraserburg, as they always had done, and the township, still home to the Coloured people of the town, was a distant, unseen hum. Change, a word often invoked, but out of reach, has a cruel ring, like the old curfew bell.

Then again, change in Fraserburg might prove even more cruel when, and if, it ever came. Just as the Karoo, once a place where little ever happened, and saved by that very neglect, may be on the point of savage alteration. It has begun to look very worryingly like a bankable proposition. Beneath the empty plains great res-ervoirs of shale gas have been identified and the oil companies are very keen to start fracking the Karoo. And if one wanted to get some idea of what this would entail, then, once again, Rhodes, his mines and his deplorable political manners are dismal examples. You have only to picture the Karoo as the new Kimberley, and treasure-hunt fever beginning all over again. The miners would move in, the eager entrepreneurs, developers, conglomerates and fortune hunters, all those who embody the spirit of Rhodes and his acolytes, would descend with cataclysmic force on the Karoo, and one of the last great lonely places would be lost.

And there is a very good chance this is what will happen. There has been an irreversible change of power in South Africa; for the first time ever a Black administration, freely chosen, has replaced a White minority regime. Yet the driving commercial forces that have the new rulers in their grip are indistinguishable from those Rhodes pioneered. The principle is the old and tiresomely simple one: there is stuff to be dug up and then sold. So let's dig it up and sell it. There are fortunes to be made, let us go out and make them, or make them for our friends and allies. The new administration, now two decades into the new century, has shown itself to be as quick as any before it to shepherd its clients, cadres and acolytes to the feeding trough.

To get some idea of what may happen to the poorest people in this great wilderness, which covers an area larger than Germany, if the mining companies take hold of it and shale gas replaces sheep as the emblem of the Karoo, consider what happened a couple of hours' drive north-west of Fraserburg, at an old fording point on the Orange River, not far from Kimberley, where, one day in 1867, a child found a shiny pebble on a riverbank.

12

wanted to go to Hopetown because one can't really understand Kimberley without it. Walking along Church Street, passing the Co-op and the bank, I found the town sleepily suspended in time, as if it could not quite shake off past disappointment or come to terms with present-day disillusion. The street was empty, muddy and cratered with potholes. The few shops were tightly barred. The early June darkness and a thin winter mist added to the weary air hanging over the town. In a dim shop doorway, a chunky cone covered in tinsel had been chained to the door. A closer look showed me it was a Christmas tree, built from stacked tractor tyres, forgotten when the shop was abandoned. Chaining it securely was necessary because, as I had been warned when I checked into my guesthouse, anything not locked would 'walk'. At the petrol station, a pick-up truck had pulled up to the pumps and bolted to the steel floor of the truck was a high-backed chair and from its arms trailed what looked like leather entanglements. It reminded me, rather eerily, of an electric chair.

There had been a time when the name Hopetown conjured up dreams of fabulous wealth. It does not conjure up much any more. Its tale is sad and familiar, haunted by those gods of irony who keep second homes in South Africa. What it once was, few can remember, and what it has become, no one I met is able to say. I have always felt a sense of kinship with Hopetown; once it was all its name promised, rich and famous and ready to dazzle the world. I shared the same name, got in the same accidental fashion, when my mother remarried after my father's death in the Second World War. The town got its name in the 1850s, on an imperial whim, to commemorate for no particular reason one William Hope, Auditor General in the Cape government. No one remembers him in Hopetown now, and of the wild excitement that once convulsed the town there is no trace.

The children of Trek-Boer families who settled in the area liked to play with what they called 'bright pebbles', on the sandy banks of the Orange River. One day in 1867, a tawny pebble a child was playing with caught the eye of a knowledgeable traveller. He sent the stone to an expert in far-away Grahamstown who identified it as a whopping diamond. Suddenly, Hopetown was on the map, its citizens dreamt of riches and fortune hunters flooded into town.

They called the first diamond ever found in South Africa the 'Eureka', a name that captured the delight of the discovery. But there were no more finds, hope faded and it seemed that the Eureka had been, literally, a flash in the pan.

A couple of years later, in March 1869, a shepherd boy of the Griqua people found a second bigger, brighter pebble and he took it along to the man who had bought the Eureka. We know the name of the sharp-eyed diamond-fancier: Schalk van Niekerk; and we know precisely what he paid the boy for the stone: five hundred sheep, ten oxen and a horse. Once again, Hopetown was ablaze with excitement and awash with prospectors from around the world. But that was the last of it. No more diamonds were found and Hopetown reverted to being what it had always been, another *dorp* in the middle of nowhere. It never did recover from its double disenchantment.

This second stone found its way to Cape Town, and into the possession of Sir Richard Southey, a British colonial official, who laid it on the table before the Cape Parliament, declaring: 'Gentleman, this is the rock on which the future of South Africa will be built.' The name the diamond later acquired was impressive: it came to be known as the 'Star of Africa'.

This kind of self-congratulatory nonsense has bedevilled the country ever since: it was the familiar and fraudulent fast-talk of successive administrations, planning to pull a fast one. The method became standard: announce a miracle, extol the benefits to the country and expropriate the loot. Hopetown and its gemstones, the governors of the time predicted, reflected the future of South Africa, where a disregarded wilderness would flower and the poor would be rich. Much the same promise has been made about shale gas of the Karoo by much the same sorts of people.

The shiny stone found by the Griqua shepherd boy triggered the frantic rush, not to Hopetown but to the immensely richer diamond fields up the road a bit, in Kimberley, when diamonds were discovered soon afterwards, in 1871. Not often remarked on is that the discovery of the Kimberley diamond fields was shot through with irony. It took the White man's servants to do the finding. A band of prospectors are said to have sent their Black cook to dig on a nearby hill, Colesberg *koppie*, in order to punish him – what for is not clear – and there he struck it lucky. Hopeful diggers from all over the world stampeded into the diggings, soon to be known simply as 'New Rush'. A few years later, when the dust cleared, Rhodes was the King of Diamonds. His company, De Beers, cornered the market and monopolized the diamond trade well into the present day. But the Hopetown diamond discoveries, and the Kimberley continuation, were never, as Southey boasted, the rocks on which South Africa was built. It could be said these were the rocks on which it was wrecked and, again, Rhodes was at the heart of it all. The diamond rush that started in Hopetown and culminated in Kimberley made him enormously rich. But the discoveries of diamonds in Kimberley and, a little later, gold on the Witwatersrand led to war, misery and subjugation, the scars of which still traumatize the country. Questions of who owned the vast wealth from mines, and who bought and sold them, became all-consuming and corruption so ubiquitous as to be practically obligatory, and it was increasingly accepted then, and now, as the traditional way of doing things.

Then again, to borrow the disclaimer the graffiti artist attributed to van Riebeeck, when he was accused of having 'stolen the land' – 'so what?' One cannot speak of wealth in South Africa without also talking of weapons. Or theft. The essential questions have always been: who has the weapons – and where did the money go? The travels of the Hopetown diamond, later the Star of South Africa, tell you nothing except the price. But to track how that price was reached tells you a very great deal about how power worked and who possessed it.

An unnamed Griqua shepherd found the stone in 1869, sold it on to van Niekerk, who sold it on, for the enormous sum of £11,200, to the Lilienfeld brokers in Hopetown. They shipped it to London, where it soon sold at over twice that price to the Earl of Dudley, who coughed up £25,000. For a while the stone was known as the 'Dudley Diamond'. It was sold again, in 1974, at auction in Switzerland for a sum that, in today's money, amounts to many millions.

If you follow the record of its price alone, the story of the Star of South Africa ends, predictably and boringly, in a Geneva auction room. But all the really exciting stuff has been left out and not even the guest appearance of Rhodes, as pantomime villain, will perk things up. It is precisely the shepherd, and the people he belonged to, that says far more about the tragic human comedy of South Africa than the British migrant who made a killing in the Kimberley diamond fields.

Who, or what, were the Griqua? The name was yet another euphemism, applied, in a rough and ready way, to a robust and rebellious clan that evolved in the Cape, in the seventeenth and eighteenth centuries, from liaisons between the Dutch colonists and indigenous KhoiSan people, and between White colonists and their many slaves.

No one was ever quite sure about the origins of the name 'Griqua'. But then this was South Africa where names have been applied, like sticking plasters, to people and to things we find unsightly. Now and then these names lift like plasters to reveal the embarrassing truth beneath. The people who came to be known as Griqua always had their own name for themselves and it was pointed and informative and thus completely impossible to use in South Africa, then or now. In a cheerful nod to their rich interracial parentage, they called themselves *Basters* – or 'Bastards'.

They were a redoubtable lot: trekkers, fighters, farmers and, deepening the embarrassment of their White compatriots, they spoke Dutch, the language of the Boers. Like the rebellious Boers, they chafed at legal restraints and to escape colonial rule in far-away Cape Town, they trekked north, into the immensity of the remote Karoo. However, the name they chose themselves, and wore with pride, was not acceptable to the ministers of the London Missionary Society who laboured to save their souls. It was uncomfortable, having to preach the Word of God to people who happily called themselves Bastards. So 'Griqua' they became.

When the apartheid regime took power, although the Basters

now had a more acceptable name, their existence did not cease to embarrass the new rulers. How they got to be who they were had sexual implications and all sex was political when it touched on race. The Griqua people were a reminder that the first European settlers in the Cape, portrayed by apartheid ideologues as lily-white, pure and pious Dutchmen (and not what a dissenting historian once called a shipload of low-lifes from the Low Countries), had mated with local KhoiSan and also slept with their many slaves. They were also a warning that some 'White' families would not stand too close a genealogical scrutiny.

It is very hard to explain to those who did not experience it how strange the old 'Whites only' society really was. But the Griqua boy from Hopetown goes some way towards doing that. The unknown shepherd is more interesting and his reality more revealing than the stone he found, or its value at auction. Because the boy who found the Star of Africa was never a South African in the eyes of those who worked and prospered in the diamond fields. To have suggested as much would have been, well, most un-South African.

13

I took another walk around Hopetown in the early morning and I spotted again the pick-up truck and its mounted chair. When back at my guesthouse I learnt what it was: the intricate arrangement of truck, chair and leather straps made a mobile shooting platform.

My informant was Theo, a very big man in a faded khaki safari suit. He was a vet in Johannesburg and his family had been sheep farmers in the Karoo for decades. Like many other farms, his was no longer workable but he came each year to hunt and used it as a base.

'It puts me in touch with my forefathers,' said Theo.

When I told him I had come to Hopetown to look around he was bemused.

'To look at what? Nothing to see.'

As his hunting party was climbing into their trucks, he waved me over and pointed out the farm on his map.

'Why not drive over later, after the hunt? And eat with us.'

When I got to the farm, it was late afternoon and the light was going. Theo introduced me to his mates, who stood around the fire. Young men, all White, all Afrikaans, they worked at city jobs which they found tiresome, uninteresting but necessary.

Evidently, it had been a successful day because a string of buck hung from the side of a truck. Some of his friends had marked on their foreheads a rough splash of blood; for first-timers it was a rite of passage, baptism into the tribe. They were not barbecuing the springbok they'd shot that day. Theo said they had reserved those for salting, drying and making into *biltong*. Instead, they were cooking thick steaks from the local supermarket and drinking beers or brandies mixed with cola.

Theo poured me a beer and we sat for a while. The sky was intensely black and thickly salted with stars.

'Are you against hunting?' Theo wanted to know.

I told him I was not against it. After all, I said, it had been going on in the Karoo for thousands of years.

For a moment Theo reckoned I must be having him on.

'Thousands? My family only got here in 1801.'

'Maybe hundreds of thousands,' I said. 'Buck have been hunted, and studied, eaten, mythologized, painted, mimicked. In the case of the eland, even worshipped.'

'Worshipped – by who?'

'By Bushmen. Who were here for a very long time.'

Theo nodded warily. 'Ah, the Bushmen. They died out.'

He seemed relieved. As if one could expect no other of such people; as if, even though they were all gone, their reputation for wilful, incurable irresponsibility still dogged them. As if there was nothing for it – but dying out.

I said: 'They got moved on.'

Theo shrugged. 'Someone had to give way. And it was us who opened up the country.'

His use of the word 'us' was loaded, as pronouns in South Africa are so often. The 'us' Theo had in mind were his Boer ancestors, who had trekked north from the Cape, into the Karoo, and shot their way through obstacles and, for that matter, any people who stood in their way. Their disappearance did not make him uneasy. He spoke lightly of 'bad luck' and of 'dying out'. As if somehow the San had contributed to their extinction; as if 'giving way' was on a par with losing a game of rugby.

It was remarkable to be so impervious. After all, Theo's own people had barely escaped being forcibly – and fatally – 'moved on'. British imperialists, in their ineffable condescension, regarded the Boers as scarcely human; a lesser breed, who would not be missed. Much as the Boers had felt about the San. But to Theo there was a world of difference: the Boers – 'our people' – had faced a deliberate massacre. Whereas the San were fated to 'move on' to make room for others; as if extinction was merely a form of crowd control. He repeated his belief that his 'people' had opened the country.

I disagreed. I said that when Theo's people at last took complete power in the mid-twentieth century, far from opening anything at all they shut down whatever and whoever they saw as a threat to their control. They set their faces against variety, reason, forbearance, love, toleration, imagination and humour. They closed schools, churches, universities and libraries. They banned books, films, plays; they expelled clerics and academics, and deported, banned, jailed or killed many who disagreed with them. During their half-century rule they put in place a system of racial intolerance so cruel, so pervasive and so murderously stupid that it blighted whatever it touched. And throughout it all, they never ceased to preach to others that they had a God-given duty to civilize Southern Africa. The assumption of moral righteousness was an imposition almost as painful as the system itself. It was a programme so destructive that only those who lived through the years of the pathological condition that we call apartheid could understand how systematized violence seeded itself into every aspect of everyone's lives.

Theo disputed this, in a gentle, mildly interested way, almost as if he no longer cared enough to be angry.

'Why should I feel guilty?' He cast a look around, as if addressing an unseen crowd. 'I was only ten when Mandela was released. You're talking about my parents' generation. Not me.'

Such conversations were familiar and futile. Talking as Theo and I had been doing was always to end by shutting down communication. We looked past each other, across a gulf of incomprehension. Neither Theo nor his parents felt bad about those years when the country was run by people who seemed, literally, to have taken leave of their senses. That was then and this was now and memories fade. It had been more than twenty years since Theo had said goodbye to all that, and embraced, like so many, ameliatory amnesia.

When the agents of the apartheid regime departed with their hands, as somebody remarked, covered in blood and gravy, and Mandela took over, the past was suddenly out of bounds. No one spoke of apartheid, no one drew attention to colour. Neither Black nor White (these were terms you stopped using pretty fast) wanted to talk about the past at all. If, occasionally, some were plagued by uncomfortable memories, these were put aside with the comforting thought that things really hadn't been all that bad. To hark back meant you were negative, an Afro-pessimist, and did not deserve to join the new colour-blind nation that had sprung into being overnight. With one mighty bound, Whites had broken free of the past and risen above their imperfections. In a gesture of magnanimity they handed over power and privilege to their former servants and were free now to go off and watch rugby, cultivate their gardens, untrammelled by guilt, doubt or bad dreams. Had you, in those heady days, gone about the country looking for volunteers, among Whites, willing to admit they had once been strong supporters of rigid racial separation from womb to tomb, you would have found very few takers. Those who, for many decades, had felt the only thing wrong with apartheid was that there wasn't even more of it, were very hard to find.

The mood at the time was a little like that which prevailed in Berlin when the Soviet system collapsed. I happened to be there in 1989, on the night that the wall came down. After the fall, a fever of unification gripped the newly reunited Berliners from opposite sides of the Wall. It became boring, onerous, even morally suspect, to hark back to how things were when the Wall was there.

So it was in South Africa. A tentative deal was struck between the White minority, who had held absolute power for the better part of a century, and the Black majority, who had been subjugated for hundreds of years. What brought about the change was not revolution; neither party had the power to overcome the other. What both sides settled for was a negotiated end to hostilities between two irreconcilable camps and agreed to find another way of running the country. It was a truce, cobbled together by the elites, a compromise hammered out by those who ran the show at the time and those who would run the show in the future. It was signed and sealed without much enquiry as to what the various followers of the two different camps might have thought about the plan. A low-grade and never-ending civil war ended with a peace treaty, packed with high-sounding sentiments, that no one had the least idea how to put into effect. And today we are discovering, as the Berliners did, that you can forget about the wall but it does not forget about you: that you can pull down the barriers and remove them but it is very much harder to get rid of the wall in the head.

If Theo was impatient, angry, dismissive, he wasn't alone. In his view, he'd given peace a chance and it sucked. The heady dream of a civil society where skin colour did not count was dead. At the end of the rainbow was not a pot of gold but a can of worms. The two sides were back in their old bunkers: at best, each showed a wary toleration of the other, but, more and more often, it was furious suspicion.

What was new was how careful people were to hide their true feelings, unless they could be certain that their auditors felt the same way. Theo had heard what I thought about the old methods of segregation and of those who, quite literally, pandered to and religiously worshipped the system. But that did not mean I might not be an ally. There were plenty of people who had once condemned apartheid, and enjoyed a brief flirtation with colour-blind freedom when Mandela had seemed like salvation, but who were reverting to familiar racial assaults on Blacks in general, as incurably incompetent and helpless corrupt. Online comments columns were filled with anonymous complainants, ready to suggest that the old system was not as bad as it was painted, or did more good than it is given credit for, or even that those who helped to undo it were traitors. Theo had to be careful – because I was rather 'foreign '– and thus hard to categorize and this made is difficult to know which form of address to reach for. Two kinds of discourse had grown up in the country – what you said to friends and family, and what you said to strangers. Whites and other minorities projected their fear and anger into the future, now looking increasingly threatening. But the language used to say what was truly heartfelt often came from the past. It was the only return still open to the way things were. Theo, like those who felt as he did, preferred not to go there except in the private company of the bitterly aggrieved. He found it too painful and too sad. For this angry nostalgia he offered no apology and would have argued that his disillusion with the current state of affairs absolved him from any need to do so.

14

There we sat, Theo and I, drinking beer. We did not understand each other and we knew it. Each attempt to explain ourselves reinforced our mutual incomprehension. But we kept trying.

'Some years ago,' Theo told me, 'I nearly killed myself. Just missed.'

It had been an accident, not a failed suicide. He had been after springbok in the afternoon, shot one and posed for a photo. The traditional pose showed the happy hunter, crouching beside the kill, often with its head on his lap, its glassy eyes pointing at the camera. He had propped his rifle on the buck's belly. Perhaps the safety catch was off, maybe the buck had the last laugh, but Theo's rifle fired and the round grazed his temple. He showed me the groove burnt into the flesh.

'If giving up means dying out, then I'm not doing it. I tried dying and it's not for me.'

His tone suggested that, somehow or other, I should relay the message. To whom, and how to do so, he did not say. I said nothing and we sat with our beers in companionable silence. We came at things from such different directions, from such contrary points of view, that understanding each other was not going to happen.

'How is it you speak Afrikaans?' Theo wanted to know.

I explained that I had grown up in Pretoria and that my family thought it essential, living as we did in a government town, that I learn to speak the local language.

'Which school?' Theo asked.

'Christian Brothers College.'

'Roman Catholic?' said Theo. 'A Roman Catholic who speaks Afrikaans and lives in France and travels around South Africa. Where did you go – after Pretoria?'

'Cape Town, Paris, London, Moscow, with time in Belgrade, Hanoi, Berlin.'

'All that moving? Anyway, now you're back home,' said Theo. 'As for me, let me tell you something, I'm not going anywhere. Dying is the last thing we'll do for them.'

He wasn't really telling me anything – he was talking to himself. When they don't prefer forgetfulness, South Africans do history in very particular, highly personal slices. History was presented not as the chronicle of theft that I had from young Blacks. Theo's version was a charge sheet, listing attempts on his life. For Theo, history was warfare. He buttressed his claim that he was not on his way out by refuting talk of extinction. As so often happened, conversation broke down into a series of battle-cries; into the war between the indispensable stereotypes of 'we' and 'them'. As for talk of 'home', that was just another shot fired into the dark.

Theo lived in a country where most people were very largely out of sympathy with those in his hunting party. Many Black leaders, when not openly hostile, were increasingly impatient with what they saw as White 'privilege'. Government restrictions on guns were tightening. The rights and privileges that Whites had commanded for so long were shrinking. The land they farmed was no longer theirs by right, or guaranteed by law or possession. Murders of White farmers in the Hopetown region, and across the country, had been increasing for years. The omens were not good.

Yet the hunters gave me the impression that they did not know; or did not care to know. They reminded me of their Zimbabwean counterparts I'd met long ago: lotus eaters drugged to the eyeballs, sleepwalking towards disaster. The bravado and the bluster were beyond obtuse. Theo and his hunters might say they were 'not going anywhere', yet they seemed to have not the least idea who, or where, they were.

When he walked me to my car, Theo suggested I take a trip. 'Do you know the camp, up the road, where they murdered our people?'

I did know of it but, once again, I did not need to say so. After a series of coded messages to each other, we had understood something of what the other was conveying, but we knew it stopped there and could take us no further.

As I reversed, my headlights picked out the day's kill. The springbok were strung by their back legs, heads down, in a tightly packed sheaf along the side of the truck. In my lights, their wide eyes flashed gentle reproach.

I knew very well what Theo meant when he talked of the 'place' where 'they murdered our people'. It had once been Hopetown's railway station and it stood some way out of town, on the south bank of the river from which it took its pleasant name: Orange River Station. After a brace of spectacular finds, although Hopetown never produced another diamond, Orange River Station became a testing ground for the advantages of railways in modern warfare. Rail was good for moving large numbers of troops, but Orange River Station also offered solutions to military planners, willing to mass-produce human misery on industrial scales.

Orange River Station was an early laboratory for an invention that became an indelible feature of the twentieth century, most notably in Germany but also in Japan, Russia, Cambodia, North Korea and many other places – the death camp.

When the Anglo-Boer War Rhodes had anticipated and backed got under way in 1899, the railways were the backbone of the British campaign. Thousands of troops, sent to relieve Boer sieges of towns like Kimberley, were bivouacked at Hopetown. It has been a long time since the last train stopped in Hopetown but you may find, even today, soldiers' leftovers: buttons, badges, coins, cups and gin bottles are scattered across the veld.

And Orange River Station was more than a staging post for troops. It was also a collection point for prisoners who were being transported to prison camps, set up along the rail line. Detention centres like Orange River Station were not the same as those we have come to think of as Nazi 'extermination camps'. Although

Boer prisoners – British concentration camp, Bloemfontein

it is unlikely this distinction would have been much consolation to the thousands of imprisoned women and children who died in the camps from disease, neglect, starvation and misery. Moreover, this idea of concentrating in such camps 'undesirable and seditious enemy sympathizers', as the British commanders called the prisoners, was one that the Nazis carried to extreme conclusions in the thirties and forties.

The British concentration camps were born out of a certain despair on the part of British generals. The Boer War began in 1899, and by 1900 large-scale battles had been conclusively won by British forces, who by that stage numbered hundreds of thousands. But there remained a much smaller, rag-tag army of farmers they could not subdue. Worse, the Boers actually seemed to relish the fight. It was General Roberts, celebrated by Kipling

Graveyard, Doornbult camp, Orange River Station

as the jaunty but remorseless 'Bobs', who came up with the idea of attacking what the Boer fighters cared for most: their farms, and their families.

Farmsteads, perhaps as many as three thousand, were systematically blown up or burnt to the ground, their wells poisoned, and livestock killed. There are remarkable photographs of British Tommies bayoneting herds of sheep. Lord Kitchener, who succeeded Roberts, refined this idea further, observing that 'the removal of all men, women and children and natives from the districts the enemy persistently occupy… [is] the most effective way of limiting the endurance of the guerrillas'. The farms having been destroyed, women and children and elderly male combatants, together with their servants, were transported, often in cattle trucks, to camps where they could be 'concentrated'. Vestiges of the old Orange River Station, its signals, rails, telegraph machinery, survived until quite recently, but were spirited away for reasons the locals cannot explain. The only records are contemporary black and white photos of long lines of tents for housing women and children, in what was once a busy place and is now empty veld.

However, on the nearby farm of Doornbult, the camp cemetery is still to be seen. Orange River Station, by all accounts, was reasonably well maintained but the mortality rate in the camps was high. Across the country it is estimated that up to twenty-eight thousand people (or over ten per cent of the republican Boer population) had perished by the end of the war. More family members died in the camps than Boer fighters on the battlefield. The great majority were children, and they succumbed to measles, typhoid, mumps and malnutrition.

Walking among the graves of these children in the concentration camp at Orange River Station is an eerie experience. They are neatly laid out stone-covered lozenges of soil, where the occasional meerkat scurries and those who tend the graveyard must sometimes restore stolen bones to their original owners. The camp has been carefully and lovingly preserved by Afrikaners who refuse to let their past fade and cherish bitter memories. An unusual feature of Orange River Station was that it was one of the few camps where the children of White Boers and Black servants were held and were sometimes buried in the same grave – an unthinkable event at any time before or since. But then, like many South African stories, much of the interest often lies in what does not appear to the eye, or in what is not said.

There were many separate camps for Blacks, along the railway line from Orange River Station to Mafeking. These were, in effect, forced labour camps and it is estimated that more than a hundred thousand prisoners were once detained in these places. In the midst of the Boer War, there was the practical and quite appalling idea that the enemy would know that normal service had been resumed when it became apparent that the mines were producing once again and, to get them back to work, labour was needed. Black prisoners were badly housed and badly fed. They were also, quite literally, worked to death. The estimate of how many died is around twenty thousand but it is all too likely that the true figure was much higher. The names of White prisoners, old and young, who died in the concentration camps were recorded and remembered. Black prisoners who died have fewer graves and scant memorials. This was a very South African situation; as familiar as it is forlorn.

When it came to fighting or recruiting soldiers, another rule applied. The last thing either the Boers or the British wanted was that either side should start arming Africans. Of course, both sides used Blacks, where it was strategic to their purposes, as

scouts, messengers and spies, but they remained shadowy, sup-
plementary and, ultimately, superfluous. What underpinned the
contradiction was the surreal belief on both sides that this was a
White man's war waged in a White man's country.

It was an illusion that prevailed. By an extraordinary sleight
of mind, Whites persuaded themselves that Africans, though
they were overwhelmingly preponderate, did not actually exist,
except as a problem to be solved, and a reservoir of labour. That
has always been the clue that gave the game away. Africans were
suddenly essential only when someone had to do the work. Blacks
who were recruited by the Boers or British, like the thousands of
Black prisoners of the thirty-four forced labour camps, so essential in growing food, in getting the mines back working again,
slipped, as soon as the war was over, into the great slough of forgetting, so deep, so comforting and so dangerous.

But all the wars, whether almost won or nearly lost, have not
been forgotten: KhoiSan, Xhosa and Zulu Wars, the Boer Wars,
both World Wars, then half a century of punitive racial separation so fierce it counted as a war in itself, these hang about
the country's neck like shrunken heads. You would struggle to
understand what made the country what it has become without reminding yourself of what Hopetown stands for, and why.
There was apparently nothing much to see in Hopetown, I had
Theo's word for it, and yet there was everything to understand.
The children's cemetery of the concentration camp at Orange
River Station speaks more powerfully than any public memorial,
and yet it is barely visible. The remains of the rail line do not
leap to the eye but they point to the inevitable destination, and
the catastrophe, that made men like Rhodes so rich and ruined
much else. It is as if nothing on the surface can help much to
clarify things in this country, that what really counts lies buried,

submerged and must be exhumed, teased out, coaxed into intelligible shape. The end of the Kimberley line was Kimberley – that was its point, you might think. But this is to be too rational, too sensible. Getting to and from Kimberley was the point of the rail line – but the Kimberley line was also a way of running things favoured by the powerful, and it endures.

15

When I was a child, on a visit to Kimberley, where an uncle was a native of the town, I was taken one day to visit Christian Brothers College, his old school. My uncle pointed to a white plaque on the wall of the main building that marked the spot where Cecil Rhodes had constructed a shelter for civilians during the Boer siege. The bunker was just inches above ground level and I could never shake the idea that those in the shelter must have been very short.

The Irish Christian Brothers opened colleges around South Africa and I was to go to one of these schools in Pretoria. The Brothers were a tough lot of fellows from Waterford and Cork, quick to use the leather strap, weighted with coins, along with the heavy cane, as anyone who went to one of their colleges will tell you. The Brothers had no sooner arrived in Kimberley, ready to educate the children of Irish miners in the diamond fields, than they found themselves stuck in a very nasty war.

My uncle always talked of the Boer War as if it had happened just the other day and I understand now why this was so. He'd been born barely twenty years after it ended and when he was at school in Kimberley he would have seen signs of shelling all over town. His reverence for Rhodes was huge. In his telling of it, the rise of Kimberley took on the tones of a creation myth. In the beginning there existed nothing but a few Boer farms in the empty veld; then came diamonds and chaos; then came salvation when Cecil Rhodes and De Beers bought the mines, owned the town and won the Boer War more or less unaided and refashioned South Africa in Rhodes' image. Rhodes had caused what had been a dusty, disease-ridden mining camp in 1870 to mushroom overnight into a town of over forty thousand people, one of the largest settlements in Southern Africa, with electric light, tramways and more diamonds than you could count. Here was a man who would have colonized the stars. What others might have seen as rampant megalomania was, to my uncle and many like him, just another day in the office for Cecil John Rhodes. Even God, when creating the world, had rested on the seventh day. The way my uncle told it, the creator of Kimberley would have seen that as slacking on the job.

I liked the fire and flash of the story but something always puzzled me. With such manic energy behind it why had Kimberley subsided into what my uncle called 'a Company town'? One that looked and felt to me like a dull, decorous half-dead *dorp*. 'Company town' was a term I grew to hate. It seemed to be a posh name for a mining camp. In a Company town every last citizen, whether miners themselves or the bankers, grocers, teachers, lawyers, doctors and preachers who serviced those who dug the stuff out of the ground, genuflected each morning to 'the Company'. Most of my family were 'on the mines', in one place or another, whether they mined diamonds or gold or platinum or coal, and they lived and worked in one or another Company town, with its lifts and mineshafts, its club and its school and its rather strange air of what I always felt was a kind of perpetual boyish relief at belonging, body, soul and Christmas bonus, to the Company. Johannesburg and its gold mines was the great, unruly

Big Hole, Kimberley Diamond Mine

example of the type but at least it never forgot what it truly was – a rough-neck mining camp. Kimberley felt dead, ruled over by the memory of Rhodes and the decisions of De Beers. Kimberley also held on to imperial pretensions, fearfully and fruitlessly, long after Rhodes had gone.

I think the adoration of the Company had to do with a need to belong to something like a family. English-speaking South Africans were, inevitably, a disconnected lot, never joined by their heartstrings to the country. Having been briefly on the side of those who won the Boer War at the beginning of the twentieth century, they spent the rest of the century losing the uneasy peace, as well as their influence. As a result, it was hard to shake off the feeling that English South Africans were perpetual *arrivistes* and unreliable patriots. It was thus reassuring to belong to something larger and more powerful than yourself, and a relief to pledge loyalty to a mining giant. The Company provided security and continuity; the Firm, the Office, the mining 'house' was where fellow members spoke and played and thought as you did and where you felt at home. For people who were no longer quite English and not really South African, and certainly not 'African', Mother Company replaced Mother Country.

At first glance Afrikaners, by contrast, seemed more real, more truly of the place. Certainly, they said so often enough and even their name, 'Afrikaner', seemed to bind them to the continent. But that turned out to be another elaborate bluff. Because if you called an Afrikaner an 'African' you risked being attacked or sued for slander. Far from being a compliment, the term was an insult. Afrikaners said they couldn't return to Europe, said so proudly and often, but seemed to ignore the fact that they hardly needed to return since they brought the place with them. They claimed to be pure-bred representatives of Western civilization whom God had settled on a benighted continent to spread His word and His ways. On inspection, even the term 'South African' turned out to be little more than a flag you flew when you opened hostilities; it was ammunition but not information. You bandied the label about, on sports fields, or at elections, or when you had a patriotic point to make. It was the boast of those who wished to feel normal. After all, you told yourself, normal people identified themselves with the name of their Mother Country. So why shouldn't we do the same?

The trouble was that South Africa was anything but normal, it was never much of a mother, and its name on the map of Africa provoked more questions than answers. Where did it begin and where did it end? Which bits of it were 'ours', and which bits of it were 'theirs'? When you looked hard at the map, it seemed to be a matter not of geography but of guns. What you meant when you said 'South Africa' depended on your skin colour and your politics. The more loudly I heard people claiming South Africa as a Mother Country, or as their 'native' land, the more like orphans they sounded. Calling someone a 'native' was unwise, because you might be assaulted; or you might see them arrested for being in the wrong racially designated zone. Perhaps that was why I had the feeling, early on, that there were no 'real' South Africans. Whites offered at best a shaky impersonation of the real thing – Blacks were refused permission to be anything of the sort.

This dislocation started under the British, who established that all genuine South Africans must be White. They left the status of Blacks undefined but allowed that they might one day, possibly, qualify as the real thing. This vague concession to good sense, this misconceived half-liberal creation, lingered on in a kind of half-life, until the mid-twentieth century when a deluded cabal of White Afrikaner tribalists, obsessed with preserving racial purity, took over the country and drove a stake through its befuddled heart.

Perhaps that's why I've always been struck by the staginess of so much South African life, because European settlement in Africa has been a long game of make-believe. Whites had to pretend, and it was a hard trick to master, that being a European was your vocation and yet Africa was your home. How was the circle to be squared? By building cities and erecting monuments that imitated the places from which you came. It meant disguising who you were, especially to yourself. A dislocated minority of semi-detached English settlers, obsessed, every bit as much as their Afrikaner compatriots, with the nuances of skin colour, language and race, closed their eyes to where they were and played a prolonged game of blind man's buff, bumping about in the dark and tripping over their own feet.

Indeed, the longer I contemplated the history of White South

Africa, the more I saw Rhodes not so much as a brutal imperialist, the favoured caricature of those who attack his statues, but as a master showman, a con artist *sans pareil*, who understood that those who admired and followed him preferred setting over substance. Africa was to be reimagined in one's own likeness, and colonial cities, monuments, laws and values were approximations of the real: pretentious enough to persuade you they counted as your very own but designed to look like they, and you, belonged somewhere else.

Matjiesfontein, the model English village concocted by Jimmy Logan, was one of these intriguing fakes but it was Kimberley that took the crown. Even its name was born out of a kind of joke, the sort of thing that amused imperial officials in far-away Whitehall. To the first diggers who came to this place in the veldt in the 1870s, the vast tented camp was known simply as 'New Rush'. But the Secretary of State for Colonies, Lord Kimberley, felt something more substantial was needed and civil servants got to work. They knew that their boss knew little and cared less about Africa and he had a particular beef about the names adopted by some African outposts that he struggled to pronounce. One of his staff solved the problem, and possibly brightened his prospects of promotion, by suggesting that the rich diamond fields in the Northern Cape should be given a name his boss would find delightfully easy to say – his own – and Kimberley it became.

Though Lord Kimberley may have named the place, it was Rhodes who owned it. When the Boer War broke out and the Boers laid siege to the town, Rhodes immediately moved back into town as soon as the shooting started. He looked on Kimberley rather as Kublai Khan did on Xanadu. Were the Boers to win it, the marvel that he had conjured up might vanish in the smoke of war.

What was to be known as the Anglo-Boer War was to Rhodes something far more serious: it was a battle to decide who would control Southern Africa, but it was also felt by those who followed Rhodes to be a decisive battle for the right to design what, even then, was envisioned as the new world order that would follow the war. Rhodes had been one of the chief manipulators of the push to war, who believed it to be essential that the right sorts of people prevailed over the wrong sorts of people, especially Boers and Blacks who were each as lamentably backward as the other. For Rhodes, and those like him, this was a moral crusade, and one he summed up in his credo: 'We are the finest race in the world and the more of it we inhabit the better it is for the human race.'

Rhodes' return to Kimberley wasn't particularly appreciated by the diggers and he infuriated the regular Army chiefs. Rhodes, massively self-certain, barely noticed their displeasure. He was not only in his element, he was in his kingdom. The Boers might rain down shells on the town, using their 'Long Tom', a formidable artillery piece. Very well, he would have a bigger cannon designed in the De Beers' workshops. It was called 'Long Cecil' and the shells that it fired back at the Boer besiegers were signed: 'With Compliments of Cecil Rhodes.'

How completely Rhodes' admirers succumbed to this pharaonic delusion is to be seen in the lines by his favourite poet, Rudyard Kipling, inscribed on the war memorial that stands on a traffic island in central Kimberley. It is known as 'The Honoured Dead Memorial' and was designed by Sir Herbert Baker, Rhodes' favourite architect. The monument's design was thought to have been inspired by the fifth-century BC tomb of the tyrant Theron, in Sicily, as well as by the Nereid Tomb, erected in the fourth century BC, for a Persian king in what is now Turkey. The

Honoured Dead Memorial, Kimberley

surviving stones of that tomb, today reassembled in the British Museum, show a graceful marble temple adorned by what may be representations of sea nymphs, whose delicate drapery seems to flow like the winds and waves they represent.

If he had in mind the Nereids, then Sir Herbert Baker's monument falls short of the original. Built of sandstone imported from the distant Matobo Hills, in what was to be Rhodesia, and where Rhodes himself was very soon to be buried, it is a top-heavy, brutal blockhouse. At its base it displays a line of shells once fired into the town by the Boers and it displays the huge cannon designed and named for Rhodes, the Long Cecil. Kipling's lines on the monument memorialize the defenders of Kimberley and remind the next generation of their sacrifice:

This for a charge to our children in sign of the price we paid
The price we paid for freedom that comes unsoiled to your
    hand

Read Revere and Uncover for here are the victors laid
They that died for the city being sons of the land

It is stirring stuff, there's no doubt about that, and the unpunctuated lines hurry the reader towards the kind of reverence Kipling aimed to elicit. It is also, like so much of the work Kipling composed at Rhodes' request, high-sounding nonsense. The repetition of 'price' and 'paid' is a bookkeeper's bloodless reckoning of real human pain. The soldiers who are interred in the monument were hardly likely to have been 'sons of the land' and they would have been fighting not for 'the city' but for Queen and Country.

Yet Sir Herbert Baker's blockhouse does have something in common with one of the classical Greek originals. It is recorded that the Nereid Temple survived for centuries and it was still standing well into the Byzantine era, when it was vandalized for its stones by local Christians. By that time the vandals would have had little idea what the temple was meant to represent. The Honoured Dead Monument is unlikely to last as long. Bits and pieces have been lost to light-fingered visitors since 2010, when the brass facings on Long Cecil were stolen.

Standing near me, among the tourists gathered at the base of the monument, a small Black boy, fingering his iPad, asked his parents what on earth the towering building was there for. His parents were at a loss to explain and I got the feeling that it would not take centuries before local citizens no longer knew, nor cared, who the memorial commemorated and began recycling it into something more useful.

What had brought the boy who stood beside me, and his family, and crowds of tourists to Kimberley were tales of diamonds galore and the prodigious chasm, scooped out by hand, in the great diamond rush and called, with refreshing understatement, the Big Hole. Years ago, a visit to the mine was trickier and it became something of a game to see how close you could get to the milky green lake that almost filled the Hole, without falling in. The Big Hole flooded in 1914, and although some mining went on in the adjacent workings, even that came to an end in 2015.

Today Rhodes' town has become what was always latent within it and trying to get out: a theme park. Theatrical sets reproduce the heat and clamour of the mine workings, and the roistering camp where diggers drank and played. There are Victorian shop-fronts, an electric tram, a pawnbroker, several taverns and, in a barbershop window, an invitation dated 1902, the year the King of Kimberley died, offering haircuts in the red leather chair frequented by 'the late Mr Rhodes'.

What visitors get for the entrance fee is the scrubbed face of a Victorian fancy. They see nothing of the diamond hunters'

Kimberley diggings, 1872; said to be the largest hole ever dug by hand

hell-hole, or the dirt or disease, or thousands of Africans who poured into Kimberley to work the diggings. Tourists are lectured on the dazzling bounty of the diamonds found in Kimberley but they will hear little of the waves of whores who serviced the diggers in dozens of brothels. Nor of the contempt that individual prospectors felt for Rhodes as he slowly but surely put them out of business. A group of diggers, furious at the careering arrogance of the man they called Kimberley's 'Diamond King and Monarch of De Beers', one day pushed to the De Beers office a handcart containing an effigy of Rhodes: their petition did not mince words. The demonstrators announced they had come to bury this 'traitor to his adopted country, a panderer to the selfish greed of a few purse-proud speculators, and a public pest. May the Lord perish him, Amen.'

It's hard to think of any summing-up of Cecil John Rhodes that has been better put and it shows that, long before the students of Cape Town University demanded that the colossus be toppled from his plinth, others had expressed the same wish, but rather more succinctly. The exasperation of the angry diggers of Kimberley endured into present times, even among fellow mining magnates. When the last large bloc of De Beers shares, still in the hands of the family that traced its connection all the way back to the founder, was sold in 2011, one diamond trader saluted the demise of what he called 'this ghastly little club'.

Kimberley was Rhodes' town: he owned it lock, stock and diamond diggings, and however understandable the anger that Rhodes evokes, it's silly to wish away history. You may as well try erasing the Big Hole. Much is made of the size and depth of the huge excavation, how it was dug by hand and prodigious amounts of soil carted away. Once again, the diamond 'diggers' were anything but that and the name describes a role not a reality, because uncounted throngs of Black labourers did most of the work. De Beers alone, at the onset of the Boer War in 1899, employed ten thousand Blacks and just two thousand Whites. What remains, and haunts, from the days of Rhodes' empire, is an enormous hole in the ground. Across the country there are countless images, effigies and memorials remembering Rhodes but none is more appropriate and more eloquent or gets closer to the great, glassy hollowness of his achievement than the yawning void of the Big Hole.

16

Nowhere are relics of Rhodes in Kimberley more palpable or intimate than in the club he helped to establish in 1881. The present club, the third and final version, opened shortly before the start of the Boer War. Limited to 250 members, all male, it evoked the London clubs to which Rhodes and his friends belonged and was to be a refuge from the seething squalor of the mining camp beyond its walls. The Kimberley Club is a boutique hotel now but remains a shrine to Rhodes and breathes the near-religious regard in which his admirers held him.

It also sums up Rhodes' belief that, if the Englishman's home was his castle, then his club was his chapel. It features the obligatory accoutrements: a billiard room, a hushed and expansive bar, bentwood chairs, mahogany sideboards, broad verandas, red tiles, cool courtyards, portraits of Queen Victoria and any number of animal heads. Its walls are thick with sketches, cartoons, effigies and busts of Rhodes, who looks, sometimes, like a rather dodgy bookmaker. Members of the club were from Kimberley society: mining magnates, colonial dignitaries, military grandees and visiting bankers. The Kimberley Club, its members rejoiced, had more millionaires per square foot than anywhere else in the world. It admitted Jews, if warily, and Rhodes lured Barney

Barnato, his great rival in the Kimberley diamond fields, to sell his holdings and give Rhodes and De Beers a near-monopoly, by promising the club would elect Barnato as a member. Or, as Rhodes, put it: 'I propose to make a gentleman of you.' It was not easy. It took Rhodes four years before he found another member willing to second his nomination of Barnato. De Beers came away with control of ninety-five per cent of diamond mining in South Africa.

In the billiard room I got talking to a young American archaeologist who was visiting Kimberley for the first time. His fieldwork took him in search of the relics of prodigious military conquerors like Alexander the Great. He had been a week in South Africa, touring the battlefields of the Boer War, and now he was in Kimberley to learn about Rhodes' role during the siege. He was impressed by what he called Rhodes' 'interesting mega-lomania' – by tales of how he would ride around town when Boer shells were falling thick and fast, with scant regard for danger. He also admired the resistance that the Boers had shown: 'Thirty thousand farmers took on the entire might of the British Empire and darn near beat them!'

The American had visited Mafeking, a town bitterly contested in the Boer War and from where, in 1900, news that the Boer siege had been lifted was greeted by scenes of wild jubilation across England. What he'd hoped to find in Mafeking was a statue of Rhodes that had stood, so his guidebook told him, near the railway station.

'It wasn't there. One day it simply took off. Folks were not happy. They said it had been smuggled – to Kimberley. And I'd find it here, in the club. I came right on over and sure enough, there it was.'

He showed me the life-size Cecil Rhodes, placed in a courtyard,

his back against a wall. This rendering showed an unusually pla-
catory Rhodes, hat in hand, as if about to ask a favour or perhaps
pleading his case. A spotlight played on his face and his stance
was unsettlingly reminiscent of a man about to be shot.

I was intrigued by his story of how the club got the statue.

'Did the people in Mafeking use the word "smuggled"?'

'Sure did,' said the American. 'Why the heck smuggle a statue
from one town to another?'

I explained that these were dangerous times for statues.
'They've been toppled, smeared with excrement, painted different
colours and set on fire. Rhodes is in big trouble.'

'But the guy's been dead for over a century.'

'Doesn't help. There are people who loathe him.'

'They still do?'

'Rhodes stands for the sins of the settlers, and their descendants. Attacking his statues is a way of making people like us look
at ourselves. And pointing up what we've done. Some Black radicals say their land was stolen by settlers and their descendants
should give it back. Rhodes was Settler-in Chief.'

The American shook his head. 'Every country had its robber
barons. People did their thing according to their times. Imagine
going back to Rockefeller or Carnegie, and asking them to say
sorry. It's history, it's past, it's over.'

I said: 'It isn't over here. It is just beginning.'

He shrugged. 'We were settlers once. Doesn't seem to be an
issue in the States. I don't see how attacking statues gets your
land back.'

I admired his equanimity and his American view of the world,
his certainty as a citizen of the great superpower. He could relate
to Alexander the Great, whose empire stretched from the Adriatic
to the Indus and who had no doubt that the Greek civilization he

imposed on those he conquered was the finest anyone could wish for. Cecil Rhodes would have felt much the same way. However, those whom Alexander invaded may have taken a very different view.

Would it not be true to say, I suggested, that in America, like Australia, new settlers from Europe had liquidated and overwhelmed the people they found living there?

'Maybe that's why you say there is no issue now?'

The American smiled. 'I guess it takes a special kind of mind to understand this country.'

I said that in fact it's probably easier for a foreigner, visiting for the first time, to see it more clearly. One of the best books ever written about South Africa was by an American: *A Very Strange Society*. It was as good today as it was fifty years ago when Allen Drury wrote it, and the country was just as strange.

'People liked the book?'

'It was banned, almost instantly.'

'Banned?'

'We had busy censors under the apartheid regime. They read everything, and anything they didn't like was suppressed. All copies vanished from shops and libraries and keeping even a dog-eared copy at home was a crime.'

He looked even more puzzled. 'This happened often?'

'It was all perfectly normal.'

He looked at me for a moment and asked me a question I had not been expecting.

'Did you once have a beard?' Before I could answer, he went on: 'I was in the Transport Museum yesterday. They have wonderful old steam locomotives on display. I noticed a big poster and on it was a poem about a guy who worked the railroad. Right alongside was a photo of the poet. Maybe I'm wrong – but something about your face gets me thinking. But this poet had a beard and looked much younger.'

The next morning I went to the Kimberley Transport Museum, located right beside the original Victorian station. Outside the museum stood gleaming steam engines, stock-still in the sun, like creatures from a lost world, ready to roll but unable to remember how and baffled into silence. The clerk behind the ticket counter told me I had the place to myself.

I made my way past exhibits of early signal systems, rail gauges, old photographs of work gangs laying sleepers, shunters at work and life-size wax models of uniformed train drivers, ticket collectors and bedding attendants from the fifties. There was a genuine sleeping car with six bunk beds that I remembered so well. The upholstery was of unyielding olive-green leather, and in the corner of the compartment was a triangular washbasin, made of steel, with a mirror-top that you lifted and secured to the wall with a leather strap.

It was all very familiar. I'd been around ten years old when I spent several school holidays on my uncle's sheep farm in the Eastern Cape. My mother would see me off on a steam train from Johannesburg, in just such a compartment of green leather bunks, and shades you pulled over the open window to block flying coal smuts from the engine. A day and a night, and almost a thousand miles later, the train paused briefly at dawn in a tiny place called Molteno, for local farmers to load their milk pails. The conductor deposited me beside the tracks, with a note pinned to my jersey, handed me my suitcase and away the train rumbled.

I soon found the poem and the photograph the archaeologist had told me about. It was displayed in a large frame behind glass and I was glad no one else was around because it was embarrassing to come face to face with this version of myself. The boy, in the narrow top-most bunk of the steam train chugging through the night towards the Eastern Cape, had changed into the bearded man who wrote the poem and, somehow or another, he had turned into me. Here was proof again, if ever I had doubted it, that South Africa was a dark and furiously funny farce, and by some fluke I'd been given a small, walk-on role.

Back in 1974, I had written a poem about the absurdities of racism and those who elevated it into a religion. I cast the poem as a mock-lament, spoken by a crippled railway worker who has lost his legs, and his job, after a shunting accident and sits in a fly-blown bar in Pretoria, cursing the ayatollahs of apartheid not for being racist – on the contrary, the old railway man is angry because they are no longer ruthlessly racist enough. It was a jaunty poem, rhymed and rhythmic, and seemed to strike a chord at the time.

In any event, it was soon banned by the national broadcaster, mouthpiece of the apartheid regime, and denounced as a calculated insult, which of course it was. Though some critics on the left later complained that lampooning a bigot from a specific ethnic group – a drunken, despairing Afrikaans railwayman – was also itself racist. In short, the poem seemed to amuse or anger people in pretty much equal proportions.

There the matter rested for some twenty years. When the new democratic government came to power in 1994, a recording of my poem, now set to music, was released and was almost immediately banned for a second time, by the same national broadcaster, now the mouthpiece of the new democratic government.

I could see why it happened. The old railway man's speech was peppered with racial epithets and insults. He spoke as many

Whites spoke, in the years when I had written the poem. A time when extreme prejudice against every 'race' but your own (and even there you had your enemies) was public policy in South Africa. But that sort of talk, once so ever-present it went unnoticed, was now *verboten*, and many people wanted it that way. Black South Africans, the customary victims of crude and vicious insults, did not want to hear them repeated. And those who once found such ways of talking absolutely natural did not wish to be reminded.

Even so, to have my poem banned once by the old racist right was not unexpected, it was the sort of thing they did all the time. But to be censored a second time, by brand new democrats, was alarming and not much help to anyone. It would merely drive various phrases and sentiments underground, where they would be reserved for saying privately what you really felt, to people you really trusted. It would also whitewash the past and make it impossible to recreate the way that, for centuries, White South Africans had sounded and spoken. It is one of those choice ironies that, with the end of the old censorship under apartheid, the defence of which was that words must be policed or they led to war, we have the beginnings of a new censorship, and the reasons given are much the same – to keep the peace it is necessary to muzzle the citizenry. The tendency in South Africa grows apace: online journals close down their comment columns lest their readers say too clearly what they feel; literary festivals 'disinvite' speakers who might say something regrettable or offend merely by being who they are; debates are chaired by *Gauleiters* ready to snatch the mike from speakers with whom they disagree; and even the national Parliament shuts off the sound when debates get rowdy. Censorship was once imposed from above, now we do it voluntarily.

I took a long look at my poem under glass, and, alongside it, at the bearded fellow whom the notice claimed to be me. I had the worrying thought that when, one day soon, the language police visited this quiet museum, the foul-mouthed old railwayman I'd conjured up, and his lament for the old days when everyone hated everyone else, would be banned once again and this time it would be forever.

I returned to the Kimberley Club for a last look at the statue of Rhodes, his back to the wall, holding up his hand as if about to say something. Reading through accounts by his contemporaries of his conversations, it is rare to find reports of anything particularly memorable he said – but Rhodes did not need to say much – his admirers were magnetized by who he was and how powerfully he played his part. A dramatic example was a photograph in the town's McGregor Museum that shows Rhodes and his staff dispensing 'Siege Soup' in Kimberley prison during the Boer War.

The convicts sit patiently on the ground. An inscription on a couple of wooden boxes, probably holding soup greens, identifies them as a gift from Rhodes' company, De Beers, and the date '1899–1900' is clearly visible; the siege of Kimberley lasted four months, from October 1899 to February 1900. The bringers of soup are White; the convicts sitting on the ground are Black. Rhodes, in pale linen trousers, lounges and looks on, his face a fleshy mask, the eyes hooded and impassive. The setting is as important as the action and all local history is in the image. Up the road was the Kimberley Club, forbidden to Blacks, Boers, itinerant diamond diggers, Asians, females, foreigners and anyone else not of the right sort. Down the road was the Kimberley jail, open to anyone who broke the rules. Rhodes did not pioneer this all-or-nothing world of polar opposites, split between pleasure dome or prison camp. Lesser versions of spatial separation began with the arrival of the first European settlers. But the Kublai Khan of Kimberley added a brutal, if seedy, grandiloquence to the way Whites saw themselves. They did not mistake the substance for the show – the show *was* the substance and they were always centre stage. Duty and destiny required that you looked the part, using whatever props were at hand.

But the show was also a bluff. A tincture of doubt often undermined what passed for unassailable superiority. What if the other side refused to play along? The fear never went away, even, perhaps especially, at a time when superiority seemed assured and eternal, even in the days when Rhodes lounged beside his soup kitchen – God in His heaven, Black prisoners at His feet.

Perhaps that was why, when at last the great change happened two decades back, when power shifted from a White minority to the Black majority, nothing much seemed to change. Loss of power brought on an identity crisis among Whites, who numbered less than one in ten of the population, because they no longer knew – not just who they were supposed to be – but what role they might play in a new South Africa. After so long in the limelight, the old ways of identifying your power were hard to shake and centre stage painful to leave. It is not all that surprising that Black nationalists still see Whites as intolerable kingpins who cling to power and command the country. They do and they don't. It is the way things look, and how things look have always been crucial for those who run the country. Rhodes, lolling in his chair with the prisoners at his feet, sums it up. That so much looks the same to so many Blacks, after a quarter-century of majority rule, is a persistent, backhanded compliment to Rhodes, the essential role-model.

Back at the Kimberley Club, I loaded my car and got ready to move on. Just beyond the front gate I found a pavement marker commemorating the spot where, at the start of the siege of Kimberley, the first Boer shell fell. At the school my uncle attended, I had seen the shelter Rhodes built for civilians during the siege. It would have sheltered only Whites. When the Boers began shelling Kimberley, the modest memorial pointed out, the first person to die had been a Black woman, whose name was not recorded.

Part 4

KNITTING SOCKS
FOR MR HITLER

17

The growing chorus of racist abuse aimed at Whites has become a feature of the times. Whether it be the self-styled 'Commander-in-Chief' of the paramilitary Economic Freedom Fighters, who offers a good line in menacing consolation when he assures his supporters that: 'We are not calling for the slaughter of White people, at least for now…' Or the lecturer in law at the University of South Africa, who declares on Facebook: 'I hate white people and [they] must go back, wherever they come from or alternatively to hell.' Or an official in South Africa's Department of Sport and Recreation, who calls for divine punishment of Whites, especially in the Cape Province, currently suffering the worse drought in decades. 'Please God,' goes the hate-monger's prayer; the drying-up dams and rivers are a gift from heaven – but to be fair, retribution in the Cape must be race-related: '…we have Black people there; choose another way of punishing White people.'

Some others, shy of singling out living beings for liquidation, hedge their bets and call for destruction of coded abstractions: 'White power', 'White capital', 'White hegemony' and even 'Whiteness' itself.

This hate-speech is shocking, and yet, in the furious reaction it provokes there is a certain *faux*-outrage. Racial venom is a very old South African trait, regrettable certainly, but it has been around for a long time. Many of the jibes and insults directed at Whites are echoes of jibes and insults once stitched into our own conversations; a linguistic orientation so natural that, more often than not, we had no idea what we were saying. We may have belonged to different language groups but we had our lingua franca, racism, and spoke it fluently. What is really surprising about the pained surprise expressed by those now on the receiving end of such crude imprecations is the surprise itself. The 'kill a White' posters and 'one settler, one bullet' jibes; the excitable Hitler groupies; all the unlovely provocations on some university campuses; these are painful but they are depressingly familiar. When I ask myself what they remind me of – it is ourselves. But this time around the abuse is coming from the other side.

There is something of the same recurring irony in the way Black firebrands pledge their troth to Hitler. Admiration for Nazi fashions goes back to long before the Boer War, when some Afrikaners took a pro-German line because Germany was an ally against Britain. The affinity was there during the First World War and, more notably, during the Second. In the thirties, when Hitler and his National Socialists won power, fervent Afrikaner right-wingers admired and emulated Nazi ideology. When the war with Germany began in 1939, signing up to fight was a free choice (for Whites) and it split the electorate. Many Afrikaner nationalists refused to enlist, preferring neutrality, and some chose to sabotage the war effort, or, as my mother put it in a homely and unlikely metaphor, 'to spend time knitting socks for Mr Hitler'. Bands of Afrikaner extremists paraded, dressed like Nazis and gave themselves names like 'Storm Hunters' and 'Grey

Shirts', and joined underground groups like the *Ossewabrand-wag* ('Oxwagon Sentinel'), dynamited bridges and railroads and attacked serving soldiers.

These right-wing Afrikaner revolutionaries were loud in their detestation of 'Jewish capital'. Their demands, as it turns out, and their prejudices, anticipated some Black radicals today, who wish to confiscate banks, appropriate farmlands and commandeer mining houses controlled by 'White monopoly capital', in which turgid phrase may be detected, once again, the unmistakable whiff of anti-Semitism. These new zealots also repudiate the vision of Oliver Tambo, as he expressed it when we talked in London long ago – of a South Africa as home to all who lived there, without regard to colour or creed. The ANC government today regards these Black ultras with the same unease as the administration of Jan Smuts felt about rebellious Afrikaners back in the forties.

But the current administration has not yet reacted in the same way as Jan Smuts, who decided these radical Afrikaners could not be allowed to wander freely and locked them up. It was to prove a fateful decision. Every ruling authority, from van Riebeeck to Verwoerd, favoured prison for those rash enough to reject the official, sacrosanct, version of paradise. When Smuts, once an Afrikaner radical himself, detained his opponents they neither forgave nor forgot, and followed his lead when they emerged from jail to become, in turn, the new rulers of South Africa.

The site chosen for internment of these Afrikaner subversives was Koffiefontein, once a promising place in the diamond fields, within easy reach of Hopetown and Kimberley. The town took its name from a spring, where the early transport riders to the diamond fields camped and brewed coffee. When diamonds were discovered in Koffiefontein, De Beers took over in the 1880s and the town soon had its own mini-version of the Kimberley

Big Hole, and a railway station. But after the Second World War Koffiefontein meant one thing only: the prison camp for home-grown Nazis and fascist Italian prisoners of war.

Driving to Koffiefontein, I was reminded again how the land-scape pretended to reveal all, to be eye-opening and honest, a sure warning always to look a little deeper. The dead-straight road from Kimberley seemed to bore into the centre of the far horizon. The sheer grandeur of the sky and the enormous expanses of veld reduced human settlements to silly dabbles on the margin of things. When Koffiefontein at last came into view, it presented a river, a bridge, a wide main street, dusty shopfronts and a giant coffee pot, the trademark of the town, suspended over a dry cement basin.

Koffiefontein's town sign

I walked over to inspect the coffee pot, and a young man, sitting on the lip of the bone-dry basin, told me that a stream of water from the spout that now and then filled the basin had been 'switched off'. When water flowed, cattle gathered on the traffic island to drink. The young man, Jakob, was lean, disconsolate and jobless, and he had been paging through a well-thumbed brochure published by the company that took over the diamond mine when De Beers sold up. Jakob had matriculated a few years before and, like half the young men in the country, he had never worked. He dreamt of a job in the diamond mine but he was not hopeful. Would I like to see the annual report?

The contrast between melancholic Koffiefontein and the gaudy shimmer of the gems paraded in the upbeat financial report was startling. There was a cruel mismatch between the optimistic pages and pictures and the sullen silence of Koffiefontein, a country town like dozens of others, where many were poor, angry and resentful and where rage erupted daily in cascades of public violence, and in femicide, homicide and domestic brutality.

'Why are you here?' Jakob wanted to know.

'To see Mussolini.'

'Who was Mussolini?'

'He was like Hitler. But he was from Italy.'

Jakob did not believe me. What on earth had Italy to do with Koffiefontein? Yet Jakob lived there and must have seen the old barracks where Italian prisoners of war were interned.

'The man with the helmet,' I said.

'Oh, Mr Dux!' said Jakob.

Jakob and I walked up the street to the old barracks, where Italian and German prisoners of war were held in the forties. A striking rendering of Mussolini, steel-helmeted, square-jawed, flanked the entrance. I understood then why Jakob knew him by

another name – alongside the portrait, painted by Italian intern-
ees, three large letters saluting the dictator: DUX.

'Tell me,' Jakob instructed.

If Jakob surprised me by knowing nothing about the man in
the steel helmet, he floored me when he told me he had never
heard of Koffiefontein's most notorious prisoner. Jakob had been
through the local public school system and emerged utterly
unprepared for anything. His was the fate of millions of kids. In
few other countries is so much public money spent on education
with so little to show for it. Of the policies of the ruling party that
may rightly be called criminal (leaving aside the AIDS denialism
of the Thabo Mbeki regime) its decades-long failure to get kids
through school heads the list.

I told Jakob the story of prisoner number 2229/42, who lived
in Hut 48, Camp 1, of the Koffiefontein Internment Camp. Along
with Italian prisoners of war, Koffiefontein also held radical Afrikaner nationalists, charged with terrorism. Most notable among
these was Balthazar Johannes Vorster, who was to become Minister of Police, Prime Minister and, finally, President of South
Africa between 1966 and 1978.

John Vorster, as he liked to be known, was interned in Koffiefontein in 1942. An unabashed Nazi sympathizer, he belonged
to the terrorist group called Oxwagon Sentinel, a name less silly
than it sounds. Vorster declared his position early on in the war
and he made no bones about his beliefs: 'We stand for Christian
Nationalism which is an ally of National Socialism. You can call
this anti-democratic principle dictatorship, if you like. In Italy it
is called Fascism, in Germany National Socialism, and in South
Africa, Christian Nationalism.'

John Vorster's imprisonment in Hut 48 was to become a badge
of honour in the White nationalist regime he went on to lead.

The camp at Koffiefontein became a place of legend, not unlike Nelson Mandela's cell block on Robben Island. There was even more to this odd pairing because the charge sheets against both prisoners were alike: Vorster and Mandela faced charges of treason and sabotage. All his life Vorster regarded himself as a freedom fighter. He considered the Boer War a smash-and-grab raid by the British Empire, determined to destroy Boer independence and capture the gold and diamond mines of Johannesburg and Kimberley. When he became Prime Minister, he was blithely unrepentant about keeping Mandela in prison. His own treatment in Koffiefontein, Vorster liked to say, had been harsher than anything Mandela had been subject to on Robben Island.

John Vorster was a lawyer by training but a thug by nature. Both roles he rather enjoyed. He came to be known as the toughest Minister of Police the country had ever seen and was caricatured wearing a policeman's helmet, carrying a truncheon, and sometimes portrayed in jackboots. The principal police station in Johannesburg, where many opponents of the apartheid regime were detained, tortured and killed, was named after him. He was, in some ways, the accidental executioner. He took over as Prime Minister when the austere ideologue Hendrik Verwoerd was assassinated. You might almost say that in the grisly pantomime of power of the apartheid decades, Verwoerd, the philosopher prince, was succeeded on stage by Vorster, the callous constable.

Vorster did at least possess a dour humour, unknown among Afrikaner leaders before him. 'Welcome to the happiest police state in the world' was the sardonic greeting he offered first-time visitors to South Africa. It was no joke. Vorster kept the giant engine of apartheid running by brute force, ameliorated from time to time by shrewd pragmatism and bushels of hypocrisy. His rule counted as the granite years, an age when those the regime could not exile, shoot or lock up, it bored to death. It was a mark of just how desperate things became that when John Vorster played golf with sycophantic celebrities, this was taken as a sign that he must be almost human.

There has been an idea put about by revisionists, with a soft spot for the old days, that apartheid was not perhaps as bad as it has been painted. In fact, it was worse than many people imagine: a system of violent repression and reaction that touched every aspect of human life from the cradle to the grave. It noted where you were born and consigned you to the place where you were to spend your life; it classified your children by skin colour and hair texture and redefined your ancestors; it decreed where you might be married or buried; and declared Blacks to be alien, hostile and primitive. John Vorster presided over a racial penitentiary where everyone not a warder was a prisoner.

Jakob listened to me as if I was telling him a fairy tale. I think he wanted to believe me but it all sounded mad. He'd been born after the apartheid years and, in a way, I envied his innocence. But I feared that knowing no history would not save him from being hurt by history.

For an answer as to why South Africa is today still such a violent place, it is to the past and to men like John Vorster that one must look. I'm not suggesting that apartheid alone was to blame for the way violence is woven into daily life in South Africa. That began long ago, as the KhoiSan people learnt to their cost. It took the arrival of the first European settlers to establish a pattern that encouraged, even demanded, the immediate resort to brute force as the normal everyday way of doing things, as a positive duty and often a pleasure. The pattern has continued to the present day.

There was not much left of the original internment camp,

though one can still make out some of the graffiti scrawled by the inmates. There was no indication of Camp 1, or Hut 48, where John Vorster was held. But his spirit lives on, and the latest youngest Black admirer of Hitler, in the Gauteng Department of Sport, Arts, Culture and Recreation, who wished to do to Whites what Hitler did to the Jews, was a brother under the skin to Balthazar Johannes Vorster, one of apartheid's chief officers and executioners. Such are the ironies, so cruel and so familiar, they may be described as truly South African.

I said goodbye to Jakob and wished him well in his hunt for a job. I took a last look at the portrait of Mr Dux, and headed out of Koffiefontein. The road runs dark as a scar, passing small termite heaps strewn across the veld, their shapes mimicking nearby hills. If Koffiefontein was a town where people remembered hardly anything, I was heading next to a nearby settlement where they forgot nothing, a place as much a shrine as a settlement, home to a coterie of believers devoted to the man whom John Vorster succeeded as Prime Minister.

In Orania, people have made memory their mission, set up monuments, collected statues and constantly reminded themselves that their destiny was to survive. They contemplated not just their superfluity in the South Africa that came into being after 1994, but their probable extinction, and took steps to resist. Their model would be the Israelites whom Moses led out of Egypt; they would gather all those faithful to the tribe, language and culture and trek into the desert. They would create for themselves what they once insisted everyone should have and live in – an ethnic enclave, what might be called an 'Afrikanerstan'. What they have made in Orania is real enough but it is also a place that feels as insubstantial as a dream. I have visited several times since it all began, and I am always faintly surprised to find it has not vanished like the morning mist.

18

'You speak good Afrikaans for a Frenchman.'

The compliment came from a man uneasy about seeing his real name in print, so I will call him Jan. On an autumn morning under a brilliant blue sky, we were sitting over a cup of coffee in the all-White Afrikaner enclave of Orania. Jan was around thirty and lived in Bloemfontein, 130 miles away. He'd been in town for a few days to test the water, and all he had seen made him keen to move to Orania.

When Jan asked me where I lived, I told him I lived in France and it drew from him the compliment on my Afrikaans. I would have explained that I went to school in Pretoria and learnt to speak the language, as everyone did, if they needed to understand the vagaries and comedies of South Africa's capital city, with its thousands of Afrikaner bureaucrats who directed all aspects of our lives. But he seemed uninterested in how it was that a Frenchman was speaking his language. France was a good place, and a republic; the Huguenots, from whom he descended, were French and, above all, France was not England.

He had been boarding with an Orania family, and liked the place mightily but for one problem.

'Not enough girls, not enough action.'

'Not enough reality, maybe?' I wondered.

He shrugged. 'Who needs reality? In Orania you don't lock your windows and won't be murdered in your bed.'

His earnest, edgy manner took me back to the sixties and seventies, when conversations quickly turned into confrontations and linguistic skirmishes. When what counted was not detail but dogma, faith not facts. Loudly repeated beliefs had been the aggressive mood music of the Verwoerd and Vorster years, and those years pressed close in Orania.

Jan was curious: 'So what do you think of us, here?'

'A lot of the time I think you're on a hiding to nothing. At other times, I'm not so sure. Orania reminds me of what I saw in ex-Yugoslavia. During the wars of the nineties, when the country split into tribal reservations, ethnic islands.'

Jan was pleased. 'They got homelands: Serbs, Croats, Bosnians and so on. Right? That's apartheid, isn't it, hey?'

I agreed that the dissolution of Yugoslavia into ethnic enclaves looked rather like the old South Africa patchwork of tribal 'homelands'. Was that what he wanted for Orania?

'We want what everyone has the right to ask for,' said Jan. 'To choose your own kind, your own family. Look at what happened in Yugoslavia, and you'd know that Dr Verwoerd was right. Mixed populations don't work. India split from Pakistan. Serbs from Croats. Czechs from Slovaks. You can't force folks to mix.'

I had been visiting Orania ever since its founder, Carel Boshoff, bought in 1991 an abandoned settlement of pre-fabricated houses near the Orange River that had once housed workers on an irrigation project. On 445 hectares of unwanted semi-desert in the Northern Cape, he hoped to establish a forward base to preserve the White Afrikaner tribe from approaching extinction. It seemed a wacky idea, like sending ill-equipped astronauts to some far-off planet. But what looked like empty veld held powerful symbolic associations. The area had seen much fighting during the Boer War. Evidence was constantly turning up: spent cartridges, gin bottles, coins, rusted bully-beef cans and cap badges and buttons of British regiments. And it was close to what remained of the concentration camp at Orange River Station.

Boshoff dreamt of a homeland where the culture, faith and language of the Afrikaner *volk* would be preserved. The idea assumed you might redeem the past by deft, retrospective surgery, slicing off bad bits, sewing on others, and serving it up as the future. Orania was separated from the new South Africa yet retained the umbilical link to the old White South Africa envisaged by Hendrik Verwoerd. The connection was not stressed but it was plain enough in the list of public holidays, some imported directly from notable anniversaries in the old South Africa, and pointedly embellished. There were coded messages behind the high and holy days listed in the Orania calendar, which initiates would understand without further prompting.

27 February: Majuba Day *(The day the Boers defeated the British at Majuba)*

6 April: Founders' Day *(Orania was born)*

31 May: Bitter-Ender Day *(Remembering those Boer fighters who resisted to the end the British usurper)*

14 August: Language Day *(The miracle of Afrikaans commemorated)*

10 October: Heroes' Day *(Saluting the martyrs who died for the volk)*

16 December: The Day of the Oath *(The day the Boers defeated the Zulus in the Battle of Blood River)*

Dr Hendrik Verwoerd, Orania

Although Orania was much mocked and expected to fail, it has survived. The numbers have never been large – around 1,400 at the last count – but it boasts a hospital, a couple of very good schools, a growing interest in green energy. It exports its crop of pecan nuts to China and it has welcomed the digital age with enthusiasm. In recent years it has added a supermarket, hotels and guesthouses. It even has a currency of its own, the Ora.

Orania won unexpected support when the ANC came to power. Nelson Mandela gave the place a bemused blessing when he took tea with the widow of Hendrik Verwoerd, who had settled in the town and became the living representative of his emblematic presence that hovers over Orania. President Jacob Zuma also visited and seemed quite impressed. Even Julius Malema, the Hugo Chavez lookalike in red beret, admired the way Afrikaners co-operated in Orania. These seemed like sensible reactions: after all, a little gathering of loyalists mounting a rearguard action against history presented no great danger to anyone, except perhaps themselves.

But while the ANC government promised to consider the dream of an Afrikaner homeland, that had always seemed unlikely. When Afrikaner nationalists ran South Africa, they did as much damage to the word 'homeland' as the Nazis once did to 'fatherland'. In the meantime, left alone and mostly ignored, Orania was getting on with the work of building a haven to which Afrikaners could retire, or retreat, if it became essential.

Carel Boshoff once explained to me his feelings about racial superiority: 'I'm opposed to White rule, I'm opposed to anyone ruling anyone else.'

He wanted the people of Orania to earn their independence. Whites would work the fields, swab out the privies, slave and sweat to survive. Blacks were not expressly excluded but Orania was run like a private club and those who wished to settle there had to pass muster before a selection committee. Citizens of Orania would speak Afrikaans and subscribe to his vision of the Christian Protestant Afrikaner nation.

This sweet reasonableness chimed rather awkwardly with Boshoff's history. He had once been a leader of the *Broederbond*, literally 'Band of Brothers', a secret society that had policed and protected the apartheid government right to the end. The Bond denounced and destroyed those who dissented or deviated from the policies of rigid racial separation and thus betrayed the divine mission of the Afrikaner *volk*, which was to spread the light of White Western civilization in darkest Africa.

Carel Boshoff had been a missionary in the tribal reservations, at a time when minute degrees of racial separation was more than a policy, it was the sign of piety. He further cemented his connection to the one true faith by marrying the daughter of

Hendrik Verwoerd. His relationship with the ideological father of systematic segregation was the key to understanding why he founded Orania. Non-racialism and multiculturalism might be admirable ideas but would never work. When a Black national-ist government took power, it would do what White Afrikaner nationalists had done, and favour its own.

It was a view at once familiar and dispiriting because so very South African; a destiny always defined by race, and skin colour, always announcing a revolutionary future that looked, on exam-ination, very like a reactionary and racist past. Your side had always to be either top of the heap or on the skids. The eternal recurrence dogged and damned every single new set of rulers. Jan van Riebeeck and his Dutch colonists wanted the indigenous people of the Cape to be enslaved, or 'educated', to meet the desires of their new masters. Exuberant imperialists like Lord Alfred Milner and Cecil Rhodes believed the 'British race' was superior to all others. Verwoerd, and those like him, designated Blacks as hewers of wood and drawers of water. With each new regime absolute power corrupted absolutely, as Acton predicted, but it also turned the powerful into bigots and bores. One sees something of the same malaise beginning to infect Black nation-alists of the ANC, who chase votes by castigating Whites, now the increasingly useful whipping boys for the failings of the present regime.

It once seemed that the pattern might be broken when Mandela was released from prison and a new democratic administration arrived. For a moment, Whites felt that by relinquishing power to the Black majority they had broken free of the past and arrived at that unlikely place, the present. Even those who had run the old system, as well as those Whites (and there were lots of them) who gained from it, felt liberated by the change. The feeling of hope flourished even more when, although everything had changed, it began to look as though everything would continue as before. There would be no pain, it was all gain, and the guys who once took charge of your gardens were now going to do the work of government. In a phrase: the henchmen of the apartheid regime got amnesty and everyone else got amnesia.

But of late, disillusion has set in and even the name of Mandela has been weaponized. Those who bandy his name about are dubbed sell-outs or closet racists by Black nationalists. Mandela, it is said, was old and far too kind; he cut a deal with the old apartheid bosses that left the poor even poorer and Blacks as much as ever at the mercy of the White oppressors who own, run and control the country. The more often Whites invoke the name of Mandela, as a mantra and lucky charm, the more it angers radical Blacks. The result has been the resumption of ancient hostilities. The war-cries of each side would have pleased Dr Verwoerd and Dr Boshoff who said ethnic groups would never rub along – they would only rub each other out.

Orania has the largest collection anywhere of statues of my old neighbour, Hendrik Verwoerd, and other political heroes, and these have been placed out of doors. That seems a miscalculation because they are dwarfed by the magnificence of the landscape. When Jan and I walked over to inspect them, I felt, as I always do when I see them, that far from inspiring respect, they inspire a certain pity. We stopped at a less than life-size Verwoerd, gazing forlornly into the middle distance, lost under the huge sky. The sculptor had captured something of his earnest, dreamy air but none of the menace. What you noticed about Verwoerd in the flesh was his rubicund face, his wave of milk-white hair, his smile that came and went, which may have hinted at a gentle, even a jolly, man – until you looked into his blue eyes and saw the ice. He was an alarming mix of ascetic, autocrat and intellectual whom even his cabinet members feared, and they confessed he reduced them to trembling obedience. After he survived the first attempt on his life, his followers were even more convinced of his super-human qualities.

But when we came face to face with him in the open veld, he looked sadly lost.

Jan agreed: 'Yes, even Mandela said he was rather small.'

But he had no doubts about the importance of Verwoerd to the tribe.

'He never forgot his own people. When de Klerk and Mandela sat down together, de Klerk, he betrayed his own people. Kicked us into touch. The Black fat cats do the same to theirs.'

There are those who ask if Verwoerd can be called a Nazi – of the sort John Vorster certainly was. Verwoerd's academic field was psychology and he may have been influenced, as a student in Germany in the late twenties, by his exposure to contempo-rary theories of eugenics. The survival of the Whites in Africa depended, he believed, on 'separate development'. Only by holding true to racial purity, Protestant spirituality and West-ern Christian civilization would the White Afrikaner survive. Verwoerd also displayed a lively anti-Semitism that would have pleased the Hitler-loving functionary from the Gauteng Depart-ment of Sport, Arts, Culture and Recreation.

In Orania's version of Verwoerd, he is a hero for fighting to win for the Afrikaner people what he freely granted to other groups: a language, a culture and an independent homeland. His policy of almost manic segregation was called various names like 'parallel freedoms' and 'self-determination' but these were euphemisms at best and the name that stuck was one he never used: 'apartheid'.

I think the really interesting thing about Hendrik Verwoerd is that he was not who he said he was, and his belief that he was the champion of the Afrikaner people, who would survive only if he walled them off from the world, was shot through with sentimentality and sheer nonsense.

For a start, Verwoerd was not an Afrikaner. He was born in the Netherlands to Lutheran parents and it is likely that young Hendrik's first language was not Dutch but German. His parents emigrated to South Africa in 1903 and spent time in Cape Town before moving to Rhodesia, where they settled in Bulawayo. The boy was enrolled in a very British college, Milton School, under the anglicized name of Harold Ferwood. Perhaps his parents were hedging their bets about which country they would eventually choose to live in. Milton School had no connection with the great poet, but took its name from Rhodes' crony, Sir William Milton, Administrator of Rhodesia, and the man behind Rhodes' decision to bar the Coloured fast-bowler, Krom Hendricks, from playing for his country. A brilliant student, the young Verwoerd, in his anglicized version, won the Beit Scholarship, funded by another of Rhodes' cronies, and took first prize in English in all Rhodesia.

It was when the family returned to South Africa, some years later, that young Verwoerd, with all the enthusiasm of a convert, gave himself to the Afrikaner cause, which he promoted and moulded with icy ferocity for the rest of his life. He excelled at his South African university and in later studies in Germany, the Netherlands and America. White Afrikaner nationalism (there was more than one kind of Afrikaner) was his passion and in Johannesburg he edited the party newspaper, a propaganda sheet of virulent xenophobia. That was at the time I lived a few streets away from him, and when we walked past his house, my Black nanny, Georgie, offered his warning about 'bad *muti*', the misfortune that he felt our neighbour portended. It was a horribly accurate prediction.

The rise and rise of this Dutch immigrant and his peculiar idea of building a country made up of many different sorts of people, by locking each group into the prison of its skin, was a catastrophe for South Africa. The effects of his policies were set in concrete, and towns, villages and cities were carved up, quite literally, into ethnic enclaves. His obsession with the nuances of skin colour ranged from the inane to the insane; from allowing Coloured ushers in cinemas to show patrons to their seats as long as they did not lift their eyes to the screen, to the death and exile of opponents.

Chief among exhibits in the museum in Orania are the clothes Dr Verwoerd was wearing on the day he was stabbed to death in Parliament, just after 2 o'clock, on 6 September 1966. It was an event of such dramatic irony that only Shakespeare could have done it justice: the assassination of an all-powerful leader, on the floor of Parliament, by a half-mad, half-White, half-Greek messenger who believed he took orders from a giant tapeworm in his stomach. Or if you used the racially biased terms Verwoerd had lived and died by, it was the murder of an immigrant of Dutch heritage, and therefore 'White', by another immigrant, of Greek and Mozambican extraction, and thus 'Coloured'. Or perhaps it was, in those strange times, an entirely normal South African assassination.

Among the oddest memorials in the veld of Orania are a group of truncated columns, pillars with their heads sliced off. They were commissioned to stand on a hill in Johannesburg, to remember the gallantry of the Irish volunteers, led by John MacBride, who fought beside the Boers. My mother took me to see the memorial when it was first erected. She took pride in her Irish republican roots, saw MacBride as a great romantic hero, not for his fighting ability but because he married Maude Gonne, the lost love of William Butler Yeats. I once pointed out to her that the marriage didn't last long, and there had been rumours later that Iseult, Maud Gonne's daughter by an earlier liaison, may have been the victim of her stepfather's advances. My mother would have none of it. John MacBride had fought for Kruger; he had been executed for his part in leading the Easter Rising in Dublin in 1916. That was more than you could say for Willie Yeats, who had never converted to Catholicism, as did Maude Gonne, and had not died for his country. 'That poor, brave man,' she would say to me, 'fought for freedom and died a martyr.' And she'd quote from Synge's *Playboy of the Western World*: 'fighting bloody wars for Kruger and the freedom of the Boers'.

The Irish monument was brought to Orania under the same shadowy circumstances as Cecil Rhodes was moved from Mafeking to the Kimberley Club. And for much the same political reasons, to save a symbol deemed sacred from those who wish to wipe away history. Another skirmish in the sad and silly, but sometimes deadly serious, statue wars.

My view of Orania has changed over time. To begin with I pictured it as a type of Boer kibbutz where, in the last instance, Afrikaners might return and live in safety. Up until now, not many Afrikaners have heeded the call. But were the threats of pogroms and forced removals of Whites to grow louder, that might change.

'It's not really a problem that only a few people want to move to Orania,' said Jan. 'The idea is to give Afrikaners a haven where they can come, if they need to do, one day. It's rather like Israel.'

Orania, at least for the moment, lacks the tragic seriousness of Israel, which offers a homeland to a people once almost wiped out. If Orania resembles anywhere, it is Matjiesfontein, where the Scotsman Jimmy Logan built an English village in the African desert, replete with pubs, cottages, Anglican appurtenances and a cricket pitch. There has always been something surreal about Orania. As if at any moment the director might bring down the curtain, the costumes be returned to the wardrobe and the actors remove their make-up. Among its props are Orania's statues. Assembled in the veld, under an enormous sky, stand images of former – and for many South Africans, half-forgotten – nationalist prime ministers, like D.F. Malan and Hans Strydom, ardent champions of racial segregation and now resident in a retirement home for fallen idols.

When not in costume, the citizens of Orania, like anyone else, went out shopping at the supermarket, surfed the internet or watched a rugby match being played in the 'new' South Africa, which must feel like the country next door. What makes Orania so strange is the way it mimicked the real world without wishing to have anything at all to do with that hybrid, pagan place. Citizens were computer friendly, embraced the world-wide web, 3D printers and solar panels and watched the latest movies. One of the popular but improbable DVDs renting well to solidly Afrikaans viewers was a very English film, Alan Bennett's *Lady in the Van*.

As we sat in companionable silence, Jan handed me a copy of a local newspaper that hewed closely to the Oranian orthodoxy in defending Verwoerd. Far from being the father of apartheid, the editor argued, he merely followed the lead given by the British who, in 1809, promulgated the Cape Native Pass Laws, which obliged non-White people to carry the hated passbook. Then, in

1894, came Rhodes' refusal to allow a Coloured cricketer to play against England. In 1913, the British administration introduced the Native Land Act, which prohibited Black Africans from owning land. Soon afterwards, lawmakers in the thoroughly British province of Natal prohibited sexual relations between the races. And all of this happened, the editorialist trumpeted, long before the word 'apartheid' was ever coined.

'You see, we weren't the first,' Jan said.

Again I heard the old music, the old songs, used to justify the way things were in the granite years of White rule.

'Maybe not. But you turned it into a religion.'

Jan said nothing but I felt silly that I'd joined in the chorus, because I had the feeling Jan rather liked the notion of tribal purity as a form of faith.

Part 5

THE WAR OF
MANDELA'S EAR

19

Johannesburg has always been an unreal city. Those of us who were born and lived on what we simply called 'The Reef' knew that our lives and livelihoods depended on what lay buried miles beneath our feet. And those who forgot were reminded by the occasional earth tremors and the mine dumps, those mountains of yellow dirt piled up around the city by human termites who slaved underground to extract the rock in which so much gold was locked.

Randolph Churchill, on a visit to Johannesburg soon after gold was discovered in 1886, surveyed the seething mining camp and saw 'folly and fraud'. Directors and managers of the mines knew next to nothing about management or mining, Churchill said bluntly. In fact, they never needed to do so. In what was then called Ferreira's Camp, all anyone needed to know was that treasure lay underfoot; everything, and everyone else, could be bought.

Cecil Rhodes, fresh from the Kimberley diamond fields, took one look at the tented dusty shambles of Ferreira's Camp and decided that what the town wanted was a decent club. And so, in 1886, he and some fellow magnates identified a patch of land and Rhodes approved: 'This corner will do for the club.' The Rand Club was never more interesting than in its earliest years. A

The Rand Club, Johannesburg

single-storey building, with the bar usefully near the front door, where the favourite whisky was 'Smugglers Brand', served by an Indian barman. The club stood among booze-soaked saloons, ever-busy brothels and the Bourse where there took place the closest thing Johannesburg had, and has ever had, to religious worship: the daily observance of share prices. The modest, original Rand Club was replaced a few times with posher edifices and what stands today is a grandiose imperial bunker, rebuilt soon after the Boer War.

This current club is another temple dedicated to the religion of Rhodes. It features a larger than life statue, reminiscent of the one smuggled from Mafeking to the Kimberley Club. The Rand Club Rhodes stands hat in hand, his free hand raised as if hailing a cab. The holy of holies was the Rhodes Room, a collection of portraits, pictures and relics commemorating the founder.

*

I was first made aware of the Rand Club in the sixties, when I was a student at the University of the Witwatersrand. I'd walk past the place each day on my way to read books, hidden deep in the cellars of the nearby public library. I was required to produce written permission from my professor before I might approach the works of Marx, or the intriguing writing of young Black writers who had worked for *Drum* magazine, until dispersed and banished to distant parts of the world where too many died from drink or despair. I'd look up at the heavy grey hulk and wonder which room had been used by the men plotting the Jameson Raid. And from which windows had members opened fire on demonstrators besieging the club in the first great mining strike of 1913. The miners had been led by Mary Fitzgerald, or 'Pick-handle Mary', named for her weapon of choice.

Years later, I was occasionally invited to lunch at the Rand Club by a rich stockbroker and met men who made the money that ran the city – bankers, brokers, property moguls and mining chiefs. No women were admitted until the early nineties and men had to be over thirty-five – perhaps in the forlorn hope that by then they might have a degree of gravitas. But this was an uphill struggle because Johannesburg remained a mining camp where the axiom of 'anything goes' was less a warning than the first commandment. Gold never led to gravitas, and the more of one you had, the less of the other. Members were very often energetic vagabonds, fortune hunters and con artists from around the world who would stop at nothing to get their hands on the loot buried beneath their feet.

Perhaps that's why the club, in its third iteration, revelled in the stilted, stultified, mock-grandeur of its furnishings: marble pillars, colonnades, crystal chandeliers, Persian carpets, stained-glass windows, the great staircase that wafted members upwards, the forests of wood that went to make the banisters, the bar and the billiard room. The Annigoni portrait of Queen Elizabeth smiled sedately down on the men heading for the Long Bar and Queen Victoria commanded the dining room. Such reassuring totems were intermingled with conventional references to 'Africa' as the sort of place where gentlemen went for a little hunting, shooting and fishing and where Black chaps did the work. Much more recently, portraits of Nelson Mandela and Thabo Mbeki were added. They always looked like afterthoughts, coming too little and too late to suggest that the Rand Club had changed its ways.

The drinkers at the legendary Long Bar, over thirty metres of it, gave off waves of well-fed self-satisfaction. They had, I suppose, at least one advantage; they were alive, or at least they were alive by comparison with the stuffed heads of giraffes, springbok, buffalo and warthogs staring down from the walls. These trophies were as dead as the authors of the elderly and seldom-read books on the shelves of the library. When I think back to those afternoon men, I have the impression of sleepwalkers, or the inhabitants of some particular dream world where reality never penetrated. Wafted each morning in a staff car to their offices in one of the great mining houses, or the stock exchange nearby. After work, after customary drinks at the club, wafted home to the genial northern suburbs, the gate opened by a Black gardener, dinner cooked by a Black maid, children bathed by a Black nanny and tea served in bed the next morning by another Black servant. And this was not in the least exceptional; it was simply the way things were. Over the heads of the sleek, pink and prosperous drinkers of the Long Bar there hung an air of invincible smugness, an unshakeable, never-questioned assumption that this was the way life must be, and deserved to be.

The Rand Club closed its doors in 2015 and will not open again in its old form. A helpful friend offered to let me in for one last time and we walked through the solitary shuttered rooms. Like its Kimberley counterpart, the Rand Club was once situated right in the best part of town but now it was marooned, beached, deserted, and for reasons that are very South African. What had been the centre of 'town' decided one day to pack its bags and leave. Jo'burg is a town that moved out of town, fled northwards to more salubrious suburbs where moneyed Jo'burg now resides. It wasn't social obsolescence that killed the Rand Club, it was White flight that did it. The bankers and lawyers and stockbrokers departed and left behind this great neo-classical nonsense to find another use for itself or another life in a city that some now called an African metropolis and others called a crime-ridden mess. Not that change would really harm Johannesburg because change has been what made it the greatest African city south of Cairo. It was changing madly, wildly, even when its robber barons, its 'gold bugs' and Randlords, got above themselves and started wearing fancy suits and exuding the ponderous respectability that hung over the drinkers gathered around the curve of the Long Bar on those long-ago afternoons.'I always used to think,' said my friend, who had been a member for practically forever, 'that members were people who, in any other society, would either have been out of a job or in jail.' I got the impression that they didn't have the slightest idea of where they were.'

The club was there to help you pretend that you lived some-where other than Africa. And, of course, so you did. Jo'burg lends itself to make-believe, to masquerade, it has always been torn down and built again. That's how it was when I was growing up and nothing much has changed. This constant alteration, this deceptiveness, is not surprising in a town whose entire point and purpose always lay hidden deep underground where, in hellish heat, men lay on their backs in narrow tunnels and chiselled out chunks of rock veined with gold. For a very large city it was always eerily impermanent, a place built, as people said, 'on spec'. Gold mines were founded, land bought and lives lived – 'on spec'. In a city so easy with fiction and fantasy, the changes now taking place in Johannesburg, where it was altering from a Chicago lookalike to an all-African city with an edgy vitality, and often menacing undercurrents, was more of the shape-shifting Jo'burg does so well.

The surface itself was pretty misleading. No one lived in the central city and what we once simply called 'town' was where people worked. Its skyscrapers were filled with banks, department stores, cinemas and offices. But by five in the afternoon, everyone fled the place and left Jo'burg largely empty. Whites went home to their suburbs, Blacks to their townships, and you sometimes felt you could have folded up the city, put it away for the night and hardly anyone would have noticed.

Then again, Jo'burg has a great gift for improvisation and survival, with no regard for architectural niceties. It has been pulled apart and rebuilt almost every decade. This is a town that erected a drive-in cinema on the summit of one of its celebrated mine dumps. Perhaps, as some hope, the Rand Club may reinvent itself: as a boutique hotel, a venue for fashion shows or publicity events. It may be so; but the Rand Club in its essence, in what it stood for and what it meant, is beyond revival. The vision that inspired it is now as widely detested as the name of Rhodes himself. What would a new generation of visitors make of its mementos, portraits, associations, relics and anniversaries? Who would be bold enough to explain why this stolid edifice was once sacred to a vanished cult that worshipped preposterous gods?

*

As I left the club I spotted two small busts: one of Mahatma Gandhi and the other of Paul Kruger. The stubborn Boer Moses and the Hindu Agitator were too important to be ignored, hence suitably small versions had been admitted and positioned so that they would not attract attention. It was another sign of the disparate universes in which South Africans once lived – and still do. Contemporary feelings about these men were as revealing as they were different. Paul Kruger was admired by those who praised his courage and excoriated by those who considered him an anachronistic Boer who detested Blacks. Gandhi was revered by some as a champion of racial justice – but was seen very differently by others.

Walking from the club, I recognized streets, squares, familiar landmarks, although these had new names and other meanings. The new African metropolis in the making was very different to the city I knew, and in one crucial way: people were living there now. That meant the return of a feature long gone from the old, mostly White, city. Near the Rand Club I saw hawkers selling everything from fresh fruit to bootleg cigarettes, hairpieces and soft drinks. Often, they piled their goods on small carts. After all those years in exile, the café de move-on was back and this time its gypsy days were done. It was there to stay.

There is another, very much larger statue of Gandhi not far from the Rand Club. This presents him as an angular, graceful figure, two and a half metres high, dressed in lawyer's robes, cast in bronze, standing in what is now called Gandhi Square. It's an entirely appropriate memorial. Gandhi lived for two decades in South Africa and practised as a lawyer. He knew the place and understood how it worked and what he discovered appalled him.

When he arrived from England, a newly qualified barrister, he quickly found out that the Whites regarded him as hopelessly inferior. It awoke him to South Africa's unique form of racial lunacy; he opposed it mightily and that struggle changed him forever.

But if Gandhi may be described as pro-Indian, he was certainly not pro-Black. On the contrary, he objected fiercely to the way Indians were treated as second-class citizens, and deplored the fact that they were obliged to live alongside Black Africans in segregated locations. When Gandhi was locked up with Black prisoners in the same cells, he protested that 'native prisoners are only one degree removed from the animal'. There are times, reading Gandhi on race and colour, when his views chime with those who designed the apartheid handbook.

Does this mean that Gandhi was a racist? Certainly, there are Blacks who think so, and who regard his views on Africans as not far removed from those of Rhodes. This memory was in the minds of those who assailed the statue in Gandhi Square, shortly before my visit.

Those who wish to sign up Gandhi to the anti-apartheid cause must perform a delicate balancing act if they wish to square racial customs of times past with political proprieties today. When the veil slips the hypocrisy on view is not a pretty sight. The South African Communist Party, at present a subservient, even slavish, element of the ruling coalition led by the ANC, does not show up very well in this dance of the veils. The distaste of the Communist Party for Black Africans was also very pointed. The slogan under which striking miners marched on the Rand Club in 1922 was: 'Workers of the World Unite and Fight for a White South Africa'. Many years later, Communists ashamed by the racialist tone of that slogan have argued it was not as bad as it sounded, that it was

Vandalized statue of Gandhi, Johannesburg

really a signal of support for White working-class miners, cruelly exploited by the rich White capitalists, sipping champagne at the Long Bar of the Rand Club. But then, in the immortal words of Mandy Rice-Davies, 'They would, wouldn't they?'

When I walked from the Rand Club to see the defaced statue of Gandhi, traces of the white paint flung at the statue still showed on the base. Reports of the attack were revealing. The attackers had driven up to the statue, spattered the figure and its plaque on which Gandhi's time in Jo'burg is commemorated and strung up a banner reading: 'Racist Gandhi Must Fall'.

Three jobless men, sitting patiently on the step beneath the statue, told me they had seen it happen.

'One guy, he had his can of paint and threw it at the statue – here.' He pointed to the plinth. 'And then another guy, he took the paint can and started climbing up the statue, like he wanted to throw white paint on the face, on the head. That's when the cops got him and took him away.'

The assailants, it was reported, were wearing ANC caps. The organization quickly denied they were members and the man the police nabbed was charged with malicious damage to property. But the notion that Gandhi was no friend to Africans was repeated by the men who had witnessed the attack.

'Indians, they didn't like us,' they said. 'Still don't.'

Behind them, a large advertisement celebrated a famous brand of local beer: 'It all comes together with a Castle', it read. This line had all the resounding vacuity of an election poster. Nothing could be less South African than this sound-good slogan. Things hardly ever came together; what they invariably did was to fly apart.

Gandhi's enthusiastic embrace of a separate development for Indians has continued to embarrass Black commentators, who argue in his defence that he was a man of his time and should not be judged too harshly. The same exculpatory line is not taken about Cecil John Rhodes. There is a vital difference: Gandhi was resolute in fighting what he regarded as the outrageous racism of the White authorities, who degraded the Indian minority in South Africa. Coming face to face with the grotesque vulgarity of White superiority, when he was thrown off the train in Natal, changed the way Gandhi thought about power, about those who wielded it and those who suffered under its sway. Rhodes, by contrast, was so sure of his near-divinity and of the imperial mission of what he called his 'race' that nothing ever altered his sense of ineffable superiority.

Even so, if the rich, smooth afternoon men at the Long Bar of the Rand Club may be called Rhodes' children, then I prefer the *pater familias* to his pink and pampered brood. Rhodes stood for something and the ferocity of the detestation many now feel for him is a measure of how profoundly he affected the life and times of the entire country, and still does. Whatever his intentions may have been when he established the Rhodes Scholarships that sent bright kids from all over the British Empire and, later, from across the Commonwealth to Oxford, his money and his scholarships changed lives. Others made fortunes from gold and diamonds, the mining magnates and corporate captains of Johannesburg and Kimberley, but left nothing behind. No libraries, hospitals, opera houses, art museums or colleges carry their names. The one university that commemorates a mining magnate is named for Cecil Rhodes.

20

Much as Whites are shifted further and further from the centres of power they once occupied, so too do they retreat from the centres of towns and cities. In Johannesburg, many now live in walled and gated estates, when they can afford it. Poorer Whites are to be seen as beggars on street corners and in shanty towns, caravan parks and squatter camps. What makes White informal settlements, as they are politely called, more noticeable is precisely because Whites live in them. Millions of Black South Africans live in shacks and they do so with a panache and a lack of complaint that have long astonished visitors. But it is White poverty that catches the eye and makes news.

My friends, whom I'll call Marie and Denys, manage to keep their very small shack fairly clean, in a shanty town outside Krugersdorp, north-west of Johannesburg. She is tiny and wears a deep purple tinge to her grey hair; her husband is as round as a soccer ball and his pronounced limp gives him a jigging gait, more bounce than walk. Years back Marie worked as a clerk in the old Johannesburg Council and Denys was an odd-job man until he injured his back and could not work any longer. They have her small pension but otherwise no money comes in. They have chosen to live in a mixed Black and White settlement rather than 'exist like gypsies', moving from place to place.

When they heard of my interest in defaced statues they took me to see those in their town. First up was J.G. Strydom, sometimes known as 'The Lion of the North' and one of the most committed designers of rigid racial segregation.

'He was covered in red paint from head to toe,' said Marie.

Looking closely at the bust of the former prime minister, I could see the traces of red. It was a most curious monument: he seemed to rise out of a cairn of closely packed stones rather like a conjurer's assistant materializing from a magic box.

'They wrote rude words on him,' said Marie.

'They painted "Fuck the Boer",' said Denys.

Next, they took me to the statue of Paul Kruger, who stands stiffly on a flat-topped pyramid, hat in hand.

'They did him in red too,' said Marie.

'And painted the same words on him,' added Denys.

'We think it was that effing lot who did it,' said Marie. 'They used a lot of red. They use a lot of red with everything.'

Prime Minister J.G. Strydom, Krugersdorp

She was referring to the love affair the Economic Freedom Fighters, led by Julius Malema, have for the colour: red hard hats, red overalls and red politics.

'Except Mao's little red book,' I said to Marie.

She smiled. 'I'm sure they are working on that.'

Marie and Denys are poor Whites now, and say as much. The term has a special resonance in South Africa where, before and after the Second World War, White Afrikaner nationalists won the crucial election of 1948 by promising to lift 'poor Whites' out of their penury. The figure of Strydom was not placed next to that of Kruger by chance: the true believers in apartheid traced a mystical line from Kruger, the father of Boer independence, to Strydom, 'The Lion of the North', who worked tirelessly to ramp up the pervasive but still messy mix of races he found when he became Prime Minister, into systematic, rock-solid segregation as a way of relieving the plight of 'poor Whites'.

The poor Whites are back again, living in backyards, shanty towns and slums. But the supremacists who once ran the country have vanished into the woodwork, or retreated to the far-right reaches of the internet, and, besides, impoverished Whites are vastly outnumbered by even poorer Blacks. Looking at the blushing figure of J.G. Strydom, I could see why Marie laughed. How does a splash of paint on a long-dead populist help anyone – when so many have no jobs and little hope, while those who run the country live high on the hog?

'Why shoot a dead lion?' Denys asked.

'Some people even lived in a graveyard,' said Marie. 'It is not respectful to invade a cemetery.'

The cemetery that Marie mentioned had been home to a group of White squatters who took it over until evicted by the town council. The point about the group in the graveyard was that the squatters were all White and not mixed, as they were in Denys and Marie's settlement.

'I am at home here.' Marie waved a hand at the wooden shacks, a duvet drying in the sun, the garbage, the occasional satellite dishes sprouting like mushrooms on tiny roofs. 'We're happy where we live. Blacks are friends. We're all just people here.'

'Some of us,' said Denys.

Marie nodded. 'At least, no one steals from us.'

'What's to steal?' said Denys.

And they both laughed.

Not far away from Denys and Marie's Black and White shanty town is Sterkfontein, a mental institution for the criminally insane and a name synonymous with madness, unhappiness and death. 'Go on behaving as you do and you'll end up in Sterkfontein,' the good Christian Brothers would warn recalcitrant students at my old school. It was to Sterkfontein that Dimitri Tsafendas was taken, after he had stabbed to death Hendrik Verwoerd.

I wonder what Georgie would have made of the killing of our neighbour. Would he have considered how one very odd individual may turn out to be the grotesque reflection of another? Would he have been alarmed or amused by the eerie similarity between Dimitri Tsafendas, a Greek immigrant of mixed race, obsessed by what he believed to be a giant, talking tapeworm in his gut that gave him orders; and Hendrik Verwoerd, a Dutch immigrant, consumed by his mission to keep the tribe from contamination, and who took his orders from the Almighty?

What would not have surprised Georgie was that Tsafendas ended up here, locked in Sterkfontein mental hospital until he died and was buried in an unmarked grave in the hospital grounds. Hendrik Verwoerd was buried in Heroes' Acre, in Pretoria, before a crowd of a quarter of a million, kept carefully segregated throughout the ceremony. Both men were subject to dangerous and deadly delusions, but while Verwoerd got to run the country, Tsafendas got life in Sterkfontein. Most likely Georgie would have known that we lived in a world so unhinged that its grotesqueries were simply the way things were, a series of vacuum chambers, or separate, sealed-off universes that might have felt strangely connected, being side by side, but bore absolutely no relation to each other.

Not far from Sterkfontein Hospital are Sterkfontein Caves, a place that calls itself 'The Cradle of Human Kind'. The sonorous title rings strangely in a country often inhuman and frequently unkind. Sterkfontein was famous for the great discoveries of early hominids made by palaeontologists like Robert Broom, Raymond Dart and Philip Tobias and it has become a popular destination for foreign visitors, if not for the locals.

Robert Broom and Mrs Ples, Cradle of Mankind, Sterkfontein Caves

In South Africa enthusiasm for our prehistoric heritage is relatively new and still rather muted, and this has to do with the way things were. There are those who do not accept the idea that humans evolved from apes. There is the further problem that, under the old regime, all history was alarming unless well policed. As little history as possible was taught and then only when heavily slanted to serve official apartheid ideology. Looking back to your antecedents was ill-advised and sometimes dangerous. You did not want to know who your grandfather might have slept with in case that liaison involved the wrong kind of 'blood', or skin colour, because such revelations could destroy a life and a career. One of the nightmares that plagued the dreams of our former rulers was waking up one morning to discover that your family was 'White' but not quite White enough. When looking back even a few generations was so scary no one did so voluntarily, the notion of looking back millions of years made everyone rather queasy. The essence of much life in this country has been not about what you wished to find out but how much you were able to hide.

At the entrance to the caves there is one of my favourite statues: it shows a man who might, at first glance, be Hamlet cradling the skull of poor Yorick. This is a bust of the palaeontologist Robert Broom, and he is shown examining the skull of a very early hominid, *Austrolopithecus africanus*, known as Mrs Ples. Broom discovered her in Sterkfontein in 1947 and she was, according to the most recent estimates, probably around two and a half million years old. Broom called her *Plesianthropus transvaalensis*, which simply means 'a near Transvaaler', after the old name of the province where she was discovered, and although the Transvaal has vanished into history and is now known as Gauteng, the skull of Mrs Ples remains in Sterkfontein, in the arms of her finder.

The forehead of Mrs Ples has been polished by thousands of hands and so has Robert Broom's face. Legend has it that to touch his nose brings luck and to stroke his right hand brings wisdom. Broom was not African; he came from Scotland, and so the statue represents not only a great scientist with his fieldwork to hand – what you see is a European with an African in his arms. What is even more pleasing is that Robert Broom and Mrs Ples have not been attacked or damaged but caressed and revered rather than carted away.

The embrace of Professor Broom and Mrs Ples is especially appealing because it is so gentle. Nothing could be further from the normal way of life in these parts. South Africa resounds with anger and South Africans are a traumatized people. Apartheid replaced compassion and civility with fear and loathing. And this was never seen as aberrant behaviour; the system required it – brutality was enforced, hate encouraged, violence applauded and, it must be said, even enjoyed. Apartheid may have gone but not the violence it engendered. It is as if, in the wish to overthrow a hate-filled past, people are now prepared to do away with each other.

The words heard most often – whether in shanty towns, cities or suburbs – are 'safety', 'security', 'peace'. As result of, perhaps compounded by, their own sense of their increasing vulnerability and redundancy, there has been a constant flight from the formerly Whites-only suburbs into walled and gated estates on the city fringes, bounded by tall walls and electric fences. Such citadels sell themselves as the answer to the Jo'burger's prayer: 'Lord grant me a life in a safe place, where no bullets fly and hijackers fear to tread.' The message reaches across the racial divide. The gunman who wants your car (every thirty minutes another vehicle is hijacked) or the burglar in the bedroom do not discriminate between White and Black. Fear rises in inverse proportion to how much security you can afford. And, for the developers of gated estates, 'lifestyle complexes' or 'security villages', it is the colour of your money, not of your skin, that counts.

But buying into the promise does not mean you get a free pass from fear, by walling yourself off from the rest of the country, because, try as you might, the country finds a way of coming to call. I saw vividly some years back, when I made my first visit to Dainfern in the northern reaches of Johannesburg, that South Africa was best understood as a series of disjointed mirror images, each an ironic reflection of another. Dainfern was the leading model of the drum-tight security complex cum golfing estate, and where Dainfern has led, others have followed. Embedded in the high walls that ringed the citadel were seismic sensors and reinforced steel bars, reaching into the earth, to deter human moles from tunnelling beneath the fortifications. An electric fence atop the wall carried enough current, a polite notice warned, 'To Cause Death'. Closed-circuit cameras and heat sensors constantly monitored the perimeter defences. In the gatehouse control-room, TV screens recorded each visitor. Rapid reaction vehicles stood ready and armed patrols glided down streets called Collingham Close and Willowgrove Road.

Outside the enclave, in the bare flat veld that lapped its walls, I happened to meet an undertaker named Lucky. His hearse was drawn up nearby. Standing in a hole in the ground, one of Lucky's workers, wearing blue overalls, was shovelling sand into a pile around the edges of what I took to be a grave. As it so happened, the man doing the shovelling was not digging a grave at all and Lucky was not burying anybody, rather he was busy overseeing an excavation. Sunlight fired the blood-red earth as the grave-digger went on lifting the soil. He was waist-deep in a trench, and when his mobile phone rang a snatch of rap jingled in the veld. The man paused, did a little shimmy while the music lasted, and went back to his digging.

This particular undertaker had turned archaeologist and the man with the shovel, digging ever deeper into the rich red soil, was searching for bones. Long before places like Dainfern had been thought of, African clans such as the Bapong, the Sithole and the Monanereng had lived on this land. Lucky was sure their remains lay buried beneath the Italian tiles, fish ponds and swimming pools of the great rich mansions behind Dainfern's long, tall wall. When I met Lucky, a court case was in progress and tempers were frayed. The developers of the estate insisted the ancestors had been exhumed, reburied elsewhere and the matter was closed. Lucky took the view that the graves deserved more respect. The ancestors were entitled to be shown a newborn child, consulted about a marriage, or soothed with a pinch of tobacco snuff.

'How can this happen,' asked Lucky, 'if you don't know where they are buried?'

While his man shovelled away, Lucky said: 'I'm not bitter, I'm very patient. The owners have legal title to this land. They have bought and developed it. But I'd say that before you and before your ancestors ever arrived in Africa, our people were here, lived here, died here.'

My friend Hugo, a Swiss migrant, had lived in Dainfern for years. He liked to call this extravagantly expensive golfing stockade 'just a ghetto for Whitey'. But then Hugo had a mordant streak of humour. 'The point of this place is that from Dainfern you can't see Jo'burg. You can't even see Africa.'

But Africa has a way of seeing you. A graceful silver pipe in the sky linked Dainfern, where residents ride golf carts, to Diepsloot (or 'Deep Ditch'), a vast Black township close by where residents ride ten and twelve in battered taxis. Diepsloot is an apocalyptic place: continual smoke, cooking fires, dirt roads, dust, buzzing energy infuse it and it grows ever larger, ever closer to the walls of Dainfern. Diepsloot houses thousands of the urban poor, looking for jobs, for hope, for a break. It may not be pretty, it isn't safe, but it's home. A silver viaduct spans the area between Dainfern and Diepsloot and, like almost everything the eye falls upon, it is not what it seems. The graceful pipe in the sky funnels the sewage of both settlements, rich and poor. Diepsloot is so close to its luxurious neighbour that it is called by some 'Dainfern Extension'.

Dainfern's bucolic illusion was achieved by brilliant recreational engineering. Within its walls lay nature trails, splashing fountains, green vistas, fish ponds, a golf course and strolling guinea fowl. Homes ranged in style and taste from the opulent to the preposterous, from 'Tuscan' to 'French Provincial' to a popular hybrid called 'African Zen'. I always had to shake my head to clear it, and then shake it a lot more, whenever I left Dainfern and walked across the veld to an even nearer neighbour, Zevenfontein, now removed, but an unforgettable place.

This sprawling settlement was home to some thirty thousand squatters – or, as the handy euphemism had it, 'informal settlers'. The people of Zevenfontein built shacks from 'zincs': often scraps of corrugated iron, cardboard boxes, plastic sheeting and, sometimes, a single file of bricks. Despite its name – 'Seven Fountains' – all drinking water was trucked in and just a few chemical toilets served the homes that stood on rutted pathways between heaps of garbage and open cesspits.

The distance from the Tuscan villas in Dainfern's 'Highgate Village' to the shacks of Zevenfontein was about half a mile, and that distance was shrinking as more people arrived in Zevenfontein. The two settlements, one wealthy beyond words and mostly White, the other dismally poor and Black, were also each other's backyards. But where Dainfern was neutered and somnolent, Zevenfontein had taverns, traders and small shops; it buzzed with vivacity and sociability. Such energy was absent in its rich next-door neighbour. Even the views of the countryside were better in Zevenfontein.

But I have no doubt its inhabitants would have opted for the walled-in delights of its wealthy neighbour; you might say that they leaned that way. The signs and signals of Zevenfontein's attachment were evident in the way its shacks mimicked the costly curlicues of its prosperous role-model. The compliments Zevenfontien's architecture paid to Dainfern were sincere: a tiny, boxy home built of planks and plastic was named 'Mon Plaisir'; an armless, plastic Greek goddess adorned a strip of bare, baked 'garden'; one entire wall of a single-storey shanty was filled with a huge picture window; a shack was plastered with advertisements and warnings discarded by Dainfern residents: 'Trespassers will be Prosecuted!', 'Beautiful Tuscan Villas' and 'Show House Open'.

Zevenfontein, the informal settlement, has since been cleared and its inhabitants moved on. But Dainfern flourishes and has easily survived the scepticism, and scorn, that it once attracted. Dainfern's achievement has been to persuade those behind its walls that this isn't a penitentiary; it is paradise. Once upon a time, only Black people lived in townships; but in the future South Africa, the planners of such fortified citadels have realized, everyone will live in townships. Those who imagined that Dainfern represented a short-lived aberration had not been looking hard at South Africa. Indeed, where the shacks of Zevenfontein once stood, a mega-citadel is being established, several times the size of Monaco, and it will make Dainfern look modest.

Somehow, though, I can't help feeling that, however paradoxical it may seem, Maria and Denys in their shack on the edges of Krugersdorp have sight of a more manageable future. So too, for that matter, do the entangled figures of Professor Broom and Mrs Ples, touchingly nose to nose. Both hint at other, better forms of belonging. Then again, I may be as mistaken as Oliver Tambo was, when he foresaw the day would come when no one would suffer a dose of the move-on blues. Maybe South Africans will have to adapt to life behind bars, in a countrywide penitentiary, and the only liberty left, for those with the money enough to spare, will be to buy a bigger cell.

21

'All you need is a bottle, petrol, an oily rag for a wick. Then what you've got is Molotov Hooch.'

This was Duane, in a flat close to the campus of Witwatersrand University, not long after three petrol bombs, unused, had been found near the Law Library. It wasn't the first time a similar discovery had been made. Duane was showing me his collection of beer bottles, each with a rag stuffed down its glass throat. He was proud of them. Not that he had used any of his weapons yet, but he stood ready.

'When called,' he said.

'Called by whom?'

He looked shy. 'By – the collective.'

'By the cadres?'

He brightened. 'Yes, the cadres.'

'And what do you do now?'

'I wait. What are you doing here?'

'This is my old university. I took two degrees here, many years back. It was a great university. Students had the cops to contend with and the cops in those days were not gentle. It could be bloody.'

Duane nodded. 'We're in the same boat. The cops beat us, shoot us, hassle us.'

I had to disagree. 'It's not the same at all. We were fighting the regime of the day – not the university.'

'The university now *is* the regime of the day,' said Duane.

There was a vagueness about Duane, and I found myself wondering if he was a freelance fanatic or really did belong to an organized grouping of serious saboteurs.

'When do you think they might be likely to call on you – the collective?'

Duane shrugged. 'When things get bad. And they are going to get very bad before they get better.'

'What would you say is better?'

'When we get free, decolonized education. Until then we need to keep some Molotov Hooch in store.'

Duane was White and being White on campus was not easy. He told me this in a rather touching mood of confession. It was hell, he said, it was hard, it was 'bloody awful'. For one thing, he stuck out like a sore thumb; for another, urged by his Black comrades, he had to keep 'checking his privilege'. As a White he had no weight, no importance. His presence was tolerated on the understanding what he wasn't really there. I had the feeling that Duane had been checking his privilege so often, in his moral rear-view mirror, that he could no longer see anything ahead of him. Duane's life had become a perennial retrospective, a looking-back life, a permanent crick-in-the-neck life. More alarmingly, to Duane at least, this new way of living meant learning a new, difficult and almost impenetrable language.

Duane talked of cadres, colleagues, comrades, structures and role-players; of 'them' and 'they'. His was a jargon studded with theories of gender, sometimes so obtuse that men and women were reduced to the coldly anonymous and eerie word 'bodies'. Duane kept checking his rear-view mirror lest coming up behind him were the gender police eager to fine him for crossing some red line, and misconstruing some precise shade of sexual orientation claimed by one sub-group or another. Somewhere, behind these abstractions, lurked real people. His talk was laced with American campus-speak. Slimmed-down, strangulated versions of original models had long been popular among students and Duane's rhetoric was flavoured with a mix of race-baiting Marxism: 'White hegemonic exploitation', and the popular local favourites: 'fallist' and 'coloniality'.

Listening to the conversations of those at the sharp end of the protests at my old university, it did not seem to matter that the jargon baffled some who used it. It served not for communication but incantation; an armoury of sacred spells to be chanted when the gods needed to be appeased or appealed to. More alarmingly, the language of Duane and his allies was superheated and often invoked death. The rhetoric was bolstered by references to notorious cases of police brutality and the shootings of unarmed protestors: in Paris in 1968, or Kent State University in 1970, in Soweto in 1976. And, more recently, and more familiar, the shootings at Marikana in 2013, where thirty-four miners died in a hail of police bullets and seventy-eight were wounded.

As an indication of what those directing the university protests really wanted, one needed to look no further than their demand for 'our own Marikana'. The ostensible reason behind the protests at the universities in South Africa began with the call for free tuition for those too poor to pay. The call was ramped up into free tuition for everyone, and then some called for martyrdom, for another Sharpeville. If you took literally what protestors were saying, you would think students had been shot to death. In fact, the cops had been using stun grenades, rubber bullets, water cannon and even paint-ball pistols, as well as a good deal of force.

The police were unruly, badly trained and prone to overreact, but the force was predominantly Black and answered to a democratic government. I hadn't the heart to remind Duane that, in October 2016, after many months of campus demonstrations, no student had died from lethal police fire.

But the temperature of the words was more important than the reality. Earlier in the year paintings and photographs had been stripped from halls of residence at Cape Town University by angry students, and solemnly burnt. The arsonists posted their manifesto on their Twitter account: 'Tonight we witness the Black psyche unleashing generations of repressed pain. 2016 is the year we no longer pander to Whiteness…'

Looking at pictures of burning paintings, the lines about the iconoclasts of Bruges came back to me:

> The Heads of the statues taken from the Town Hall were brought to the marketplace and smashed to pieces by people who were very angry and embittered. They also burned all traces of the hateful devices that had previously served the Old Law, such as gibbets, gallows and whips. Throughout these events the whole market square echoed to the constant cries of the assembled people: 'Long live the nation! Long live freedom!'

Between the angry demonstrators at Cape Town University in 2016 burning paintings, and the revolutionaries of 1789 torching gibbets and gallows, it was very hard to see any comparability. The former seemed only a faint, and farcical, echo of the latter. What struck me too was the difference between the pettiness of the actions taken and the large and woolly phrases used to justify destroying paintings. 'Black psyche' and 'generations of repressed

Paintings being burnt, Cape Town University campus, 2016

pain' and the constant use of 'Whiteness' were terms too hollow to mean very much. High-sounding gobbledegook was used to dignify what were often extremely undignified and often equally ugly feelings of rage and the desire for revenge. There were those for whom being furious was simply not enough, hence the stores of Molotov Hooch that Duane had shown me. I'd seen at first hand, a few days before I met Duane, what happened when words failed. It was the discrepancy that I could not get over. All that fire and what you ended with was ash.

I had also visited the site of the fire that gutted the handsome auditorium of the nearby University of Johannesburg, and for which a group of students, suspected of having links to the arsonists, had been suspended. The ostensible target of the arsonists and their petrol bombs was not the blackened wreck. Through their incendiary rhetoric one could dimly make out the real target: sometimes called 'the West', 'Colonization', vaporous

194

abstractions, euphemisms for the real enemy. What was remarkable was the unwillingness to come out and say who that enemy was. It was difficult because that way lies racism and in South Africa most people recoil from open expressions of race-hatred, as unabashed admirers of Hitler have found to their cost. So those leading the assault, eager to wound but afraid to strike, veered away at the last minute, and pointed not at 'White people' but at that guilty ghost in the Aryan machine – 'Whiteness'.

But when you're left only with inanimate or symbolic targets to attack, action is constrained. Those who firebombed the auditorium at the University of Johannesburg, which was funded by a large insurance company, also miscalculated. Far from eliciting sympathy for what those who burnt paintings on the Cape Town campus called 'generations of repressed pain', this act of arson drew scorn for its stupidity – and dismay at the sheer waste of money. After all, this was Jo'burg, a mining town where money talked and where 'moral outrage' sounded like some funky disco.

Indeed, the eager arsonists seemed unaware of the contradictions in their position. Among the objects burnt by the iconoclasts of Cape Town University was a painting entitled *The Extinguished Torch of Academic Freedom* by the Black artist Keresemose Richard Baholo, some five of whose works went up in flames. Baholo's painting recalled protests by White students at Cape Town University, in the sixties and seventies, who rejected apartheid and drew attention to the injustices faced by all-White universities, where the struggle for the free expression of ideas, along with the great dream of admitting students whatever their ethnic background, was emphasized, year after year, with stubborn courage. Baholo's painting celebrated this defiance but went into the flames nonetheless. In such bonfires of the inanities, there were no winners.

How things repeated themselves. Listening to Duane among the petrol bombs, I had a vision of what some White students, in various universities, were increasingly succumbing to; constantly checking their privilege, wishing for a part in the proceedings but forced to be content with small backstage jobs. Doubtless, given the vaulting arrogance of many Whites in the past, this might be a useful corrective. Perhaps some felt rather lucky. After all, they would be reminded frequently that there was a war going on, but it was not their war, they were actually the enemy. It was only through the magnanimity of the true resistants who were running the revolution that they were permitted to supply a little aid and comfort. It was only by displaying their willing subjugation that they might give those who did the real fighting a little brief pleasure – a role reminiscent of the 'comfort women' in the Second World War who supplied sexual solace to Japanese soldiers. What a fall was there – from one-time kings of all they surveyed to camp followers.

It is notable how often echoes of the Second World War have floated across the noisy battlefield of the 'War on Whiteness'. The leader of the students occupying the campus of the University of the Witwatersrand reinforced those echoes when he declared his 'love' for Adolf Hitler, an affection apparently bolstered by Hitler's 'charisma' and his organizational capabilities. 'We need more leaders of such calibre,' he said. It would have done little good to point out to this man that Hitler had murdered millions of Jews. He had already dealt with that question. Jews, he said, were 'devils... working behind the scenes to subvert society'. The Legal Department in his own university was full of Jews, and its mission, he announced, was to 'protect White minds,

White bodies and Jewish philosophers'. The Vice Chancellor of the university, who was in fact a Muslim, he declared to be 'a Jewish puppet'. Not long after my conversation with Duane, the campus was again locked down, and I watched the Hitler-loving student leader, wearing what looked like a Lenin cap, declare he had found a novel way of dealing with the recalcitrant Vice Chancellor's failings; he had fired him and nominated himself for the job before an enthusiastic crowd.

The self-proclaimed new Vice Chancellor lacked the sash of office and may have worn a Lenin cap and not a top hat, but the easy way he took to the pedestal brought to mind another autocrat, who stands in Pretoria Square, whom I'd glimpse from the bus each day after school, and whose effigy had been among those recently attacked: the Boer leader – Paul Kruger. It must be something to do with hats and sashes and pedestals and preening – but the despots of our country have a most eerie way of echoing and mimicking each other.

22

I lived for ten years in Pretoria and spent my school days there. The giant bronze Paul Kruger, on a plinth on Church Square in the centre of the city, had survived the statue wars but it had not been easy. It had been necessary to fence him off to save him from iconoclasts who tried several times to spoil his top hat and smeared green paint on the four Boer bodyguards who sit at his feet. In response to the attacks, Afrikaner loyalists chained themselves to his four bodyguards and there was a minor riot.

Pretoria was, and is today, a government town, still strangely itself, even though the name, like many others, has been changed. Throughout my school days in Pretoria, I took the bus to the library nearby the statue of Kruger, and the solid figure, in top hat and sash of office, was as familiar to me as it was to the pigeons settled on his shoulders. I'd see his portly person from the bus as we circled Church Square; droves of civil servants in regulation safari suits scurried here and nothing ever seemed to happen.

Pretoria is now known as Tshwane, at least by some, and the government in Pretoria is controlled by Black, not White, nationalists. While the city that had been Boer, then British, then White and now Black, may have acquired a new name, it has remained stubbornly itself. Under the former regime, it was a town where

Paul Kruger behind barbed wire, Pretoria, 2015

you did nothing on Sundays, because your religious faith forbade it; and you did cruel things for the rest of the week, because your political philosophy demanded it. A government town where our rulers never cared about healing a fractious nation and preferred crafting fresh offensives on the recalcitrant citizenry. The capital has a new name but cannot kick old habits and, when night falls, and the silence thickens, I swear I can hear the bump and grind as separate universes and contending furies that make up what is vaguely called South Africa brutally collide and recoil, and the next day seem as far apart as ever.

I paid a visit to Kruger's effigy after the attacks. The green paint had gone but the fence was there still and I spoke to a woman sitting on the steps, beside one of the armed figures at the base of the plinth. She wore a lace cap and long skirt. These women were members of a group known as the *Kappie Kommando*, a patriotic platoon who turned out in traditional Voortrekker dress at political rallies. She was over sixty, I'd say, with silvery hair. Her eyes, which would once have been sky-blue, had faded a little but still opened very wide and she had a piercing look. She was, she told me, a custodian or a 'watch-keeper', ready to sound the alarm if the 'defacers' ever showed up again. But she visited only now and then because it was dangerous to be out on her own.

'I remember the *Kommando*,' I said.

That pleased her. It meant, among other things, that we were both the same sort of age. What you remembered revealed who you were, and which side you were on. The watch-keeper remembered very different things and we came from very different sides but what pleased us both was that we knew what those differences meant.

She pointed across the square, towards two large buildings.

'That was the Palace of Justice. I don't know what it is now.'

The Palace of Justice was where Nelson Mandela had been tried for treason, in 1963, and sent to Robben Island for nearly three decades. When I pointed this out, the watch-keeper was unimpressed. What was significant was the squalor of the square, the flecks of paint still visible on the Kruger monument, the barbed-wire fence, the snoozing office workers stretched on the grass. She summed up, in her defiant Voortrekker costume and her quiet despair, the quandary faced by an older generation of White South Africans who never imagined things would turn out this way. And that drew me to her. She saw so many things very differently yet she reminded me of myself.

'Do you recognize the building next door?'

She nodded. 'It was some old bioscope. I don't know what it is now.'

It wasn't surprising that the watch-keeper was dismissive. The crumbling pile had been the flamboyant Capitol Theatre, designed in the Italian Renaissance style, intended for live performances, but it soon became a cinema or 'bioscope'. Her loyalties would have been with Paul Kruger and John Calvin and even the name of the Capitol would have suggested to her a heathen temple to false gods. And, in a way, so it was.

As bemused, delighted teenagers, flocking to the Capitol, we were in love with those false gods. Throughout the fifties the Capitol was the best and raunchiest movie house in town, the first in Pretoria to show Elvis Presley, Little Richard, Chuck Berry and Bill Haley, exploding on screen. Glorious extraterrestrials had come among us to make us happy and to make us different, and come all the way from America to Pretoria, where nothing moved and nothing exploded and happiness was always discouraged and being different meant trouble. The usherettes would patrol the dark aisles, the beams of their torches slicing through the cigarette smoke, calling out loudly: 'No dancing in the aisles – or we will throw you out!' But dance we did because, lost in the darkness of the Capitol bioscope, we were happy and we were different.

All of which meant very little to the watch-keeper, who kept her eyes on Paul Kruger. What I was talking about, she told me, were simply 'old buildings'.

'Don't you care about the history of your town?' I asked her.

She shrugged. 'History is just full of dead people.'

'Maybe they keep an eye on us, the living?'

She liked that and she pointed to the statue of Kruger behind his protective fence.

'And we keep our eyes on them, too. They were our people and we must look after them. The crazies want to drive them away, did you know that? And they want to drive us away too. But we are not going anywhere.'

'Who are the crazies?'

'The red berets. Do you know who they are?'

She turned her pale blue eyes on the statue behind the fence and without warning she began to cry. Her tears left shining trails on her cheeks, and because I could think of nothing else to do, I took out a tissue and wiped her eyes. She didn't appear to notice. She was referring to the storm troopers of the Economic Freedom Fighters, who claimed to have attacked the statue of Kruger, and when the city threatened to charge them, rescinded their claim yet cheered the attack anyway.

But if I knew who 'they' were, the question then was: who were 'we'? Our conversation was in Afrikaans, both of us were White, and she assumed, naturally, that I knew who 'we' were. But the 'us' to whom she believed we both belonged, I did not recognize. Like her, I had grown up in Pretoria but as a Roman Catholic of Irish descent and I spoke English at home; she was a Calvinist of Dutch descent and spoke Afrikaans at home. The tribes from which we came feared and detested each other and were mutually appalled at the other's manners, culture, religion and politics. We saw eye to eye on nothing – except perhaps our rather hazy European identity, which we looked back to for status and validity. Crudely put, and nothing was cruder than the old racial obsessions, our colour told us who we were.

But looking back would not help us any more. That world she and I had known was being dismantled, bit by bit, as the signs and symbols that helped us to identify ourselves were recast, renamed or effaced. The best hope left for 'us' was not rebellion, as those who chained themselves to Kruger's sentries and spat defiance had pretended, but, perhaps, a managed redundancy.

That was what made assaults on effigies not only pointless but misguided. It might be best to treat these memorials, from Rhodes to Kruger, with care because, without them, how were we to remind ourselves of the way we had been? Removing every last statue changed the past not one whit, because those they commemorated still remained, for good or ill, aspects of ourselves. And in a country so given to amnesia we needed all the memory we might save.

The Capitol bioscope closed decades ago and became a parking garage. Only the shell remained but there were few who knew or cared what it once was. The city was no longer Pretoria, the province of which it was the capital was no longer the Transvaal and, soon, few would know why the fierce, blue-eyed watch-keeper dressed as she did, or why the bronze statue in a top hat stood in what used to be called Church Square. Everything once familiar was turning into something else.

But of course it had always been doing so. From its beginnings, 'Pretoria' had been a fantasy, dreamt up by the Boers, revised by the British, refashioned by the old White nationalists of the apartheid regime in the middle of the last century, and now being profoundly reworked by the new Black nationalists of the ANC, who had joined the magic lantern show and were busy replacing the old Boer-British creation with one more to their liking.

Outside City Hall, just across the square from the Paul Kruger memorial, there is now a handsome statue of King Tshwane, after whom the region and the city have been renamed. The legendary chief is cast in bronze and stands over three metres high. He was believed to have ruled the area around Pretoria in the seventeenth century, before the first European Trek-Boers arrived.

From the start there has been trouble with the king's statue. Back in 2006, after its unveiling was delayed several times, the sculptor urged the city council to hurry things along because, under its plastic wrappings, the bronze was turning green. There was also some doubt as to whether King Tshwane ever existed. There were some, from the royal houses with roots in the region going back centuries, who disputed the name and lineage of King Tshwane, and claimed never to have heard of him. Perhaps it did not matter. The tall bronze figure reminded everyone that there were Africans in this region long before the first White trekkers arrived in the eighteenth and nineteenth centuries.

Things went little better when the statue was at last unveiled. In an incident that uncannily anticipated the unseating of Cecil Rhodes nine years later, Chief Tshwane was attacked one night and the culprits, presumed to be right-wing Whites, daubed his breechcloth in blue, white and orange, the colours of the apartheid-era South African flag. They urinated on the plinth and added the letters BB, which might, it was suggested, stand for 'Black Bastards'.

The renaming of streets and suburbs in Pretoria after the Boer War ended was a form of warfare by other means and one with which South Africans have long been familiar. Having captured Pretoria from the Boers, and dispatched Paul Kruger into Swiss exile, the British conquerors were remorseless in their desire to extinguish all infidel nomenclature and went about with a will renaming towns, gardens, suburbs and streets until what had been a Boer citadel looked and sounded more like a decently named British garrison town.

When I lived in Pretoria, my home was in Duncan Street, named after the former British Governor General of South Africa, Sir Patrick Duncan. Duncan was a protégé of Lord Milner and admired his chief's unabashed 'race patriotism'. He would have shared Milner's vast imperial ambition, as well as his belief that the superiority of the true-born Englishman was heaven-sent.

When White nationalists retrieved Pretoria in the election of 1948, they were just as eager to put their stamp on the capital city. It is something of an irony that their descendants now complain bitterly when the new Black nationalists who rule Pretoria do much the same. Yet one name they let stand, despite what would have been a natural dislike of all Sir Patrick Duncan represented. It was left to the Black ANC administration to do away with the name in favour of a more suitable hero.

I walked down Duncan Street, where jacaranda blossoms on the pavements had faded to match exactly the pale blue eyes of the watch-keeper I'd met at the foot of the Paul Kruger statue. I passed my old house at number 671, and I remembered my telephone number: 45675. The neighbouring suburbs had wistful and misleading names: Hatfield, Hillcrest, Arcadia and Sunnyside, which they had retained after the Afrikaner Nationalist resurgence. Duncan Street was a major thoroughfare in the suburb of Brooklyn, an allusion to New York nobody can explain. I picked out the familiar topography of my childhood; corner shops, public swimming pool, police station, and Duncan Street itself still looked vaguely related to the road along which I walked and cycled thousands of times, half a century earlier.

But Duncan Street was now 'Jan Shoba Street', named for a notable member of the Pan-African Congress, the rival liberation movement that competed with the ANC for Black support in the struggle against apartheid, and was much less effective. Jan Shoba belonged to the armed wing of the PAC, the Azanian

People's Liberation Army, another wonderfully vacuous appellation, all sonority and no sense. There was never an Azania; the 'people' never backed the PAC with any enthusiasm or in any numbers; its 'Army' was a derisory mess whose models were the Maoists of Nepal and the Tamil Tigers of Sri Lanka; and, worst of all, it liberated no one. Instead, PAC bombs blew up worshippers in churches and it was credited with inventing the slogan 'One Settler, One Bullet'. Shoba's career was memorable for just two events: he spent six years imprisoned on Robben Island and, on his release in 1990, he was murdered outside his home by persons unknown but it was thought his assassins might have been members of his own party.

The ANC detested this rival organization and reduced it to an angry groupuscule on the far edges of power, where it remains to this day. But those who get to change the names of suburban streets felt obliged to throw a bone to their old enemies in the PAC and offered, as they always do, the usual polysyllabic impostures: 'inclusiveness', 'transformation' and 'reconciliation'. Sir Patrick Duncan was out and Jan Shoba was in. The street that had memorialized a British civil servant now commemorated a freedom fighter. And quite right too, I thought – until I thought a little more and the usual confusion overtook me. Names and words came at a price and when you got them wrong they extracted their revenge.

If Sir Patrick Duncan *père* was not especially memorable, then his son, also named Patrick, was a rare and remarkable man in whose memory you night name boulevards and airports. When the Nationalist government took charge in 1948 and declared apartheid to be the will of the almighty, young Patrick Duncan was galvanized into revolt. He spent the rest of his life fighting racism and he paid dearly for it. Duncan was deeply influenced by Gandhi's notion of non-violent resistance, *satyagraha*, and as a young man he joined the Defiance Campaign, the mother movement of all subsequent civil resistance to apartheid. He was accepted as a member by both the ANC and the South African Indian Congress. When he led a march to an African location to point up the chasm between the lives of Whites and Blacks he was carted off to jail; the first of many such arrests.

Patrick Duncan joined the Liberal Party and defended its belief in equality for all, regardless of race. He started his own newspaper to promote this idea, for which in 1961 he was arrested again, banned, placed under house arrest, banned again in 1962, and fled into what was then Basutoland (now Lesotho). Duncan was also the first White to join the Pan-African Congress – the organization to which Jan Shoba had belonged, without remotely approaching Duncan's distinction or originality. Duncan was the PAC representative abroad, speaking for both the organization in America and at the United Nations. As a result, he was refused permission to re-enter Basutoland and was to spend the rest of his life in exile.

Before long he proved too hot to handle, even for the PAC, and was fired. Duncan, who was now living in the UK, switched gear. He turned ecologist and argued, in articles and books, that people needed to live with, and not against, the natural world. When he died in exile in 1967, he had anticipated by decades the relevance of such ideas. Had the municipal name-givers of Tshwane left the name of Duncan Street exactly as it was, they would have honoured a heroic critic of racial hatred and a rebel as remarkable as any the country has produced.

23

Around the corner from my house in Duncan Street was the Brooklyn Police Station. I used to pass it day after day as I rode my bike to serve early morning mass at the nearby Catholic church. Known to all simply as 'the cop shop', it was a forbidding place, notorious for the murderous assaults on Black prisoners by two of its officers, back in the fifties. Sergeant Arlow and Constable Hattingh were legends for their brutality, a reputation they enjoyed. In a dozen years in the police force, Arlow was reported to have shot dead thirteen men. This was a time when assaults by White policemen on Black people was a matter of gruff humour and some considered Arlow a hero. Yet so flagrant was one particular attack that the authorities had little option but to act. In a rare show of justice, both cops were charged with murder. Although their guilt was proven, they escaped with fines so derisory that many White South Africans, inured though they had become to the violence routinely meted out to Black Africans by the police, were scandalized.

Brooklyn Police Station never shook off the ghosts of Black prisoners murdered in the cells. Sergeant Arlow expressed the prevailing view of the times with great concision when he once said: 'I only talk once to a Black and then I shoot.' That sort of pre-emptive brutality was much practised and it was much praised. It is also a continuing way of thinking and acting. Sergeant Arlow regarded himself as invincible with his revolver. Many years have passed since the trigger-happy days of the fifties, when the enthusiastic response of small-time cops at the Brooklyn Police Station to any kind of resistance by a prisoner was to assault him. What hasn't changed, however, is the way endemic violence is woven into everyday life, much as it always was.

It was to Brooklyn Police Station that Oscar Pistorius was brought, after shooting his girlfriend, Reeva Steenkamp, on St Valentine's Day, 2013, claiming he had mistaken her for an intruder. Oscar Pistorius, the blade-runner who won races on his bionic legs, who went a step further than simply exulting in the way that many South African matters are settled by the fist, the boot or the gun, when he declared himself to be 'the bullet in the chamber'.

Brooklyn Police Station

Pistorius lived not far from Duncan Street, in a walled and gated high-security enclave. I went to school no more than a bike ride away from what is now the Silver Woods Country Estate, where the shooting took place. In a time before Silver Woods was built, there were no woods and certainly no silver. I remember the stretch of bare and stony veld that has been buried under a sprawl of security estates, golf courses and shopping malls, where the middle classes of Pretoria make their homes.

Guns are as central to everything as they were when Sergeant Arlow celebrated how quick he was on the trigger. Government regulations have made it increasingly difficult to get a firearm licence, but as long as guns confer power, prestige and protection, people are going to get their hands on them. There are an estimated six million firearms in private hands – one for every dozen people. Pistorius used a 9mm Parabellum pistol when he shot Steenkamp four times, with hollowed-out 'dum-dum' bullets, as she hid behind the bathroom door in his apartment. It was the only gun for which he held a licence. It turned out that Pistorius kept an arsenal of other weapons for which he had applied, but not yet been granted, licences. These included two revolvers, a powerful hunting rifle and three shotguns.

About a month before the murder, Pistorius took his girlfriend to a crowded restaurant and played a game of pass-the-pistol. One of his friends had a revolver with him and Pistorius wanted to handle it; while he was examining the gun, he fired a shot. Happily, the bullet narrowly missed diners at the same table and a friend loyally took the blame for the shooting. What struck me as extraordinary, and typical, was that none of the diners reported the incident and the restaurant owner preferred not to say anything about it, perhaps because Pistorius and Steenkamp were good customers. As things turned out, he was being unusually modest in calling himself 'the bullet in the chamber' during his Olympic heyday. He wasn't just the bullet in the chamber, he was the four fired through the bathroom door where his girlfriend was hidden.

There were several statues I wanted to visit in Pretoria. Top of my list was the Mandela colossus outside the Union Buildings, yet another sandstone pile designed by Cecil Rhodes' preferred architect, Sir Herbert Baker. The Mandela statue is cast in bronze, stands nine metres high and shows him arms outstretched in a welcoming embrace. But I was also after the rabbit.

The wraps came off the statue in 2014, less than a year after Mandela died. It's hard to say exactly what those who arrange such things are after when they turn a real person into marble or metal and stand the figure on a plinth or a pedestal in a public

Mandela at the Union Buildings, Pretoria

place. But one thing seems sure: the bigger you make the figure, the more likely it is that you are in the deification business. Much in the way that the apartheid regime used to boast that the dams it built were the biggest in Africa, so in the gardens of the Union Buildings, the tourist publicity assured me, there stood the largest bronze Mandela in the world. Everyone liked it, until one day, deep inside Mandela's right ear, someone spied a rabbit. It is not a large rabbit, indeed it was so tiny you needed binoculars to spot it hidden deep inside the ear canal, but it was to cause no end of trouble.

The two sculptors who had fashioned the statue were Afrikaners; tastefully chosen, it was said, from the tribe that had once been the enemy and Mandela's particular gift to the country had been the way he embraced, without qualm, enemies as well as friends. When Mandela had died on 5 December 2013, the sculptors had been under enormous pressure to finish the work so it could go on display. They had hoped to sign their names on the giant's trousers but the request was turned down. So they placed the minuscule rabbit in Mandela's ear, thinking it would never be spotted. The word in Afrikaans for rabbit or hare is *haas* – to be *haastig* means to be in a hurry.

The officials who had commissioned the statue were adamant: the rabbit had to go. The men with the angle-grinders were sent for and the rabbit was excised from Mandela's ear. But it was not destroyed. The kindly people at PETA, People for the Ethical Treatment of Animals, offered the creature a home and pointed out that Mandela had been fond of animals and would have approved. But the offer of asylum was declined by those in charge of the project, who insisted that this giant figure, opening his arms to all, was the personification of a titanic battle for freedom, and rabbits had played no part in that struggle.

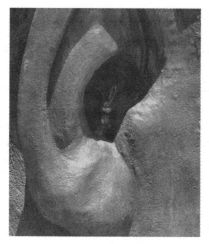

Rabbit in Mandela's ear

I stood beside the giant shoes of the statue and I noticed a White woman, dressed in jeans and a blouse, sitting cross-legged on the grass looking up at the statue with a reverence that was really very captivating, if slightly disconcerting. Every now and then she took a picture with her phone, but she didn't photograph Mandela, she took shots of the visitors.

When I asked her if she was taking a survey of tourists, her answer was surprising. 'In a way, I guess I am. I'm an early warning system.'

'What are you warning about?'

'They talk of attacking him.' She nodded towards the statue.

'Who talks of attacking him?'

'I've heard it myself. You see, I speak Sesotho. Not many White folks around here do. And from time to time these guys come here and, because I'm White, and they speak in Sesotho, they think I don't know what they are saying. I've heard them joke about the rabbit in Madiba's ear and how Mandela sold people short. Twenty years after liberation, they say, they have no land and no jobs and no hope. But the Boers – they're sitting pretty. Mandela must fall, they say. It's time for action. White men must go. They killed us. And Mandela, he let us down. Throw Mandela on the scrap heap, they say, with his rabbit.'

It was a message I had heard before, a steady drumbeat, the rumble that warns of the approaching storm. But how seriously was one to take this sort of rhetoric? Certainly it fitted the pattern that I'd been finding around the country: pull down the false gods, deface the statues, destroy the symbols, bury the emblems. But how confident, or capable, were those who said these things of moving from what was violent play-acting to real pogroms? Watching the baying crowds at one or another ritual defacement of one or another statue, it was hard to resist the feeling that the actors in these dramas had trouble convincing even themselves. In fact, it was sometimes difficult to tell the difference between those who were angry with the enemy and those who were simply sorry for themselves.

'What would you do if you saw people coming to attack Mandela?'

She shrugged. 'Not much. But at least I could try to warn someone. Maybe I'd call the police. I come here when I can, just to check that he is still okay. When he was here, we were moving forward, there was hope.'

The elderly woman in Voortrekker costume, defending Paul Kruger, and the younger woman in jeans, watching over Nelson Mandela, both made a cult of their heroes. Much as the people of Orania had done with Verwoerd. They saw their sacred figures as representatives of happier times, they believed in fairy-tale thinking, that by weaving a powerful spell you could change the past. But the nostalgic defenders had very little support, even among those who should be their natural allies. Young Blacks increasingly resented the appropriation of Mandela by White liberals and some branded him a sell-out. Few Afrikaners believed the old Boer republics could be revived, or migrated to Orania. Yet the iconoclasts assaulting the effigy of Cecil Rhodes were in the grip of the same magical thinking: just pull down the image of the wicked wizard and all his works would be abolished.

I took a long look at the giant Mandela. He was dressed in his trademark silk shirt, traditionally designed by Surtee, his favourite tailor. In the fifties, Surtee was the hippest designer in Johannesburg and his fame spread to Pretoria. I remembered how Surtee's style was mimicked by Indian tailors, working at the lower end of Church Street, who sold flash gear to kids like me, drunk on rock 'n' roll movies and the gear we saw on screen: long loose jackets, stove-pipe trousers, fluorescent pink socks, shimmering silk shirts, often cheap copies of Surtee's work.

But the flowing shirt on the giant figure looked much more like a tunic, or a Mao jacket, once popular with revolutionary figures from China to Vietnam. It was all very South African. You give two Afrikaans sculptors their heads, ask them to memorialize a man who embodied the spirit of freedom and democracy, and what do they come up with? A gargantuan figure straight out of the North Korean playbook. I had to wonder whether it might not have been cheaper to go straight to the source. The sculptors of Pyongyang apparently ran a profitable industry, supplying towering effigies of dead dictators at bargain prices. The Democratic Republic of Congo had commissioned a ponderous effigy of the late, lamentable Kabila *père*, who was succeeded by his son, Kabila *bis*, as they call him in the DRC. Equatorial Guinea, Ethiopia and Togo had bought effigies of their strong men from the

North Korean masters of Ozymandian overreach. It is rumoured that two very large Robert Mugabes await shipping.

But what do the South African sculptors give us? The only flash of originality was a rabbit in Mandela's right ear, and even that glimmer of defiance had been surgically removed. The illicit rabbit has gone the way of so many opponents of the North Korean leadership; the bunny has been 'disappeared'.

24

As a boy I'd visited, once or twice, the cemetery in the centre of town in what used to be called Pretoria, and in what used to be called Church Street. But I'd never been to that section of it known as Heroes' Acre; I'd heard it described by distraught friends as a wreck, sad, depleted and neglected, and I wanted to see it for myself.

I was driving along what used to be D.F. Malan Drive, named for one of the more disagreeable of the old White prime ministers, but now known as Es'kia Mphahlele Drive. This in itself was an odd sensation and rather alarming, because I'd known Mphahlele briefly, and those who knew him had always called him 'Zeke'. As a teenager I got my hands on his much-admired memoir, *Down Second Avenue*. The opening lines of that remarkable book, banned for decades in the old South Africa and its author pushed into exile, always stayed with me: 'I have never known why we – my brother, my sister and I – were taken to the country when I was five.'

Mphahlele's memoir echoes, from first to last, with the only question worth asking about South Africa: where are we going, and why are we going there? The question has been asked again and again in the knowledge that whatever answers we got were bound to be wrong.

In central Pretoria, or Tshwane, on an early Sunday morning there was no movement. The almost empty streets looked much as I remembered them. The capital may have morphed from a White Calvinist encampment to an African city, but the silence of early Sunday mornings still obtained and when I arrived at the cemetery I found the gates firmly locked. But a cheerful, thin man, wearing a red bandana, offered in nicely formal terms to help me.

'You would like to see Breaker Morant? Dr Verwoerd? Paul Kruger? Who is your delight to see today? Tell me. My name is George, the locked gate we care not about. There are other entries into this place and George will be your guide.'

And so I found myself, after many decades, once more being shown the things that lay beneath the skin of life, in a very strange town, by a guide named George.

He took me first to the grave of Breaker Morant, assuming that I was Australian.

'We get lots here,' said George. 'Looking for history.'

Morant's grave lay in a rather neglected section of the cemetery. The gravestone carried the lines from Matthew, Chapter 10, Verse 36: 'And a Man's foes will be of his own household.'

George traced the letters with his finger. 'It means he was shot by his friends.'

'And that still rankles in Australia,' I said.

'What is "rankles"?' George asked.

'It means such things go on hurting.'

'History is hurting,' said George.

Breaker Morant had been among the Australian contingent fighting with the British to subdue the recalcitrant Boers who knew they were beaten but would not give in. Morant had been undone in a moment of murderous rage, after a close friend was killed in an attack on a Boer position. On Morant's orders, twenty-two Boer prisoners of war and a Dutch parson were shot. For this Morant was court-martialled, found guilty, and executed by firing squad in Pretoria in the early morning, on 27 February 1902.

It is the familiarity of what happened that I found so haunting. The essence of it was – killing and lots of that, by all sides, in a country where history, as George reminded me, was 'hurting'. Breaker Morant's rush of blood to the head was of the same order as that of Sergeant Arlow, the terror of Brooklyn Police Station, who disposed of Black prisoners as if swatting flies. Oscar Pistorius, another noted denizen of Brooklyn Police Station, ran to form when he repeatedly fired heavy calibre dum-dum bullets through the bathroom door, behind which cowered his girlfriend. It was brutal and brainless but by no means exceptional in a land that, from its very early years, was convulsed by violence.

The Boer prisoners Breaker Morant had executed were regarded by many on the British side as a primitive species. Doing away with those not regarded as fully human, 'useless appendages' in a phrase from the apartheid era, was a long tradition. Under the old apartheid regime murder moved from being a freely available option to something close to an obligation. Arlow summed up the general rule: when provoked – open fire. Breaker Morant was charged, much as Arlow had been, not because what he did was of itself out of the ordinary but because it was so flagrant and caused so much fuss it could not be overlooked.

George walked me next to that section in the centre of the cemetery known as Heroes' Acre.

'It is all being stolen,' George told me sadly, 'very, very quick.' He pointed to the bust of Paul Kruger and said: 'Oom Paul.'

I was rather touched to hear him use the familiar Afrikaans

nickname for Kruger, and his tone of affection. Kruger's bust showed him bearded, be-medalled and square-shouldered, with the air of some stoic Roman Caesar, which seemed about right.

Next George took me to see 'the English Prince'. The Prince was 'English' in that distant way of the British royal family, the son of Princess Christian of Schleswig-Holstein, fifth child of Queen Victoria. His names were a regal drumroll: Christian Victor Albert Ludwig Ernest Anton of Schleswig-Holstein-Sonderburg-Augustenburg. Around his grave grew yellow cat's tails and purple vygies, and they brightened when sunlight splashed the headstone. The thirty-three-year-old prince died of enteric fever during the Boer War and was buried in Pretoria in 1900. It had been a grand affair. Troops lined the funeral route for two miles, the pall-bearers included Baden-Powell, and among the chief mourners was Lord Roberts, who was to be rewarded for his role in defeating the Boers by having an entire suburb named after him. I used to play as a boy in Roberts Heights but the name was revised to Voortrekker Heights when the triumphant Afrikaner Nationalists won power. Lord Kitchener was also among the mourners, a man who, in later times, would have been charged with war crimes for his scorched earth programme and his enthusiasm for concentration camps.

We moved on to the grave of Hendrik Verwoerd. I had seen photographs that showed his bust on the tomb. But this was missing, spirited away, perhaps, by devotees.

'I think Verwoerd was no good,' said George. 'What do you think?'

I did not know what I thought. Was Breaker Morant, who murdered prisoners in cold blood, and was shot after a rigged trial, a war criminal? Or was he a man driven beyond endurance, sacrificed by his hypocritical British commanders? Many people thought so. Was Paul Kruger a narrow, stubborn racist, or was he a hero who resisted to the end a shabby war launched by British imperialists to rob his country of the gold that lay beneath the earth? Millions thought so. And what about Hendrik Verwoerd? He thought deeply, and carried out his absurd and unworkable racial theories with appalling results. A few weeks earlier, a commentator, forgetting that the space for free discussion is closing fast in South Africa, called Verwoerd a 'clever' politician. The commentator was lynched in the media and obliged to recant and apologize. Was Kitchener 'no good'? More Boer women and children died in his camps than Boer fighters in the war. Was he worse than Cecil Rhodes? Were they all beyond the pale – or were they, no more and no less, creatures of their time and place?

In a country given over to brutality, where the rule has been that there were no rules; where the elite, then as now, enriched themselves, all the time claiming to be on the side of the angels, who could answer the question?

But George asked again. 'What do you say?'

'I think he was bad *muti*,' I said to George. Using the words I had heard from that other George, when I was a boy walking past Hendrik Verwoerd's house, and we crossed the road to escape his spell.

When I told George the Second that I was heading next to the Central Prison, he shuddered. 'So much rope.' He advised me to drive there rather than walk. There were hijackers beyond the cemetery walls but on a Sunday this was less of a danger than the muggers around the Kruger statue, in Church Square.

'Thank you for visiting my office,' George said when I handed him some money and we shook hands. 'Come again soon, and I will be here.'

At the rate it was being pillaged, I doubted there would be much of the cemetery left. An air of dereliction hung about the place, graves were awry and the silver crosses that signified the status of those buried in Heroes' Acre were going fast. It wasn't really surprising because the graveyard held attractive loot. Even less notable graveyards were reporting that fresh flowers, left by mourners, were being resold outside the walls. Heroes' Acre was crumbling away, and not only because bits and pieces were pilfered. Time was doing the real damage; history was being effaced in what felt more like a fit of absent-mindedness.

Driving the short distance to the prison I was reminded again how many public buildings had the form of stolid fortresses, as if the ideology that made the city the capital of apartheid was mimicked in stone. I used to get the same feeling in central Moscow in Soviet times, or walking along Karl Marx Allee in the old German Democratic Republic. Architecture was a series of brutal statements in concrete and matched the only language spoken; power was set in stone.

Pretoria Central Prison was once called the 'hanging jail'. The practice was abolished in 1995 and the gallows, where up to seven people could be hanged at the same time, became a museum. Fifty-two steps led up to the execution chamber where a line of seven nooses dangled over the drop. A telephone stood ready for a call from the president that might bring a reprieve, but it was never known to ring. The execution chamber is a silent and sombre place.

In the main, those commemorated in the museum were active in the Black Liberation Movements and this seems proper. But the hangman did not discriminate. Some 3,500 people, from all

Gallows, Pretoria Central Prison

walks of life, were hanged in Pretoria's jail. Sometimes an execution took place every two or three days, a rate exceeded only by the busy hangmen of Iran. I could not help noticing the intricate, rather shapely, shadows cast on the walls by the hangman's knots in the dangling nooses.

No statues or effigies or marble memorials distracted and interfered with the stark silence of the gallows chamber. The difficulty, as it were, of bringing people back to life, in bronze, or stone or marble, is that so much can go wrong. Not very far from the jail a new venture, the National Heritage Park, contains dozens of big bronze statues. The entrepreneur who established the park told the press that there were lots of White men on plinths around the country but a scandalously few statues of iconic Blacks. He planned to repair the omission by populating the park with indigenous, home-grown heroes. Statues included anti-apartheid icons like Oliver Tambo (not a particularly accurate representation but cheerful enough) to an athletic Steve Biko, and a phalanx of distinguished Black men and women who changed the history of South Africa. His plan was to grow the number of historical figures from the present fifty-five to around five hundred. The theme was a freedom marathon, with each figure handing on the baton of liberty to the next.

I was particularly interested in one of the first Khoi rebels, known as Doman or Damon (the name given him by the Dutch), who fought what came to be known as the first KhoiSan war against the incomers. Many wars against the Dutch were waged by the KhoiSan before they were suppressed and extinguished, and Damon is rare that in his lifetime he became, and remains, a legend. There can be few individuals more worthy of commemoration precisely because we know so little about him.

Of course, no records show what Damon looked like, but that was fine. I didn't go along with those who insisted that if you did not know what someone looked like you could not create a likeness. Many of the statues I had come across on my travels had turned out to be just one version of the 'real' individual. And the history in which the legendary person was embedded was often less than accurate, false or invented. The making of graven images really seemed a kind of story-telling, to be taken with a large pinch of salt. So I was particularly keen to see how the artist had depicted Damon.

Unfortunately, he was not to be found. When I asked in the park where he might be, I was told that Damon had been stolen. Although the park was floodlit and guarded day and night, daring thieves had arrived after dark with an angle-grinder, carefully removed Damon from his base, loaded 150 kilos of brass onto a truck, and vanished. A reward for Damon's recovery had been offered and from then on, I was told, a tracking chip was installed in the base of each of the statues in case another one was stolen.

I felt sorry for Damon, but sorrier for the KhoiSan who vanished from the map of the country and when, at last, one of their leaders was celebrated in public, he went missing. It was a very South African phenomenon. History hurts, as George had reminded me, and does so all the more when its wounds are salted with irony.

As I left Pretoria a long line of cars, at the end of Es'kia Mphahlele Drive, blocked the way. I noticed a black saloon stranded between the traffic lights, with its boot open. It seemed that some driver had overshot the lights. At the roadside, a burly barefoot White man in shorts was talking in a very agitated way to a newspaper seller, who nodded in sympathy. So absorbed were they that neither saw the Black man, perhaps the driver of the damaged saloon, cross briskly to the stranded car, reach into the open boot and pull out a golf club. Whirling it overhead to get the weight of it, he ran at the White man. His quarry spotted him at the last moment and fled, thudding up the road in his bare feet, just ahead of his pursuer with his club. The two of them passed so close to me I feared for the wing mirror of my rented car, and then vanished. The line of stalled traffic surged forward and carried me away from what might have been a very bloody scene. The show was over. No one stayed to see what happened or tried to intervene. It was as if an angry man with a golf club, murder-bent, was the sort of thing you would see in downtown Pretoria on a Sunday morning.

I scanned the papers in the days that followed but there were no reports of assault or homicide – but it was not very likely the news would have made the news. Thinking about it later, I reflected that what I had seen did suggest one essential change since democracy dawned in South Africa. In the old days, a White man armed with some weapon and in hot pursuit of a Black man was the order of things. This time, the man running for his life had been White and that signalled something of a change.

25

There are monuments that strive to make you remember and then there are those you cannot forget. In the dusty graveyard of a little settlement called Tweefontein ('Two Springs') a few hours north of Johannesburg, there is a remarkable memorial to a boy who went by the name of Happy Sindane. The black granite tombstone is imposing and its size and design set it apart from the forest of simple wooden crosses and unmarked mounds of red earth that are the many paupers' graves.

Happy was not his real name but then very little about the boy buried in Tweefontein could be called 'real' – except his suffering, his humour and his hopes. He had another family name and the gravestone records that he was also known as 'Abbey Mzayiya', and he will be remembered, promises the message etched into the polished stone of the tombstone, by the trustees who administered a fund set up in his name, as well as by his extended families. This is the sort of wishful thinking that I guess Happy might well have approved of – but it says nothing about the extraordinary young man who is buried here.

What Happy did was to remind the country of how deeply, perhaps permanently, the abiding obsession with race and skin colour has damaged so many lives. There was a brief, euphoric moment, with the arrival of the 'new' South Africa, when it was believed, by Whites in particular, that the nightmare was over and racism was on its way out. Anyone who suggested it might be so threaded through the national psyche as to be nearly ineradicable was seen as a very bad sport and unpatriotic to boot. There were even some who said that perhaps apartheid had not been as bad as people made out, certainly no more awful than the sort of thing that went on in the segregationist states of the USA.

Anyone who lived in the heyday of apartheid knew this was nonsense. The zealots who wrote the rules were obsessed with the purity of 'blood' and tribe. In their monomania they thought of little else: race infected everything from hair texture to heart transplants; it reached in to love affairs, it pursued you to the grave. The country was a giant menagerie where zoo keepers who claimed to be divinely appointed presided over less-than-human others, who were locked into the prisons of their skins. That is why Happy Sindane lies in what is still a segregated cemetery, in a segregated village, in a segregated country.

But for me his life and death is the ultimate South African story in all its mad, sad, bitter comedy. But then perhaps I would think this way because my first novel, promptly suppressed by the old regime, was about a boy called Harry Moto who could not make up his mind what colour he was. But the real-life tragedy of the lost boy who is buried in the Tweefontein graveyard easily outdoes my imaginary tale. And besides, what Happy did was to invent his own life as a very South African fairy tale and, for a while at least, he almost got away with it.

Happy was born in 1984, or so the best guess has it, in a suburb called Fourways, on the northern edge of Johannesburg. When he was about six, the boy and his mother went for a walk and they met along the way, not a man selling magic beans, or someone who could turn straw into gold, but a fairy godmother. Her name was Betty Sindane, and Happy's mother asked her if she would mind the child for a few minutes, and when Betty agreed, Happy's mother disappeared into a liquor store and was never seen again.

Betty Sindane reported what had happened to the police and she was asked to look after the boy, at least until things had been sorted out. But things were never sorted out and Betty took over as the boy's mother. She had trouble with his name so instead of calling him 'Abbey', she settled for calling him 'Happy'. They must have been very close, the boy and his adopted mother, because when Betty died ten years later, Happy would go to her grave and weep. He was placed next in the care of his 'grandfather', a man called Koos Sindane, who did what he could for the boy but the two never got on. The trouble was all in the skin – Happy was pale and this made him stand out in school. He was teased by his township classmates who saw him as a misfit, a 'White' boy in a Black world.

Happy had now lost his mother twice over but he still had some faint memory, or had heard tell, of the man who was his 'real' father. He began to build this figure into a hero who was rich, powerful and, above all, White. The trigger for what Happy did next seems to have been a television programme that he saw about babies being stolen from their prams. Suddenly he knew what to do. He would find his father again, regain the world he had lost, and live happily ever after.

One day in 2003, into the police station in Bronkhorstspruit, a town not far from Tweefontein, there walked a teenage visitor with a very strange story. Happy, who was now nineteen, told the officers that he was a White boy who had been stolen when he was a baby and raised by a Black family who put him to work as their slave. He said he'd been half-starved, made to live rough and now he wanted to find his true parents.

The story caused a sensation. Ten years in to what must be very loosely called the 'new' South Africa, the country now had its very own Mowgli. There was talk of Hollywood movie contracts, there were appearances on radio, and White couples whose babies had gone missing now came forward to claim this 'slave boy' as their own son. My guess is that by now even Happy believed his own story; and so did sponsors and well-wishers. He began appearing on television wearing new clothes and expensive sunglasses. The pauper had turned into the prince.

But not for long. When DNA tests showed that Happy was the son of a shadowy German immigrant with the unlikely name of Henry Nick, and his Black housekeeper, Rina Mzayiya, the excitement slowly ebbed away. What Happy had been doing used to have a name, back in the bad old days: it was called 'trying for White'; but in 2003, no one wished to remember any longer the bad old days. People felt let down. Happy was not the son from a rich White family, who had been stolen by the maid. He was the son of the maid. Far from being a slave-child raised in the wild, he was a boy of mixed race, like millions of others. And that was when the fairy tale came unstuck and the interviews and the movie deals all went out of the window. The ugly duckling never made it into a swan; Cinderella kept being hijacked on her way to the ball.

It's never easy to explain to others the intense, ruinous fascination with skin colour that has for so long haunted this country. It was evident in the manner that people in the country responded to the story of the stolen White child. At a time when colour was said no longer to matter, the truth turned out to be that it counted more than ever. A national paint manufacturer ran an advertisement showing Happy's face above the tagline: 'Any Colour You Can Think Of.' Almost a decade after South Africa had apparently rejected race as being the tell-tale sign of who you really were, here was a joke that everyone was expected to find wonderfully apt.

Happy did not see the funny side of the joke, sued the paint company for using his picture without permission and was awarded substantial damages. The company also offered to paint a children's home, of Happy's choice, any colour he could think of. The joke was far from over.

The money he got went into a trust and one of the first things Happy Sindane did was to erect a decent tombstone to his lost stepmother, Betty. But his adoptive family also wanted a share of the money and very soon, with the demands they made, there was no cash left and Happy ended up in a children's refuge, resistant to attempts to help or train or comfort him. And yet Happy went on attracting friends, two of whom tried as best they could to save the boy.

'Happy longed to know who he was and he wanted to meet his father. He believed he was rich and wanted his support.'

That was the view of Father Kuppelwieser, a Catholic priest who gave Happy a home in the Sizanani Children's Home, a refuge for severely disabled boys and girls that he had founded.

It didn't help very much. By the time he was eighteen Happy was drinking a great deal and when he hit rock bottom he was inclined to wander out into the road, lie down and dice with death.

'I only drink when I try to forget my past,' he told a local newspaper. 'It haunts me no matter how much I try to forget.'

. He found another friend in the examining judge, Martinus Kruger, who oversaw the DNA tests that showed that Happy Sindane was really Abbey Mzayiya. The boy had not consciously misled the court, the judge said, but he'd been overwhelmed by his dreams and his hopes. With help, the judge hoped, Happy might finally be happy.

But things were simply going from bad to worse. Happy found the temptation to go out into the road and lie down to be almost overwhelming. One day the suicidal game turned bloody when he was hit and run over by a minibus taxi as well as the vehicle travelling behind it. He was put on a life-support system in hospital, expected to die but astonishingly he pulled through.

After a succession of no-hope jobs, Happy found himself back where he had begun, in Tweefontein, the place he had tried so hard to flee, living again with his adopted family. When I talked to some of the drinkers in the JZee Tavern where Happy liked to hang out, they said he was known for two things: getting drunk and being famous. One morning, after one of these mammoth drinking sessions at the JZee Tavern, Happy's body was found in a ditch not far from the bar. He had been beaten to

Happy's funeral, Tweefontein, 2013

death and a fellow drinker from the tavern was charged with his murder.

A local funeral company covered the costs of his burial and another donated the grand memorial gravestone. If you were to add the price of the gravestone announced by the donor in a PR release to the burial costs, the sum amounts to much the same as that which Happy was awarded by the paint company that had once found him such a funny fellow.

After he died, the jokes still went round: 'What is better than being Happy? Being White.'

When Happy looked at himself in the mirror I think he was faced with a fatal question: on which side of the Black and White divide did he stand? Try as he might to choose one or the other, in the end he was both, and that was a very bad place to be. In the world on the other side of the looking glass, the new South Africa looked alarmingly like the old.

In the JZee Tavern, the young men were amused to see me back again when I called in. Yes, they still remembered Happy, and yes, they were still sad at the way he died. Why would anyone harm a boy so quiet? I had no answer to that but I was intrigued by something one young man said.

'He tried for White. Why do that?' He looked at me with some scorn. 'What's good about being White? Maybe it was once, but now?'

When I came back to visit Happy's grave, little had changed but for a fresh forest of wooden crosses. Funerals are frequent in the area and AIDS, poverty, murder and despair carry off people all the time and in great numbers. Happy's tomb towers above all the other memorials, impressive but troubling because nobody visits it. The lines cut in to the black granite speak of the way that Happy will be remembered by his extended families, but both families fell out before he was buried, both demanded sole possession of the boy and his legend. As for the trustees of what used to be known as the Sindane Trust, they had long since disbursed all the funds. Nothing on the tombstone is accurate, except the website address of the stonemasons who donated the memorial and which is incised at its base.

An over-large monument in a far-away country graveyard, to a boy whose story seems slight. But he is more important in the history of the country than either Rhodes or Kruger or any of the proliferating images of chiefs and charlatans now in vogue. Because Happy goes to the heart of the matter. He is who we are; or he is what we have done to ourselves. I remember his funeral years ago and the hundreds and hundreds of mourners, many of whom really did not seem to know why they were there, except that they wanted to be present. The judge who had befriended Happy spoke well that day and he likened Happy to a fire on a winter's night: 'He was a warm and lovely boy and to see him laugh was something I loved.'

26

The 'White Cross Memorial' is to be found on a farm in the province of Polokwane, some hours north of Pretoria, in a place called Ysterberg, and it is a strange sight: hundreds of white wooden crosses in serried ranks, marching up and over a low hill. The impression made is one you might have on first seeing, in France, the military cemeteries of the First World War. The crosses commemorate murdered White farmers and many carry the names of the victims. Other crosses are blank. The reason was explained to me, as I walked among the crosses, by a woman whose husband was among the dead: 'These empty ones are made ready for the next to die. We know it's going to happen and we prepare.'

I first saw these crosses years ago, along the national road that leads to the Zimbabwe border, when they were tied to the fences and seemed to stretch for miles along the national road. After objections from the authorities in charge of national roads, the crosses were moved to a privately owned farm.

White farmers are four times more likely to be murdered than anyone else. The period 2016/2017 saw 357 attacks and 74 murders on farms. Some reports put the total number of White farmers murdered since 1990 at an astonishing 1,700. Investigating officers I spoke to in police stations, in places like Witbank, say that most of the attackers are young, semi-literate Black teenagers, often with no jobs and no prospects. They were after money, cell phones and guns, and it is believed farmers have these in quantity. The victims tended to be over fifty, and soft targets for brutal attackers. My companion, pointing out the blank crosses, was correct in her mournful expectation of murders still to come.

But the figures are disputed all the time because when you talk of murder you are soon talking of race, history and politics. Even the term 'farm murders' is said by some to be divisive because it implies that victims of attacks are always White farmers. Those troubled by the phrase point out that Black farm workers, too, are attacked and murdered, sometimes by White farmers, who have earned a reputation for brutality that goes back centuries. The White Cross Memorial is a reminder of why the whole subject is so contentious. The field of crosses has been reserved for Whites, and those who oversee the rededication of the crosses, in a ceremony that takes place each year, have declined to permit victims from other 'ethnic' groups to be remembered on this hillside.

This is a pity but it is also very South African. In the decision to keep the place segregated, the memorial had become a contested site, a place of defiance and anger. It draws to itself fans and far-right groups, so extreme that to call them 'right-wingers' is to malign sensible conservatives. These people are openly and enthusiastically racist, as well as deeply nostalgic for the old ways and days. What is heartfelt pain at the disproportionate and brutal killing of so many White farmers has become shrouded in tacky conspiracy theories, which I have heard across the world from the Balkans to Bloemfontein, and which always seem to involve the same suspects – a cabal of international and cosmopolitan conspirators plotting the end of the White 'race'. This theory has gained much traction now in the United States, and local groups derive comfort from international allies, especially from America, where way-out conspiracy theories have gone mainstream.

Some who gather each year for the White Cross Memorial rededication embody the exuberant race-hatred of those who once believed in apartheid. They include exotic groupuscules such as the *Boerevolk-Geloftevolk*, the Boernation Heritage Foundation and the *Volks Kommando*, as well as outfits with names such as Genocide Watch and Stop White Genocide SA. These groups parade under the old South African flag, sing the old South African anthem and exhibit much the same yearning for a familiar, fatherly fascism as the Russians who wept for the vanished Stalin, or Spaniards who paraded for Franco, or the nostalgic Nazis who met in Jo'burg taverns, on the anniversary of Hitler's birthday, and sang the 'Horst Wessel' song.

In large part they fear that Whites are being moved to the margins of power and importance. There is certainly evidence that this is happening, but to maintain that some shadowy force, Freemasons, Jews, Illuminati, or New World Order is out to destroy the Afrikaner people is to believe that there are those who are organized, disciplined and bright enough to make this possible. But travel the country as I do, again and again, and there is scant sign of anything like it. Quite the reverse, in fact. In the twelve-month period 2016/2017 there were 19,016 murders in the country, or over 50 each day. South Africans are in far greater danger from each other than from the malevolent masters of the universe.

On the hill of white crosses there is one today that carries the name of Eugene Ney Terre'Blanche, leader of the Afrikaner Resistance Movement, and the date of his death. On the one hand I can understand why the keepers of the crosses would have wanted him within the field of martyrs and he certainly qualifies. He was a White farmer, murdered as he slept, like many of the others. But I knew him well and I don't think he would have been very happy with this inclusion. Because what it does is to fly in the face of everything he imagined he stood for; he was, in his eyes, the unique one, the leader, he always wanted the leading role in any production in which he appeared. What Terre'Blanche possessed, in heady quantities, was exactly what infects the South African scene: a love of being centre stage, a theatricality, a rising anger, and a willingness to revert to violence whenever it served his ends.

Terre'Blanche liked to tell me that he would die facing the enemy. But his end was not one he imagined. On Easter weekend in 2010, he was bludgeoned to death in his spartan bedroom, on his farm near his home town of Ventersdorp, a tiny farming village north-west of Johannesburg. Ventersdorp is set in a flatland of red soil streaked with blonde vistas of endless maize fields. It has always been an Afrikaner farming town, a Boer redoubt, with streets broad enough to turn an ox wagon. It is an uneasy, testy little place where big men, Black and White, stare straight past each other, and the steeples of the three Dutch Reformed churches that were once temples of the White Nationalist party at prayer stab the skyline.

Those charged with his murder were two of his workers: an illegal Zimbabwean immigrant called Chris Mahlangu and a fifteen-year-old boy who slept in squalid quarters in the barn. Terre'Blanche had not paid their Easter wages and they were angry about that. Instead he had bought them lots of booze and then he went to bed alone in his farmhouse. A few hours later, the man and the boy forced a window open with a heavy iron bar and, using that bar and a large bush knife, they hacked and bludgeoned their sleeping boss to death.

Terre'Blanche hankered for a return to the Boer republics of the Transvaal and the Free State and warned of plans to get rid of White Afrikaners. What one hears at the White Cross Memorial is a version of Terre'Blanche's demand, presented by younger Afrikaners, who will gather around the statue of Paul Kruger in Pretoria when it is splashed with paint, chain themselves to the base and promise to defend their language and their culture with their lives. Terre'Blanche's demand to be allowed to return to these lands of lost Boer content is echoed by some, who do not brandish pseudo Swastikas, wear silly hats or fall off horses, but also demand their country back. It's a poignant but perfectly useless cry because the old South Africa has gone for good.

And yet, in a funny way he pointed to the future. Terre'Blanche's private army, the Afrikaner Resistance Movement, was a tacky travelling circus, and its faux-Führer liked to pose as a Boer patriarch. But the leader anticipated the rise of someone who might be a clone of the late White demagogue: Julius Malema, self-styled 'Commander in Chief' of the Economic Freedom Fighters. He shows a fondness for red berets rather than black shirts, delight in military regalia and a taste for violence directed against a lengthening list of enemies, from Boers to banks, and it connects the EFF with Terre'Blanche's ARM. Malema leans to Chavez and Terre'Blanche to Hitler but they echo each other in their deliberate cultivation of violence.

Just as Terre'Blanche's men unnerved the last apartheid regime, the EFF present themselves as the true liberation movement, betrayed by the ANC. Their slogans are notorious: 'Kill the farmer, kill the Boer' is probably the best known but there are others: 'To be a revolutionary you must be inspired by hate and bloodshed,' or its chilling variation, 'A revolutionary must become a cold killing machine motivated by pure hate.' These are sentiments Eugene Terre'Blanche would have understood. That is why I think placing his cross among the forest on the hillside misrepresents him. He was more than a bygone voice in a sepulchral chorus. He points, very alarmingly, towards things to come, a time when superheated threats lose potency and desperate people then turn to fire, even if it is they who burn.

I moved north again, into the province of Limpopo where, in a little place called Vuwani, upwards of twenty schools had been burnt to the ground and no one was able to say why people, with so little, were setting fire to their places of education. Enquiries had been going on for weeks but no one had any clear answer about who was setting the fires. Except, as one witness told me, the school was 'there', and that the government paid no attention to the people of Vuwani until 'we burn things'.

My guide on this melancholy tour I will call Joshua. The explanation that Joshua did his best to give chimed with much that was going on in the universities and in the townships and in the shanty towns where hospitals, clinics, libraries were frequently set on fire and where the identities of the arsonists seemed to remain unknown and were called simply 'they'. The burning of these clinics, libraries and schools was explained by those who suffered most from the burning as being the only way of attracting attention from the far-away authorities in government offices who, like the perpetrators of the fire, were also 'they'. Joshua was himself a teacher and he looked at the burnt-out buildings with the same dismay as I did; it hurt him terribly, this destruction. I went to elementary schools, tiny country schools, often a room or two – desks, papers, books, blackboards, all of them charred and reeking of ash. These schools no longer possessed any records, no pencils, no equipment, no life. They were their own funerals, cloaked in mourning.

Standing in the charred ruins of a village school, the question struck me as it had done when I watched in Cape Town the students of the university attacking the statue of Cecil John Rhodes. What did it mean? The iconoclasts of Bruges had destroyed gallows, gibbets and whips, and all they found 'hateful' and they called out for 'freedom'. But village schoolrooms? I hoped that Joshua understood why it was happening. But when he tried to tell me, he ended up shaking his head and saying nothing, not because he would not say but because words failed him.

Ministers from the distant capital arrived, promised money and mobile classrooms, then went back to the big city. Newspapers reported the fires but offered no explanation or sought to discover why schools were burnt, or at what or at whom this anger was directed. The state-run television service, a minion of the ruling party, compounded its failure to inform and explain by declaring it would no longer show pictures of burning buildings because this only encouraged people to go out and torch a few more.

As I left Vuwani, I heard news that the students of the Nelson Mandela Metropolitan University, 950 miles away in Port Elizabeth, had a more interesting idea than burning their college to the ground. Their campus happened to be on a private nature reserve, where wild animals roamed. The students issued an ultimatum: if the university did not attend to their protests, they planned to take action, as they explained in a voice-file posted online: 'Every day we take one zebra and then we tell management, if you don't do what we're telling you, we will deal with those zebras accordingly…'

Perhaps without intending it, they had chosen a symbol that stood precisely for the struggle taking place across the country, or more accurately, taking place in the hearts and minds of the student demonstrators. They had chosen an animal that symbolizes precisely the line between the races, between Black and White, an animal that could not change its stripes, an animal that would have served perfectly as an emblem of the old apartheid state: two exclusionary zones, one Black, one White, and never the twain shall meet. What, I wondered, did these students propose: to kill and cook one zebra a day until… what precisely? Until, one assumes, the people who ran the country capitulated and could no longer bear the sight of zebra steaks sizzling on the revolutionary barbecue.

But then South Africa is a country where sad charade and tragic farce may replace one another so quickly that no one can keep pace. Because there was, once upon a time, a case very like this. Years ago, in Mozambique, I paid a visit to a zoo where most of the animals had been eaten by starving villagers, some of whom had also moved into the cages once occupied by lions and tigers. They had no option. The civil war had been savage and the countryside around the zoo was mined. Theirs, however, was a practical reality. South Africans do not deal much in reality. What they do rather well is to entertain the idea of parallel universes, and of living at the same time in both. One world is the truly sad, summed up by the empty zoo in Mozambique and the animals that went to feed the starving. Then, alongside it, is the absurd world of the students who wish to barbecue zebra. What everyone does not get wrong is power and the violence that goes with power. The only question is: who will be the victims and who will be the winners? That is what lay behind the toppling of the first of many statues, the unseating of Cecil John Rhodes. For the most part these were a series of skirmishes in a phoney war and would not change for one moment the moods or the manners of those who run the country. That was what Rhodes understood as did the ineffable autocrats who built the apartheid state.

It was also understood by a man who used power to build a nation and create his own homeland. This man was Shaka, King of the Zulus, the creator of one of the greatest empires in Africa. A commemorative statue of the king was erected in Durban some years back, but no sooner had it gone up, with much fanfare, than it vanished from its place of honour and it has not been seen since.

Part 6

THE BATTLE OF
RHODES' NOSE

27

I knew the road to Durban well enough and I lived in the city for some years when I attended Natal University. What I'd never seen before, as I reached the outskirts, was the small herd of stone elephants on a traffic island. Later, I found out I had witnessed something of a second coming; these elephants had inhabited the island in an earlier life. An artist had sculpted the impressive creatures from local stone, shaped within wire mesh, and set them on the traffic island shortly before the start of the soccer World Cup, in 2010. But before he was done, the ANC authorities in the city ordered him to stop work. An elephant trio, it was claimed, was the trademark of bitter political rival, the Inkatha Freedom Party. The elephants thus abandoned on the traffic island were soon vandalized, daubed with red paint, and when the steel netting containing the stones was stolen, the sculptures fell to pieces.

There the fragments rested until, years later, the authorities had a change of mind and the artist resurrected his trio on the traffic island. To be on the safe side he added a fourth elephant. He had never intended, he sadly explained, that his work should be anything other than an innocent memorial to the elephants, once plentiful in Natal, 'until they were all killed by hunters'.

But in a post-Rhodes world there were no innocent memorials.

Any or all might be revised, removed or recast. The stone elephants that came and went were pawns in a characteristic game of
competing, made-to-measure myths. Rewriting history required
time and effort but remaking images needed only a can of paint,
a hammer or a smelter, or the whim of some functionary who did
not like what he saw.

The Afrikaans sculptor who cast King Shaka in bronze, to stand
outside Durban's international airport that bears his name, was
to find this out around the same time the stone elephants ceased
to be. Shaka was a military tactician of genius, an African Napo-
leon who, in the early nineteenth century, founded and ruled a
great Zulu empire. But his reign ended in blood. After the death
of his mother whom he revered, Shaka seems to have gone mad
and, in 1828, he was assassinated, probably by his half-brothers.

Much is uncertain about Shaka's life and no reliable portrait
exists, so the artist played safe in the version of the Zulu monarch he chose to create. He depicted Shaka in a peaceful rustic
setting, surrounded by a ring of Nguni cattle. These striking
animals with their curving horns, multicoloured skins and black
noses are indigenous to South Africa. So far so good, you might
have thought. Shaka had an affection for Nguni cattle and bred
them for their looks as well as for their military symbolism. The
formidable warrior regiments, or impis, of his conquering army
displayed regimental colours on shields made of Nguni cowhide.
His praetorian guard alone was permitted pure white shields,
woven from the hides of Shaka's royal herd.

While many see Shaka as an inspired leader who built the
Zulus into a formidable people, some see him as a brutal warlord
who annihilated all who opposed him. By showing the monarch
at peace among his cherished herd, the sculptor may well have
believed he had found a way of squaring the circle. But this was

Statue of King Shaka, International Airport, KwaZulu-Natal

South Africa, where many good ideas go to die. The current Zulu monarch, King Goodwill Zwelithini, liked the statue but had doubts about exhibiting Shaka outside an airport. Some in the royal household felt that setting the king among his Nguni cows portrayed him as herder rather than martial hero.

The statue was barely in place before the men with the angle-grinders moved in, once again, and Shaka was removed for transformation, in 2010. Optimistic officials promised that a new and better version would be back in a month but, in the meantime, the royal cattle would stay.

By 2014 the king had still not reappeared. The artist pointed out that the circle of Nguni cows without the king missed the point of the work. But the officials in charge of the transformation project reported that a new statue, some five metres high, was on its way.

When I visited the forecourt of the airport, I found the Nguni cattle where they had been, arranged in a peaceable circle, awaiting the return of the vanished king. I couldn't help noticing, yet again, how curiously joined things are in this country. The cows stand beside a busy steakhouse and some irreverent soul had drawn, on the flank of one of them, the outline of a steak. A foreigner visiting the airport for the first time might have imagined that the bronze cattle in front of the airport terminal were really no more than an extravagant advertisement for the nearby restaurant.

We all have our personal memorials, and they are not in bronze or marble. Driving back to Durban along the coast, I passed Umhlanga Rocks, a seaside resort that I knew as a child. In those days it boasted the fanciest hotel anywhere in the country, the Beverly Hills, a name borrowed, as is so much in South Africa, from the United States, which is constantly viewed by many who have never been near the place with either delectation or detestation. The room prices of this towering pillar of pleasure were so eye-watering that the locals called it 'The Heavenly Bills'. It was a joke that my uncle, who lived nearby, liked to repeat and it is he whom I recall when I pass Umhlanga Rocks and 'The Heavenly Bills'.

It was on a beach not far from the hotel that he launched his double suicide attempt, some years ago. I'd been to see him a short time before and found him a little depressed but courteous and gentle as always. I realize now that he would have been very much advanced in the plans he was making. One day, soon after my visit, he walked down to the beach, walked into the waves and kept walking, through the foaming breakers into the Indian Ocean. A couple of kids out surfing saw this man, fully dressed, moving into the waves at a slow and steady pace, paddled over to him and somehow or other got him back to the shore. He let them reassure themselves that he was okay, waited until they had moved far away and walked back into the sea and this time they did not reach him in time.

Why he did it no one was ever sure. But it moved me to think of him taking his last walk, not once, but twice. There was a certain poetic quality about his death, as well as a quiet and steady determination. Not that Uncle Don was at all poetic. He was a chartered accountant, the first in the family to go to university and the youngest in the country to pass the board exams. For some reason, perhaps because they began in South Africa as impoverished Irish immigrants, or perhaps because it wasn't a talent that many of us possessed, his head for figures was hugely prized in my family. My mother's greatest source of pride was to tell me that she'd mastered double-entry bookkeeping. It was with a double-entry that my uncle closed the books on that beach, north of Durban. There is nothing to be seen but I've always regarded that stretch of sand and sea as his memorial. It's often what you can't see that stays with you.

When I lived in Durban I used to swim off the beach in Umhlanga and at the far end of the pristine sands, close to Heavenly Bills, stood a notice that read: 'This beach strictly reserved for Whites Only.' At the time no one gave it a second glance. No one White, anyway, because such notices were everywhere, they were woven into our daily life, they were so familiar that we did not need to read them to understand what they were saying. Such notices have been relegated to museums that record the weird world of apartheid but those signs and notices are still there in the heads of many of us.

The pain of those on the receiving end is something that Whites struggle, and fail, to comprehend. Will the effacement of signs and symbols, or statues, do what is hoped? And how long will it take? The ever-present notices commanding Blacks to move on and out are long gone, so is the statue of Cecil Rhodes; but the wounds are deep. And yet it is a paradox that, in the main, those who suffered most, unlike our past and present hate-mongers, remain astonishingly generous and forbearing.

28

C onsider the full-length statue of the portly moustachioed
monarch, King George V, which stands on the Natal
University campus, gazing out to the Indian Ocean. He
was a familiar stone effigy we students passed without a second
glance and few could have recognized the grandson of Queen
Victoria or named his sonorous titles: 'King of the United Kingdom, and the British Dominions Beyond the Seas, Defender of
the Faith and Emperor of India'.

King George V, who reigned from 1910 to 1936, was magnifi-
cently dull; he knew no passions greater than philately and his
biographer remarked that the young prince liked nothing better
than to 'sit in his study and look at his stamps'. The future king
once described himself, rather endearingly, as 'a very ordinary
sort of fellow'. But history caught up with this very ordinary
fellow and, as King George V, he presided over momentous events
of the twentieth century, from the Russian Revolution to the rise
of Adolf Hitler.

No doubt loyal locals paid for the royal effigy. Natal was a
feverishly royalist province, proud to be mocked as the last of the
British colonies. That sort of boasting annoyed the Boers who
had once ruled Natal when it had been their republic. The Boers,
in turn, annoyed the Zulus who had ruled the territory before the

Boers. Both Zulus and Boers had, in turn, fought bitterly against the British in a number of wars, and the graves of members of all three tribes were to be found scattered across the length and breadth of Natal. King George V dropped in to see his Natal colony once or twice, notably after the Boer War, when he handed out medals to soldiers from both sides. The visit didn't go down particularly well because the king was accused of squandering money that might have gone to rebuild a shattered country.

A short while before I arrived in Durban, King George's statue had been attacked by students, daubed with white paint, and

King George V, Natal University, Durban

around his neck they hung a sign that read: 'End White Privilege'. Now it was certainly true that King George V was White, and very privileged, but I doubt that those students who defaced his statue had any more idea of who he was than we did. He would have been to them, as he was to us, familiar campus furniture. But in the present state of heady ignorance, the history and background of those you attack is not something you need to know much about. It was enough to select your targets by the colour of their skins. Only someone who has lived under the former White regime, which thought exactly along those lines, would understand the shock that one feels to have seen the country travel so far away from the warped and stupid notions of the old South Africa, only to arrive back in a position from where it all began and where ethnicity and skin colour are the beginning and the end of everything.

There was a heady period, after the release of Mandela from jail, when South Africa had ahead of it a non-racial future where, as Oliver Tambo had repeated to me, the country would belong to all who lived in it. That dream is over. There is a sizeable minority of South Africans who are, increasingly, not wanted on voyage. But until people come out and say so, and back their words with actions, defacing symbols of the oppressor is all the iconoclasts can do. It is a game anyone with a paintbrush or firebomb can play, and in a society where politics is the continuation of war by other means, your sacred icon may be my arch-enemy and vice versa.

The Durban campus, perched on a ridge overlooking the Indian Ocean, was always a sunny subtropical domain, but shadows are falling fast. My guide took me from the painted statue of King George V, something that merely flaunted the excitable ignorance of its attackers, to the Howard College Law Library, where things had turned serious. A few nights before, the library had been torched and fire had destroyed old and historical law books, some irreplaceable.

I was assailed by the same acrid stench I had smelt in the charred schools of Vuwani. Those had been small classrooms with very few books. The Law Library housed dozens of tightly packed volumes. Some had been gouged by the flames, some mildly scorched, some melted in the heat, and the reek of soot and ashes was stifling. Such was the general dismay that the ruling ANC put out a statement warning that burning books was an attack on reason and common sense, and pointing out that the attack mirrored what the Nazis had once done in Berlin, on Kristallnacht when they fed to the flames books by Jews, liberals and Communists. This was all unusually strong stuff and very welcome. But those who backed the burning of the library defended the fire in a defiant tweet: 'That Library hadn't even a single Black author, maybe there's 2 but the rest was all colonial Dutch-law bullshit that came [sic] 1652.'

When I looked at the figures, I realized that burning libraries has become something of a growth industry. Between 2005 and 2013, fifteen libraries had been burnt, including local and community libraries that had been partially burnt or destroyed, some serving thousands of people, where the destruction involved not only books but computers, as well as copying and fax machines. The figure was regarded by other researchers as conservative and library burnings have accelerated.

It's a sad business and some quoted the poet Heine, who observed that those who begin by burning books ended up by burning people. This prediction turned out to be eerily true in Nazi Germany. But such perceptions, however worthy, simply don't meet the standards of absurdity, irony and pathos that are the norms in South Africa. In the townships, in the years leading up to democratic rule, people considered to be 'sell-outs' or 'traitors' to the struggle had tyres filled with petrol draped around their necks and they were burnt to death. Winnie Mandela's clarion call for human bonfires echoed across the land: 'With our boxes of matches and our necklaces we will liberate our country…' So you might almost say that, in reversing the order of Heine's prediction and by moving away from burning people to burning books, South Africans have taken a small step forward and that was perhaps as much progress as we may expect.

It is wrong to imagine that by overturning idols, we can prevent the past from haunting the present. Because without useful, though painful, reminders of where we came from, how are we to begin even to have any idea of where we wish to go? Deeply repressive societies, in the Soviet Union or Eastern Europe, have been ardent about re-engineering the past but failed. No amount of name-calling or name-changing gets rid of the past. Re-education of the transgressing classes, however expertly and forcefully administered, will not do the trick. Even state-sponsored ignorance, so popular in the old South Africa, is no protection against returning demons. Effigies and idols, after they have been forcibly 'disappeared', have ways of reappearing to remind us they were once intimate, if embarrassing, members of the family. Rather than covering them up or trucking them off to the scrap heap, it seems to me that they have something to tell us, and it pays to hear them out.

On my way out of Durban I drove along what used to be known as Point Road, once a dockland underworld, notorious for its sailors, booze, drugs and streetwalkers. In the sixties, I used to go drinking in a pub called the Smuggler's Arms with Douglas Livingstone, one of the finest poets the country ever knew. Livingstone was a diver, surfer, boxer and late-night carouser. But deep down he was a scientist, a bacteriologist who preferred gritty common sense in politics to the rebellious rapture that many of us were given to, back in those strange days.

Livingstone died tragically young, in 1996, and a bust was commissioned by an admirer, mounted in a public space in a shopping centre and much appreciated. It was not a very good likeness, but it caught something of the swashbuckling character of the man. Then someone stole the bust and when the theft was reported, the police declared themselves uninterested in hunting down a lump of metal, dismissing the theft of a poet as 'low priority crime'. Things have changed: the assault on statues has moved from low priority crime to high priority protest.

We did not expect to see the bust again. Then one day, trawling through junk in a scrap metal dealer's yard, a fan of the poet came across a familiar face and, once again, another long-lost Dr Livingstone had been found. A label around the neck of the bust, listing its copper, lead and brass content, suggested it had been rescued at the last moment before it vanished forever into a furnace. Admirers donated the bust to Livingstone's old school and there it rests. I was surprised to find it was an unexpectedly posh alma mater for a street fighter. I guess that was why he never mentioned it to me. He would have been shocked had he known he would be cast in bronze but deeply amused to know his bust had been stolen, found, and returned to the school he'd last seen as a boy.

I could find no trace of the old Smuggler's Arms in Point Road. In fact, I could find no mention of Point Road at all because the run-down area had been given a facelift. Point Road had been renamed Mahatma Gandhi Road, to commemorate Gandhi's time in Durban, and no doubt Durban town-planners felt that the Indian community would appreciate the compliment. They were wrong about that. Some in the Asian community felt that naming a thoroughfare in a neighbourhood long known to Durbanites for girls and ganja was no compliment to the abstemious and austere Mahatma. Neither the facelift nor the name change have done much good anyway, because guidebooks still warn tourists against a visit, persist in calling the avenue 'Point Road' and its brothels are as busy as ever. As his paint-splashed statue in central Johannesburg had warned me, even being Gandhi is no protection these days, as the hunt for past oppressors gathers pace. You may change the name, it seems, but that does not change the game.

29

The road from Durban runs along the Natal south coast, and it passes seaside towns where I spent summer holidays as a child. I was aiming for a little village called Nkantolo, in the rural Eastern Cape, where Oliver Tambo was born. I'd been there a few years before and come face to face with Tambo, some thirty years after we met in London and he had cautioned me against the move-on blues. In his home village Tambo had been commemorated by a bronze bust. It is odd to come across people you once knew in the flesh recast as street names and statues and airports.

The names of the Natal south coast villages along the national road, Margate, Ramsgate, St Michael's on Sea and even Trafalgar, speak of a world of British settlers, with their Winston Churchill Drives and Sir Harry Smith Avenues, with their Closes, Copses and Crescents. Sounds of home; echoes of an empire that felt close and comforting – however far it might be from the banana trees, sugar cane and subtropical nights of African Natal.

Such illusions fall away once you leave the Natal south coast and swing inland, you meet the immense plains of Eastern Cape, where the pointed thatched roofs of the huts seem sometimes to mimic the peaks of the mountains, and you know you could be nowhere but in Africa. Oliver Tambo died soon after his triumphant return to South Africa in 1993. His home village in rural Mbizana District had the idea of building a memorial garden in his honour as well as a craft centre, and also on display was a bronze bust of the famous son of the village that I'd seen some years earlier. It was a very good likeness of Tambo, with his large specs and mild professorial air, even if it missed the steel beneath.

When I got to Nkantolo and looked for the memorial garden and craft centre, it wasn't there and nor was his bust. They had been burnt, some time before. Villagers told me this with a mixture of embarrassment and perplexity, as if the shock was still with them. And I could understand why that was. After all, Tambo spent decades in exile leading the ANC in the struggle against apartheid, and returned to South Africa in triumph, only to die soon after he got back. And yet when his friends and family erected a memorial to the man in his home village, someone torched it. His nephew summed up perfectly the distress and dismay the family felt, when he told a local newspaper: 'Burning the bust means they are burning Tambo himself.'

I asked people in Nkantolo if they knew why it had happened and I got a number of answers but one detail was emphasized over and over. There were not enough new houses in the neighbourhood. The blame for the destruction of the memorial was laid squarely on people from the nearby village of Silangwe, from where Tambo's mother had come. It was said that people there felt aggrieved that Nkantolo village was getting all the attention and all the money from the government. They had even been given a monument to Tambo. There were whispers in Nkantolo itself that Tambo's family had objected to the small size of the bust, a mere head and shoulders effigy, like a playing-card king. It would not have escaped attention that Nelson Mandela was immortalized in nine metres of bronze in Pretoria and, even in death, Mandela outshone his senior colleague. Others I spoke to told me that the government had understood their feelings. New roads were planned for Mbizana District, more houses were to be built and a revised and much grander effigy of Oliver Tambo was in the making.

But there was another question that puzzled me almost as much as it did the villagers of Mbizana worried over the destruction of the garden of remembrance. 'Where will it stop?' a villager in Nkantolo asked me and I would have liked to have had an answer for him. If the statue of Oliver Tambo, a leader who ranked with Nelson Mandela, might be attacked and destroyed, where was this going?

Perhaps it was mistaken to look for direction in a trail of destruction because, rather like a forest fire, it might be accelerated by any fierce wind, and move in any direction. It had no programme; it was simply all appetite and did not ask: where next? What it wanted and needed and what it took was, simply, 'more' – more images, effigies, symbols, relics, pictures, photographs. What began with the removal and incarceration in some secret location of the statue of Cecil John Rhodes, followed by assaults on effigies of Jan van Riebeeck and Paul Kruger, was followed by the disfiguring of Chief Tshwane and Mahatma Gandhi and the immolation of Oliver Tambo.

In the wake of the fall of Rhodes, the sniffing out of seditious symbols had begun. Various artworks, deemed doubtful, were stripped from the walls of the University of Cape Town and carried off to a place of greater safety. An announcement from the university authorities that managed to be po-faced and menacing all at once declared that a task team had 'begun the process of interrogating all the artwork and photographs in public spaces', in order to decide which were safe and acceptable for preservation. Evidently, we had arrived on a linguistic funny farm where words had lost their meaning.

Perhaps this was to be expected, given the phantasmagoria in which the statue wars began, with students solemnly assaulting, and then acting out a mock-lynching of a statue, before setting off for a beer in a seaside entertainment mall. When statues were 'executed' and paintings marched away for interrogation in back rooms, then the sense of words had fled. When Oliver Tambo's nephew remarked that 'burning the bust means burning Oliver Tambo himself', I heard what was said but the meaning had vanished. Tambo was not burnt for being who he was; the burning was meaningless. Tambo had become, in his own birthplace, a weaponized word in a local war; he was just more fuel for the fire.

What was once said of Ulster politics may be said of South Africa; those who said they knew what was going on were very confused. It took an American, Allen Drury, visiting the country for the first time, fifty years ago, to register just how weird we were. 'I hope you understand us,' some nameless functionary in the ruling party confided to Drury, adding, 'I don't.' Drury's travels, recounted in *A Very Strange Society*, expressed a heartfelt bewilderment so appropriate and embarrassing that the censors banned his book almost immediately. Those in charge who spoke to Drury display the crusading ignorance, happy vacuity and deadly homicidal tendencies that summed up the national character. They also sound today strikingly like our contemporaries and every bit as unhinged. Self-delusion is what we do well – when we're not busy doing each other in. The immolation of Oliver Tambo and the removal of Cecil John Rhodes from his plinth in Cape Town seem unlikely to change much, any more than the removal of the body of Lenin from Red Square would erase the history of Bolshevik Russia.

And a further question arises: if Lenin were to be removed, would somebody offer him a good home? Do fallen idols deserve a retirement home of the kind now to be found in India, Hungary and Russia where they can be housed pending some change in their fortunes? I recall in the nineties, in Moscow, how often I passed the enormous statue of Felix Dzerzhinsky, close to the Lubyanka building. After the Russian Revolution, 'Iron Felix', as he was known, was appointed by Lenin to direct the Bolshevik programme of 'organized terror' and he proved an enthusiastic executioner. I'd look up at his massive effigy outside the KGB headquarters, and remember the bitter Muscovite remark that only a Pole could have hated Russians enough to murder so many in the cellars of the Lubyanka. His statue was toppled in 1991, after the failed coup against Mikhail Gorbachev, and he was carted off to a park for retired idols. But nearly half of the Russians polled recently now wanted Iron Felix back on his plinth. Might someone offer a similar refuge to Cecil Rhodes, while he waits out the verdict of history? And what would be a better destination than a town named for the exiled imperialist?

If you take the road from Tambo's native village it's around four hours to the hamlet named Rhodes, high in the mountains by the Lesotho border. It is a delightful little place and dates back to the 1890s, when Rhodes was Prime Minister of the Cape. The villagers hoped that by flattering the great man by naming the village after him, Rhodes would shower cash on the community. Rhodes never saw the town but he sent what was then a lot of money, a donation of some £500. No sooner had the cash arrived from the capital than it vanished – a disappearing trick long favoured by many towns and cities, and still spectacularly evident today.

The real attraction of the little town called Rhodes, down the years, has not been its interesting accounting procedures but its location in the highlands of the Eastern Cape, at the southern end of the Drakensberg Range. It is high enough and cold enough for some mountain peaks to show snow in many months of the year. The village lures those who want to walk in the mountains, fish for trout, or ski when the snows fall. As winter comes on, the light turns icy clear and mountains and sky merge in shades of blue and russet. As with many towns, it is possible to read in its topography the old history of the country. You notice, for instance, the inevitable disparity between the pretty Victorian cottages, owned mostly by Whites, and the flimsy shacks of the local people, mostly Blacks, for whom jobs are scarce and ill-paid.

The hospitable owner of the local hostelry, the Walkerbouts Inn, knows how hard it is to create jobs for local people. Because Rhodes lies in a fragile river valley, it was decided to pay people to root out alien species of vegetation, like black wattle, that have long been choking the river. It turned out to be easier said than done because only the accessible wattle has been controlled but hard-to-reach sections, where the river bends and buckles, have not been touched. The result has been to reduce the amount of firewood available and so people increasingly take firewood wherever they find it – 'and who can blame them,' said the innkeeper, 'this is a very chilly part of the world.'

But the innkeeper's chief contribution to the sanity of the country might be his willingness to provide a home for the Rhodes statue, banished from the Cape Town campus. The innkeeper exhibits an indomitable breeziness about war and peace, as befits someone who has seen so much come and go, and shares his favourite quotation with his guests: 'It's never too late to have a happy childhood...'

It would be appropriate if Rhodes took his place in the garden, not just because the town carried his name as a reminder that the conflict between Boers and British that he had done so much to initiate was by no means over. 'The Boer War continues around here,' the innkeeper told me cheerfully as I left town.

He was right. In South Africa wars do not end but peter out into uneasy truces, only to flare up again when least expected. Travelling further through the Eastern Cape, heading towards the sea and Port Elizabeth, it was war and memories of war that haunted the landscape and the memory. As you approached the coast, the feeling increased because this was once settler country. A contingent of British emigrants was not so much planted as dumped in the wilds of the Eastern Cape in 1820, to strengthen the border against the local Xhosa who had been there for centuries and took a very dim view of the British interlopers. So too did local KhoiSan. Just as the KhoiSan had felt about the first Dutch settlers who arrived in 1652, the Xhosa dreamt of driving pale-skinned invaders into the sea from where they came. The desire sharpened when the British tried to extend their Cape Colony eastwards and Xhosa and KhoiSan resisted. The British governor decided a human buffer would hold off the belligerent Xhosa and encouraged a plan to lure British immigrants to the Eastern Cape. They would be settled in large tracts of the region, between the Fish and the Sundays rivers, a region that colonial officials convinced themselves had 'the appearance of unoccupied land'.

On paper it looked like a cunning plan. At the end of the Napoleonic Wars, many in England were without work or housing or hope. It seemed a fine idea to add this 'surplus population' to the Cape Colony, where they might be useful, productive and feed themselves, as well as holding the line against the Xhosa. The idea was applied again in the following century when the apartheid government shunted what were called 'useless appendages' to the tribal reserves. The English migrants of 1820 were often tradespeople who had no idea of farming and were quite unprepared for Africa and its hardships. They were soon to find that the 'unoccupied land' where they were to make their homes was already home to others who bitterly resented the intrusion.

Our school history books made much of the 1820 settlers, of their bravery, prowess on the sports field, fighting skills and down-to-earth British ways. Much of this was nonsense. The settlers were deceived from the start and many chosen for the passage to the Cape would have preferred migrating to the United States. But the government wanted them in South Africa and it was suggested in the House of Commons that those who did not go freely might be transported. Those who volunteered for the passage were assured that the Cape Colony was a place of peace and plenty, sunshine and serenity, where crops, cattle and sheep would thrive.

The conditions of service were harsh. Fearful that settlers might abscond, the 'pass' system was introduced to bind them to their new homes. Colonial officials admitted privately that the indigenous tribes would do all they could to get rid of the migrants. Even so, the hostility of indigenous people in the Eastern Cape, astonished officials reported to superiors in London, was based on the delusion that they were 'the original possessors of the country'. Settlers were warned to keep their guns ready, and to use watchmen against Xhosa cattle rustlers, or they were very likely 'to be plundered by their restless neighbours'. But the belief persisted, in the face of all evidence, that settler solidarity and superior weapons would take care of the native problem.

The settlers and the British Army had the firepower but the Xhosa had the numbers and no fewer than nine frontier wars were fought on the Eastern Cape border. There was carnage, pillage and conflagration and the settlers were cruelly hounded and harried. More forts were built in the Eastern Cape than you could shake an assegai at, and their names make an eerie music that haunts the lovely mountain passes, in what is still known as 'border country': Fort Beaufort, Fort England, Fort Waterloo, Fort Misery, Fort Luxury and, still there of course, Fort Hare, best remembered because the university established there would one day accommodate Nelson Mandela and Oliver Tambo, and where Tambo was to get to hear for the first time the heart-sore music of the blues.

If it was in the countryside that British settlers often failed as farmers, it was when they began moving to the coast and the growing cities of East London and Port Elizabeth, where they might use their trade skills, that they thrived. The frontier wars against the Xhosa, like the Boer War, never really ended, but subsided into 'a grumbling peace'. However tightly successive White regimes nailed it down, and damped revolt, revolt sooner or later broke out once again in the Eastern Cape.

Not surprising, then, that in Port Elizabeth, in 2015, the new iconoclasts attacked a monument erected soon after the Boer War to commemorate hundreds of thousands of horses that perished in the conflict. It was a powerful memorial. Kneeling before his mount, a British soldier holds up a pail of water. The attackers,

Horse Memorial, Port Elizabeth, after the attack, 2016

dressed in red, arrived in a car, pushed the soldier from the platform where he knelt, and fled. They failed to dislodge the horse but the trooper lay on his back, as if shot, one leg pointing stiffly at the sky in an attitude reminiscent of rigor mortis.

There was pain and anger when the Horse Memorial was attacked. What next? people asked. Would someone assault Queen Victoria, whose statue stood in front of the public library? It might have been a mistake to bring in Queen Victoria because, a few days later, she was showered in dark green paint.

But she got off pretty lightly, compared with the assault that took place in the nearby city of Uitenhage where I stopped in the market square to see a monument that had suffered an attack unlike any other. This memorial to a soldier of the Boer War had been 'necklaced'. A tyre filled with petrol was strung around the neck of the figure and set alight. Those who carried out the attack, all red-clad members of the EFF, were unapologetic about their action: 'We put a tyre around the neck of that White statue and we put it on fire...' They filmed the flaming pyre on their phones and, in a nice change of tone, someone put out a tweet praising the recent performance of Arsenal football club.

30

There is a village named Rhodes and there is also a university that still carries his name, although that is likely to change before much longer. The university is in Grahamstown, a pleasant place, once a redoubt where English settlers found shelter from the attacks of hostile tribes but now best known for its schools and colleges and for the National Arts Festival. A large ungainly memorial planted on a hill overlooking the town commemorates the same 1820 settlers who had such a hard time of it. A plaque inside the building reads: 'We must take root or die.' It's a nice thought, but it seems more useful to reflect that some did take root, and die.

The town is filled with disconcerting evidence of former British ways. It is not just its colleges and churches, it is the kind of dreaminess that characterizes many White South Africans, descendants of those 1820 settlers who, for a very long time, have never had to ask themselves who they thought they were, and what they thought they were doing in Africa, in the heart of border country. Rhodes University was begun not by the man himself but by his faithful friend, Leander Starr Jameson, who channelled the necessary funds its way, back in 1905.

When I reached the campus, I found the town was once again a battlefield, just as it had been in the bad old days of the frontier wars. Rhodes University has become unsure of who and what it is supposed to be and was now being referred to, by students I met, as 'the university currently known as Rhodes'.

I met with someone I shall call Thandi, a second-year student in a faculty she preferred not to identify – the degree of paranoia seemed to step up each time I listened or spoke to students. She showed me the 'rules for journalists'; a stern document that allowed next to no news-gathering and certainly no pictures.

'In a world where everyone takes pictures of everyone all the time,' I said to her, 'that isn't going to be easy to stop.'

'No pictures,' said Thandi. 'You can't take any without prior permission and there's no filming, that's the rules. That is our strategy.'

'What does your strategy stand for?'

She shook her head. 'I'm not allowed to say and even if I told you, you wouldn't be allowed to publish it. We warn journalists about this.'

'But I'm not a journalist.'

'You're a writer, it's the same thing. You need to be aware of attitudes.'

'Whose attitude?'

'Ours and yours. Especially yours. You need to be sensitive and humble and remember that students have their dignity. Don't write about them in some hard way.'

'This is a bit like being sent to a re-education camp.'

She was intrigued, almost as if it sounded like rather a good idea. 'What's a re-education camp?'

'The sort of thing they went in for during the Cultural Revolution, in China.'

'What was the Cultural Revolution?'

I didn't think we were really on the same wavelength but I was going to try.

'What is it that you and your colleagues want?'

What she and her generation wanted, she said, was '…everything. And we want it now. If they go ahead the way they are at the moment, we'll stop the exams at the end of the year and some people will even burn the place.'

'When you say everything, what does everything mean?'

'We want free higher education across the land. And we will get it, and then we will take the country.'

'Take it where?'

'Take it back. Take it over. Take it for us and make it free.'

'Free for whom?'

'For all Black people.'

'For rich Black people too?'

She hesitated. 'For all Black people.'

'Then, it is a race thing?'

She shook her head. 'No. It's an economic thing.'

'Would you say that there are those here who hate Whites?'

She thought about this. 'Some, yes. But it's not the Whites themselves – it's what they stand for.'

'What do they stand for?'

Thandi thought about it again. 'For everything.'

It was apt that we were having our talk outside the student residence named Olive Schreiner House. Schreiner saw more clearly, and much earlier, than anyone where the fault-lines lay. She wrote in a letter to a friend back in 1896: 'There are two and only two questions in South Africa, the native question and the question – Shall the whole land fall into the hands of a knot of capitalists?'

When I repeated this to Thandi, she nodded. 'Yes, we want to take the land back, it is time. And we want Black economic power... and we've put our Black bodies on the line for that.'

But why, I wondered, would the acceptable colour of power be Black? Why would it be any kinder than its paler mirror image? To date, the rising Black capitalists in the country have shown themselves as dedicated to profit as anyone else.

Thandi shrugged. 'We have to hope.'

What I didn't ask her was something that profoundly puzzled me; who did she think she was addressing when she asked questions or threw down challenges? Who was she speaking to? What I heard in her tone, and I'd heard it from others, was not only anger, it was a demand for sympathy invoked by references to 'our Black bodies', to 'our pain', to 'our struggle', as if recognition was not enough for those who paraded their hurt and their anguish, they demanded pity and wanted it from the very people they were supposed to be fighting.

But there was only so much I could keep in my head without writing anything down and I wanted to remember as much as possible. Thandi talked for some while, passionately and eloquently, but her language had become so clouded that when, a bit later, I did write down what I could remember, I could not make much sense of it.

As I walked through the town centre I passed a platoon of school kids from one of the grander colleges, drawn up in two lines, all so perfectly orderly, so kempt, so well behaved, and, mostly, so White. And I felt then something of the pain that I knew Thandi felt. That pain is real but then so are the numbers, and the notion that the White kids leaving the Anglican cathedral and heading back to their college represent somehow the real power in the land is, simply, wrong. Most students at university are Black; the present administration is Black; almost all of the police, whom Thandi calls servants of the state, are Black; those who administer every government department are almost all Black; and overall income of the rising Black middle class has outstripped that of the Whites. And yet it seems as if the old White apartheid state haunts the land, its power lingers, like the ghost of Rhodes, and the very fact that it does not any longer exist makes it essential that it should be reinvented.

I had the same problem with Thandi's passionate beliefs as I did with the guardian of the Molotov cocktails whom I had met in Johannesburg, on the campus of the university. These weapons were aimed in the wrong direction – at libraries, lecture theatres, statues, paintings. Still worse, the war was paltry. To anyone wanting real change, it was a mistake and a disappointment. Indeed, between the grandiosity of the ambition, which declared that all shall burn and that this was a revolution, and the evidence of a few broken windows and a gutted storeroom, a burnt auditorium, Duane among his petrol bombs, there was an aching, embarrassing gap, a profound failure of achievement.

But there was something more – for Thandi and her cohorts the language they used was fizzy, woolly, vague, not because the right words couldn't be found, but because those full of such intensity preferred, for the most part, not to use the blunt words that spoke what they meant. So they talked about 'Black pain' and 'Black economics' and deplored 'White capital' and 'White power' and even 'Whiteness', when what they really wanted to say but somehow could not quite bring themselves to do was what it said on the T-shirts that I'd seen on some of the university campuses: 'Kill All Whites'.

Things had come to a pretty pass when, after all this time and so many promises of having put all the old insanity behind us, the country was fast returning to the drear business of colour-coding everything and, inevitably, everyone.

'Where are you off to now?' Thandi wanted to know.

'Cape Town. I want to see where it all began.'

She nodded. 'Yes, it all began with van Riebeeck.'

Yes and no. I stopped, as I always do, on my way from Grahamstown to Cape Town at a little town called Hankey. I always stop there because it houses a monument to the Khoi, or Hottentot, woman who was taken to Europe, perhaps freely, perhaps not, and paraded as a freak, the 'Hottentot Venus', in the salons and circuses of London, Ireland and Paris where she died aged twenty-six, in 1815.

Her remains were brought back to South Africa and buried on a hilltop in Hankey, which was more or less home to her. I go

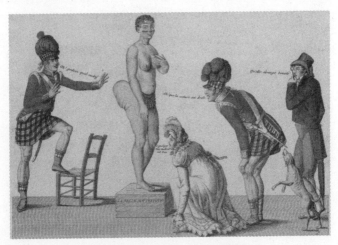

Inspecting the Hottentot Venus

back because the monument, once the scene of much public reverence, when she was repatriated, is now almost unapproachable. The tomb is guarded against vandals by a steel fence and, more recently, it is being enlarged or altered or transformed – and you cannot now visit the monument at all. Yet an entire district of the Eastern Cape, measuring hundreds of miles, has been named for her – but her small grave is now out of bounds. Sarah Baartman was the real thing – but is invisible. Her name is on all the signposts – but her grave was vandalized soon after it was dedicated. Interest has waned and next to no one I spoke to in Hankey could say who she was.

31

I planned to end my trip around the country in the place where, as Thandi said, it all began – in Cape Town with van Riebeeck and his Dutch settlers. But I stopped about an hour from Cape Town, at the university town of Stellenbosch, because the moment you indulge in the local popular games of muscular myth-making and arguing about how good or bad your chosen hero or my villain may be, you are spoilt for choice. It's in hypocrisy and not history where we excel.

Simon van der Stel was another of those early Dutch settlers who, in 1679, gave his name to the town of Stellenbosch and was always presented as an enlightened and effective governor of the colony. And so indeed he seems to have been. What was not said, however, was that Simon van der Stel was never entirely 'White'. His grandmother had been a slave named Monyca de Costa, from Coromandel in Southern India.

Such considerations seemed far away from the busy campus of Stellenbosch University, where I met someone who spoke to me in Afrikaans, with great conviction, about stamping out Afrikaans in the university. She was slight, dark-haired, intense and I'd say around nineteen or so. We sat at a coffee shop, at a table that she chose, well clear of the other patrons, because what she said was to be private. She did not want me to know her real name and she told me that the only proper way to spell her gender was 'womxn'. I said that made it unpronounceable, and she seemed rather pleased.

She set out firmly what were to be the rules of engagement. I might refer to her as a 'Cadre', the term that was preferred by 'The Collective' to which she belonged. 'Cadre' has something of the cachet of 'comrade', except that it's somehow more cool than the other wispy identifiers preferred by those who talk about campus politics using hoary abstractions like 'role-players', 'stakeholders', 'structures' and 'formations'; terms so airy they float before your eyes or slip into one ear and out the other without ever engaging the mind. It's odd that 'Cadre' should be hip because everywhere else in the world, except perhaps North Korea and Cuba, 'Cadre', like 'comrade', sounds creakingly old-fashioned. On the other hand, it is impersonal, free of gender, anonymous, and it signifies membership or 'co-ownership' of a secret, subversive grouping. It is a title, a teaser, a trademark – or all three. It is felt, by those who belong to 'The Collective', to be 'somehow less aggressive' than the terms used by fellow followers in what the Cadre refers to as 'intersectionality'; feminist activists who refer to themselves as 'Bodies' or 'Allies'. The Collective to which the Cadre belonged opposed all forms of what she called 'Western White Patriarchal Capital'. She was a philosophy student with a special interest in the works of Nietzsche.

'Afrikaans must go.'

'Altogether?'

'Altogether. Please remember, I'll talk to you on condition that you don't say who I am or repeat what I've said.'

I told her this wouldn't be possible. I was happy either to make notes of what she said or to put it down on tape and I was prepared to disguise her identity, and even to paraphrase what she said to me, but without being able to report what she said it was silly to talk to her.

'Why would you have agreed to talk to me anyway?'

'Because they say you are all right. That you are known. And that you are not from here, you've come from overseas.'

I found it particularly painful to hear myself described as 'not from here'. At least she did not refer to 'overseas' in the way we once did, under the old White Nationalist regime, as 'the outside world'.

'So tell me,' I asked her, 'what does your Collective wish to do?'

'Burn things,' she said. 'This place included, if it comes to that.'

This 'place' was the University of Stellenbosch, which takes up much of the very pretty town with its Cape Dutch houses, creamy gables and oak-lined pavements thronged with students. Almost everything and everyone is related to the university, which was founded in the later nineteenth century and benefits from being a

Plaque commemorating Hendrik Verwoerd being removed from the Stellenbosch University campus, May 2015

world away from cosmopolitan Cape Town. It was for a very long time the college where many leading politicians were trained. It was once also exclusively White and Afrikaans-speaking. What made it special was that it was the guardian, the sacred dwelling place of those most pure, most devoted and most loyal to the philosophy and religion of the old White Nationalist government. They believed in it as a religion, as a philosophy, as a way of life, and as a way of speaking, because the Afrikaans language was often referred to, with a proprietorial fondness, simply as *die taal* – the language. It was Hendrik Verwoerd's alma mater.

Then the country changed. Mandela was released and everyone of whatever colour might go to any of the universities. The Cape is a very large province where most Coloureds and Whites speak Afrikaans at home; it is the patois. But Afrikaans was also the language of those who, for far too long, had things all their own way. And what was the point, Black students who did not and would not speak the language wanted to know, of change – if nothing at all changed? People of mixed race, like the Cadre, wanted Afrikaans either to be abolished or radically reduced as a teaching language, and if it didn't happen, then, she told me quite plainly, her colleagues had sent word to the university authorities that they would torch the place.

In anything like a normal country, the threat of arson would be a matter for the police but this is South Africa and nothing is normal and the police are not to be counted on and the idea of burning down buildings had been presented, even by those in charge of Stellenbosch, not as a crime but as part of the political conversation. This, naturally enough, was a rather disturbing idea both to the parents of students in the university and to those who taught them, but the university had been living for some years with violent clashes, sometimes involving students, sometimes between students and the police, both on and off campus. Disturbance was the order of the day and so too, for that matter, was burning things.

'We need to hit back, to make them aware. So we send out word to all; to the Cadres, to our allies, to our family, that we would march together.'

'Family?'

'I mean people who are with us. Family. We want to end colonial brutality, we want to stop oppression by the patriarchs and the racists. We want to live freely in our own land. We march not for us alone but also for our mothers and fathers.'

'More family?'

'I don't mean it literally. I mean the workers in the university who are kicked out of their jobs, which were privatized. We want the workers in-sourced again, because these workers are our mothers and fathers.'

The terms, the words, grow ever more vague, need more and more explanation, and in the end they mean less and less. What counts are the threats of action. But even the threats are often not what they claim to be. There have been fires on the campus, an office or two has been burnt and the authorities were quick to issue an almost triumphant statement – 'very small fire… no casualties'. A month earlier an entire building went up in smoke. Small fires no longer made much news at a time when hashtags on Twitter celebrate arson, and when 2016 was named 'the year of fire'.

The Cadre told me, with a degree of envy, that the office of the Vice Chancellor at the University of Cape Town had been firebombed and that was really serious stuff. All they'd managed to do at Stellenbosch was to take down a building here or an office there and she really felt they could have done better.

What was notable about this war talk was not really what it said but how far short of anything like reality it fell. No one who has seen serious fire damage would think of it as either interesting or worthwhile or pretty. I said so.

'But we need to make our presence felt,' the Cadre insisted, 'and if they won't listen to us, what option do we have?'

'Who are "they"?'

She shrugged. She lifted an ironic eyebrow. I got the impression that she regretted what she had to say next, as I was included, and indeed complicit, and she did not want to offend.

'The White world… Whiteness… what else?'

The question she asked was empty of meaning. Whose attention did she wish to attract? She talked as if the old apartheid regime was still in place, that amalgam of 'the White world', the Western world, the capitalistic world, which, awful as it was, at least provided a clear and visible target. It was very hard to attack and destroy an abstraction, so ways must be found to make real and concrete the true enemy. And in desperate circumstances any available enemy would do. That is what the students with their buckets of human excrement in their lynching party were trying to do at the University of Cape Town; they wished to lay hands on a scapegoat, a culprit and since a suitable White sacrifice was, for the moment at least, not available, then another token must be found.

The students of Cape Town University who removed the statue of Rhodes and consigned it to the outer darkness made a pile of paintings and photographs they found on campus and ceremonially with much cheerfulness set them on fire. They were, they explained, 'burning Whiteness'.

The Cadre's chagrin was understandable, in the face of a competitor college's superior fire-raising ability. But the complexity of who to attack, what to destroy, how to go about it, and when, deepened on the campus of Stellenbosch University. It was not just words and images and language and skin colour that haunted and troubled many of her colleagues; there were practical and immediate dangers: the campus must be open to all but how was 'all' to be measured?

'What we face on campus is a culture of rape. And it's ironic that we see some protests against rape being led by men. Even though most of the power is held by men and most of the physical attacks on us are by men. It's as though Black bodies are the playthings of males.'

I saw what she meant. But when you wanted to open the college as widely as possible to everyone from all backgrounds and genders and ethnic mixes, you had to include men.

'I know that this is not just here, in the university, where we've had any number of rapes. I also know that it's a very small thing compared to the overall picture in the country. Some say there are over half a million a year, and then there is the rape of children and even of babies. But a lot of those who want to open Stellenbosch to the world tend to be men and they also tend to paint us out of the picture. And if you're not easily definable, as with gender, you get painted out even more quickly and brutally.'

When I left she asked where I was heading to next and I told her I was driving back to Cape Town, where I'd begun my trail of the assaulted effigies. She nodded and repeated the mantra I had heard so often:

'Cape Town – where it all began.'

32

Walking along the foreshore, within sight of the docks, I stood beneath the statue of Jan van Riebeeck. He no longer carried around his neck a large notice that read: 'I stole your land. So what?' I was sorry about that. It had shown a lightness of touch, even a trace of irony lacking from other insults scrawled on despoiled monuments. Literacy beats eschatology. But again I was plunged into the familiar well of absurdity. Van Riebeeck and his small band of Dutch colleagues landed in the Cape in 1652, we were taught, and founded White South Africa. His handsome face with its flowing locks of chestnut hair was pictured on banknotes and the arrival in South Africa of the doughty settlers became a creation myth, taught as gospel truth in school history books. But van Riebeeck was no founder, he was an ambitious functionary in the Dutch East India Company, sent to the Cape to provision passing ships. He had his sights set on the riches of the East, and dallied a while on the tip of Africa before high-tailing it east to Malacca, money and promotion.

The furious reaction of Black students to the venerable lying machine that had been 'national education' was understandable – if misdirected. We needed our statues and legends, however false, because they stood to remind us that, when the powerful erect memorials, these tell only one side of the story. We needed to know the other side and the other way of telling, and even then to treat both sides with caution. How are we to measure the depth of the deception unless we keep those statues standing?

As it turned out, almost everything we were taught about the early White settlers was wrong. Even the defaced statue of van Riebeeck on the Cape Town foreshore is a fake. Those who strung a placard, demanding the return of their land, around the neck of the dashing figure, gazing out to sea, had the wrong man. The fellow on the banknotes and the tall figure on the plinth are modelled not after Jan van Riebeeck, but after a man named Bartholomeus Vermuyden, who was better looking than the orotund and homely original. In short, van Riebeeck, as remembered and immortalized, was not van Riebeeck at all. His portrait was a charade, and the story spun around him as founding father of the nation, and to which we pledged allegiance on pain of being expelled from the tribe, was the founding fraud at the heart of our history.

Although this was not unknown at the time, few said so aloud, and for good reason. Portraits of the Dutch settlers of the original Cape Colony were rare and much disputed – but in the apartheid years, there were other reasons for not looking too hard at Dutch settlement. Many families, classified as 'White' Afrikaners, descended from unions between early Dutch, Belgian and German settlers, and their slaves; or from liaisons with indigenous Khoi-Khoi people of the Cape. The chequered pasts of many White citizens were not discussed; it could be painful, dangerous and even fatal.

Yet we needed the van Riebeeck impostor standing at the gateway to Cape Town, if for no other reason than he helps us to understand the web of deceit and delusion that was the stock in trade of some South African historians. Van Riebeeck on his plinth reminded us that people in power bend the truth to suit their needs and insist that everyone else believe it. Every statue, every image made in bronze or marble, like every election promise, was useful because it provoked a vital question: how were we to know that we were being lied to unless we listened to the story being told and made up our own minds?

I set off on a walk through Kirstenbosch Botanical Garden, on the slopes of Table Mountain, looking for a hedge, or the remains of a hedge, that van Riebeeck had planted, over three centuries earlier. Newly arrived in the Cape, he faced a spot of bother with the local Khoi and the San, who objected to the way settlers helped themselves to whatever they liked and stole their cattle. In 1658, the governor erected a wooden fence to keep the unruly KhoiSan smugglers at bay. He built a second barrier a couple of years later, planting a wild almond hedge to make the boundary of what, for the moment at least, the settlers regarded as the extent of their colony. The barrier was never very successful because cattle had to be kept on the further side of the hedge and the smugglers liked that. The question was: on which side of the hedge did the real thieves live? A leader of the Khoi, a certain Autshumato, put the question to the colonists and van Riebeeck recorded it in his diary: 'Who should rather in justice give way, the rightful owner or the foreign intruder?'

The question is as fresh today as it was in 1660 and it has received no satisfactory answer. It was as a result of this disenchantment that the aggrieved Khoi and San people launched a series of wars against the Dutch interlopers; wars that lasted well over a century, and even though the original people have vanished it is true to say that the wars have not abated. The remains of van Riebeeck's once thick and thorny hedge in Kirstenbosch

Hedge planted by Jan van Riebeeck in 1660, Cape Town

Botanical Garden is a lasting testimony to the hedge in our own heads.

What is striking about the present state of the statue wars is the way some people seem to be determined to replant, all over again, the thorny hedge that keeps people apart. They exhibit the resurgent obsession we have lived with for a very long time: the belief that race and skin colour are everything. It is a belief that would have delighted the man who was once a neighbour of mine: the apostle of apartheid, Hendrik Verwoerd.

This obsession has taken a further lurch into unreality recently, as the statues came down. Nowadays colours are attached to abstract nouns like 'White' power, 'White' capital, and even 'White' mathematics. Those who colour-code these abstractions demand that oppressive readings and contexts must be eliminated and that there should arise in their places 'Black' equivalents, free of colonial trappings.

You might say that there is something reasonable in this view; people are entitled to oppose 'Whiteness', just as they may oppose globalization, carnivory, patriarchy or the overweening power of the banks. But if you go down this path, the question is: why stop there? If you reject, as an anti-Rhodes protestor has recently done, Newton's law of universal gravitation, for its perceived bias towards 'Whiteness', should you not apply the same colour-cleansing to German cars and Korean phones, to Russian ballet, Chinese cuisine and German barbecues – should you not 'decolonize' and recolour the rules of soccer and Scrabble?

And if you do go down this path, don't you have a good deal in common with the theories of Hendrik Verwoerd, who systematized racial separation? His teaching holds that each ethnic group, sect or clan must define itself, its culture and beliefs in its own homeland. Self-determination equals liberty, Verwoerd taught; each 'nation' must be sovereign but separate in order to be free. Do you then believe, as Verwoerd proposed, that skin colour assigns your destiny and cultural traits are inborn and eradicable? In short, that tribalism is freedom?

The answer is that we have tried it more consistently than anyone else. For decades the most brutal, obsessive racial partition took place in South Africa. And it did not work. Worse, it was a sham and a charade. It was built on lies and it could be maintained only by overwhelming force. The separated racial 'homelands', 'tribal reserves' and 'independent mini-states' of Verwoerd's dream were kept in line by police officers and soldiers and hangmen, all White, who banished, jailed or killed those who opposed them. Apartheid had little to do with freedom and everything to do with brute force. It was, in the end, a mad circus that relied on thugs and bullies to keep order. It is not surprising that thugs and bullies, who preach the new religion of race and colour and the manifold sins of the skin, favour force as the way of getting things done. They just come at it from the opposite direction.

The more recent colour-coding occurred when I was back in Cape Town, as I went looking at van Riebeeck and his hedge of bitter almonds. In April 2016, a Black student detected a phenomenon he dubbed 'White tears'. It occurred when Black activists from the 'Rhodes Must Fall' programme confronted a White waitress in a café in Cape Town. When she brought their bill they handed her a written demand: 'We will give tip when you return the land…' The astonished waitress burst into tears; her harriers announced on Facebook that they were amused to see the waitress weeping 'typical White tears' ('…like why are you crying when all we've done is to make a kind request?').

What was notable about their language and their laughter that day, in what I think of now as the Café Lachrymosa, was its mock-jocular tone. One waitress was to answer for the fact that the country had been stolen by Whites, *en masse*, as if they were an indivisible bloc or sect, and the weeping waitress of the Café Lachrymosa represented every last landowner.

'Go to your fellow White people,' her tormentors instructed, 'and mobilize for them to give us the land back.'

Dr Verwoerd would have loved it. All members of a particular group are thus defined by their race and, to the leaders of the lachrymosal liberation brigade in pursuit of the lone waitress, all are guilty simply by virtue of their skin colour.

It would do no good to point out that, the last time I looked, tears were colourless. For those of the Verwoerdian tendency, all is colour-coded and they would argue, and have done so, that the phrase had nothing to do with weeping, in and of itself. Indeed, those who made the White waitress cry denied a single tear fell – though she confirmed that she wept. But then, it was never really about whether drops of salty water coursed down her cheeks. Like the skirmishes against statues, this was a prelude to the real battle.

Anticipating that some might argue you can't tar all Whites with the same brush, the race-baiters were ready with a rebuttal: 'We are tired of "not all White people" and all other bullshit. We are here and we want the stolen land back.'

The prose of the race-mongers is pockmarked with capitals and exclamation marks, as if by heating up the words, they will blare and deafen. But written words don't lend themselves to the sort of aural assault that you get from a good public address system by cranking up the decibel level, or when a drill sergeant barks out marching orders, or from noisy speakers at fascist rallies, for whom individuals must be welded into an obedient mass whose only significant feature is party loyalty and tribal affiliation and who will believe what you say as long as the orders are loud enough.

The ultimatums of the new race-obsessed are noisy with capitals: 'NO White person will be out here living their best life while we are out here being a landless and dispossessed Black mass. NO White person shall rest.'

It is a warning as familiar as the veld. When words will not work, then fists, boots and bullets are next, because violence is the reliable route to victory.

I visited the café of the weeping waitress and wondered aloud which had been the table where 'White tears' fell. Those who work in the Café Lachrymosa were not keen to talk about the incident. That was a pity because the phenomenon aroused interest all over the world. In Catholic countries it is generally the statues of saints or portraits of the Virgin Mary that suddenly and mysteriously begin to cry. In South Africa it is waitresses. A shrine might have been good for business – and attracted pilgrims from far and wide. The Café Lachrymosa might consider one day commissioning a plaque and screw it into a table top, to indicate where the first tears fell. Or better still, a water feature, a fountain, a well, a spring, or even a tap, that patrons might turn on and off to commemorate what happened that day and name it something like 'Tears Must Fall'. Then again, the morals committee from the nearby university might carry away the offending artwork for interrogation, in one of the cellars where confiscated artworks are held. You can't be too careful.

It's a dismal discovery but perhaps not much of a surprise to find that, inevitably, Nelson Mandela is increasingly blamed by those discontents who believe in making waitresses weep. He is regarded by such people as an appeaser, an ally of White people; he is, they say, the 'White people's Black darling... whose status as the voice and God of all Black people before the altar of Whiteness dwindles by the day'.

It's difficult to know which is the more dispiriting, the convoluted prose style or the unwarranted insult. Whichever way you look at it, it's all too familiar because it was where the whole story began, when Georgie and I went walking through the neighbourhood where I grew up, carefully crossing the road when we passed Dr Verwoerd's house. Dr Verwoerd, who believed in much the same rigid wall between White and Black and whose faithful followers spent the next half-century painstakingly building barriers until they had constructed a grand asylum of absurdity in which everyone was forced to live. Where, and even now as I write this, I find it hard to believe that I'm reporting facts and not inventing a scene from some bitter comedy, ophthalmologists seeking transplants for Africans were obliged to advertise for 'Black eyes'; cinema ushers who were Coloured were permitted to work in White cinemas, as long as they did not watch the movie; and people found it natural to worry, when the first heart transplants were pioneered in South Africa, that White patients might receive 'Black' hearts. It was the sort of thing that George had called 'bad *muti*', and it poisoned the lifeblood of the country.

The University of Cape Town had formally declared that the statue of Rhodes was not coming back to the plinth. One had to assume that the interrogation committee had handed down its judgement and 'effigy effacement' was in full swing. I had harboured the faint hope that the now redundant Rhodes might be sent to the little town of Rhodes, where the innkeeper of Walkerbouts Inn had offered it political asylum in his garden. But he told me he had no reply to his offer.

However, the university had decided to retain the plinth the statue had once occupied. The block of stone seemed to have taken on something of the quasi-sacred powers once attributed to the seated Rhodes. 'There is something about the heightened space...' the university explained, as well as its elevation that made 'the performative space so valuable because it stands out above road level. It means you are very visible whatever you are doing.'

I remembered how, after the statue of Rhodes had been trundled away, dancers had taken over the plinth. I was curious to see what performances were now playing on the plinth, and went back to the campus to take a look.

33

I f it looked like anything, it was a tombstone, a blank slab, or an empty altar, as flat as the top of Table Mountain. It was even more compelling without its statue, and more eloquent. It spoke of what had gone and not of dancing to come. Sometimes removal achieves the opposite effect to that intended, making the memory of what has gone even more vivid and mysterious. The bronze effigy of Rhodes may have been banished but the empty plinth hinted that he had taken to haunting the mountain.

Of course, his spectral presence would vanish and few would remember whose likeness had once occupied the empty plinth, or why it had been removed. Rhodes had been moved on. Another window in the collective memory of the country, already much weakened, would have closed. History would have slipped back into its base position, a way of defending the prevailing prejudices of whoever held power.

Perhaps, then, I was not too surprised to discover that the cry of 'Rhodes Must Fall' was neither original nor new. It turned out it had been a repeat performance and not a revolution. Back in the fifties, Afrikaans undergraduates at Cape Town University demanded the removal of Rhodes' statue and had their reasons for doing so. Had he not been promoter of the Boer War, eager colonialist, insufferable imperialist and sworn enemy of White

Afrikaner independence? The Nationalist government of the day, all White Afrikaners to a man, sympathized with the student demands – and ignored them.

Passing the tall classical columns of the neo-Grecian pile known as Jameson Hall, renamed Memorial Hall after the fall of Rhodes but rumoured to become Sarah Baartman Hall at some later date, and watching the blue Jameson shuttle buses rumble by, I reckoned it would take more than demonstrations to exorcise the ghost of Rhodes. As I crossed the main campus, I saw what a long hard job purification would be if it was to be done well. A start had been made with the removal of dubious 'White Colonialist' paintings and photographs for 'interrogation'. Others had been torched. When a representative of those who fed the bonfire was asked if burning paintings was part of the 'decolonization' project, he replied: 'Yes, it is, intrinsically.'

But you might remove every offending painting or photograph and still the campus was saturated with Western symbols and colonial hangovers. Rhodes had fallen, but dozens of imperial nabobs remained, their names inscribed on halls and residences. After the names had gone, so must the symbols, the Grecian columns, the sash windows, the gowns and mortars of graduates, the libraries named for donors and scholars and lots of books. When the removals are complete then the renaming may start. It will be a long business.

Strangely enough, there had been no protests aimed at Leander Starr Jameson, Rhodes' dearest friend and with whom he had a relationship so close it might be called a love affair. Jameson took the blame for Rhodes' scheme to draw the British Empire into a war against the Boers. He led the raiding party into Kruger's

Transvaal Republic, failed spectacularly and was captured by the Boers but stayed resolutely loyal to his chief. The farce of the failed raid played havoc with Rhodes' political fortunes and he resigned as the Premier of the Cape Province, though soon enough he got the war he wanted. Jameson's fidelity to Rhodes was very likely the inspiration behind Kipling's poem 'If' – that summation of Victorian virtues.

There is a haunting photograph of Rhodes and Jameson disembarking from a liner in Cape Town at the end of the Boer War. In dress, girth and headgear, as alike as Tweedledum and Tweedledee, they march in step along the quayside. In a few months, Rhodes would be dead. He was buried on a hilltop in Rhodesia, the country he once owned and named, and what is now Zimbabwe. Beside him lies Leander Starr Jameson. Robert Mugabe, who fought to free the country from the colonial yoke, wisely left the arch-imperialist and his beloved friend in peace in the Matobo Hills.

Once all traces of colonialism, imperialism and capitalism were wiped away, what was to be done with the spaces left behind? Unless you filled the gaps they might haunt the landscape, like the empty plinth. Removals could actually reinforce memories you wished to pension off. This had happened when the suburb of District Six in Cape Town, where Coloured people had lived for centuries, was cleared of its residents by the apartheid planners, bulldozed and proclaimed 'White'. Such assaults on its own citizens was the daily work of the old regime. The policy assumed that you could preserve Cape Town as a White redoubt by destroying what made the city vigorous, mixed and inimitable. The merciless moving on and out of the Coloureds of District Six was a crime – but it was also a bad mistake. Something vital died. Cape Town without its Coloureds was like Vienna without its Jews. The naked scars on the mountainside, where District Six had stood, have haunted the city ever since. It was no longer there, but its nothingness weighed terribly, and its non-existence made it unforgettable.

Georgie, or someone very like him, had waved to me on that day I watched the removal of Rhodes. Then Georgie, or the man I took to be Georgie, had moved away before I could reach him and walked up the road that leads higher up the mountain, towards Devil's Peak, where I knew there was another, more formal, memorial to Rhodes. It did not matter if I was hallucinating, or plain wrong, about the figure in the crowd. Georgie always had a way of waking me to new discoveries and to my own ignorance. So once again, as I'd done as a child, I followed his lead.

The steep, winding road to Devil's Peak took about half an hour of stiff walking before I arrived at the Rhodes Memorial. I'd not been to see it before and it fitted well with Rhodes' fondness for high places and commanding views. The granite prow of the memorial, pointing northwards, is a lunging horseman by George Frederic Watts, representing 'Physical Energy'. Forty-nine steps, cut from Cape granite, one for each year of Rhodes' life, flanked by eight great bronze lions, led up to the memorial itself, where the bust of Rhodes reposes, chin in hand, as if dreaming Africa into existence. Close by there is a delightful restaurant. This twinning of quasi-mysticisms, mingled with commerce, the temple and the tearoom, seemed apt. Unveiled in 1912, the Rhodes Memorial was another landmark designed by Rhodes' favourite architect, Sir Herbert Baker. The inscription reads: 'To the spirit and the life work of Cecil John Rhodes who loved and served South Africa.'

Looking up at the head of Rhodes, the first thing I noticed was the hole where his nose had been. It had been cleanly removed, leaving a perfectly shaped nasal aperture. Hostile graffiti writers had been busy: 'Your dreams of empire will die,' read one line, and another, to the right of the noseless head: 'Racist, thief, murderer…'

The assault seemed a half-hearted, unfinished job; part and parcel of the fatuity of these iconoclastic times. The theft of Rhodes' nose made the head even more powerful and the vandalism more risible. If this was the worst angry young South Africans could do to one of the few really world-class villains, you had to wonder if they deserved to have any.

But I can see why people might hate the image. Here is Rhodes as Ozymandias and Kublai Khan rolled into one. The memorial, it was said, had echoes of a classical Grecian temple. But the one genuine Greek quality about the memorial was its hubris, and in Kipling Rhodes found his court poet.

Noseless Rhodes on Devil's Peak, Cape Town

> The immense and brooding Spirit still
> Shall quicken and control.

Kipling's lines, cut into the stone, reflect awe-struck reverence for the colossus of the continent. Rhodes was not simply being memorialized on Devil's Peak, he was deified. In Kipling's panegyric, Rhodes' presence and power suffuse all sub-Saharan Africa, from the Cape of Good Hope, to Lake Victoria and beyond. Death would not diminish his imperial reach – Rhodes would continue shaping the continent from beyond the grave:

> It is his will that he look forth
> Across the world he won –
> The granite of the ancient North –
> Great spaces washed with sun.

Rhodes becomes a kind of substitute religion, a pantheism for patriots; the equivalent of a Cape Town cargo-cult.

> Living he was the land, and dead
> His soul shall be her soul!

Kipling's lines, however silly and embarrassingly over the top, have a memorable sonority. They foresee the range of Rhodes' influence throughout the twentieth century. Similar sound-good sentiments, devoid of Kipling's genius, would be trumpeted in school assemblies, boardrooms, churches and sporting clubs for decades to come. Those who challenged the idea of Rhodes as touched with divinity and anointed by the god of bankers would have been seen as odd, even irreligious, as well as downright seditious.

*

Standing at the Rhodes Memorial, where the vandals had attacked the head and knocked off its nose, I felt strangely relieved. The memorial on Devil's Peak is preposterous, but it might have been worse. There was once a plan to erect on the mountain an immense Rhodes who would tower over the city, rather like Christ standing guard over Rio de Janeiro. The dark comedy of South African life often provides some respite. I felt grateful that we had on Devil's Peak, instead of Christ of the Cape, a man missing a nose.

I hope the noseless Rhodes survives. It so eloquent and unforgettable and portrays something of who we are and how we got this way. The scar left on the landscape, and the soul, when District Six was 'removed' says all that is needed about, not only the cruelty, but the stupidity of apartheid, based as it was on the belief that by knocking down people's homes and demanding they live out of sight, at least by night, you could re-engineer reality. It was an idea even more foolish than claiming that by toppling effigies you did not like you could rewrite history. We should preserve embarrassing monuments – bad memories can be a precious resource.

We have had enough amnesia and careless forgetfulness. What you may see at the Rhodes Memorial on Devil's Peak is not just the man with a nose. You can also see Robben Island, where many prisoners have been locked up over the centuries – from Damon the Khoi rebel to Nelson Mandela. The view was available during the years Mandela was on the island but few locals would have pointed it out. Had I sat in the tearoom beside the Rhodes Memorial in the eighties, or even the early nineties, and called for the immediate release of Mandela, assuring my astonished audience that Mandela was the president the country needed and that they would weep when he died and wish him back again, I would have risked being led away in suitable restraints.

As I looked up at the noseless Rhodes on his temple mount, a young Black man came and sat beside me and also looked up at Rhodes. I asked him whether he thought that this Rhodes would follow the statue down the road, away to the garden of fallen idols.

'For sure,' he said. 'Can't be stopped. It's the endgame.'

It was disconcerting meeting a chess player on a mountain-side. I heard what he said but I have always been suspicious of large generalizations, especially those designed to make my flesh creep. South Africans, until now at least, have never been good enough at being bad enough to bring about an endgame. Besides, the extraordinary grandmaster we face has an absurd, sometimes cruel sense of comedy.

On another part of the mountain, and on another significant peak known as Lion's Head, in April 2015, when the statue wars had just begun, a small, bald, pot-bellied golden manikin, quite naked, suddenly made an appearance. The sturdy little troll, said to look very much like President Zuma, carried in his right hand a large pink plastic dildo. The little statue was entitled 'Swordsman of the Nation', a disreputable joke at the expense of the libidinous president. The priapic golden gnome was quickly carted away by the Parks Board staff who patrol the mountain, and never seen again. It was a pity to see him go because such cheerful sacrilege is all too rare.

Looking left from Lion's Head I could see Clifton, its beach and the evening sun sliding like a drop of oil into the calm blue sea. To my right was Table Bay where, President Zuma reminded us, one day in 1652 the first White adventurers arrived and stayed and ruined everything they touched. But what is everything? And who is everybody?

I remembered my conversation with Oliver Tambo and how he assured me that, when freedom came to South Africa, it would belong to all who lived there. That had been the pledge of the ANC he led but it had become today the sort of talk that got Black leaders written off as 'White men's darlings'. It sounded comforting, but it was not much help. The ruling party continued to repeat the old mantra, but with diminishing conviction. Whites were less and less wanted on voyages and faced their own redundancy, and they were frequently reminded of it by an assortment of oddly allied race-baiters; the new Verwoerdians who, once again, saw everything in Black and White.

You might say, of course, that Whites had it coming and you may be right. But if South Africa ever had any real gift, it has been precisely in the rich, messy mix of its people: a multiplicity of Blacks, a congregation of Coloureds, fundamental admixtures of KhoiSan, Asians, Chinese, as well as a handful of Whites, and a good many of others who have always been simply unclassifiable. The challenge has been to strike a tolerable and tolerant balance. To those who say the idea would never have worked, I'd say it has never been tried – but for a brief, exuberant moment in the Mandela years.

It is not that pogroms are on the way, though there are some who would approve. When I hear that the hate-mongers have been busy at Witwatersrand University once again, scrawling 'Kill A Jew' on walls and running away, then I tell myself that the only thing to be said about this latest call to execution is that it is, at least, modest, and a one-at-a-time murder rate is somewhat preferable to wholesale holocaust.

There are others, notably among those who make the return of 'Black' land a priority, who show little of the same restraint and whose tweets and bleats grow more frenzied.

'I have an aspiration to kill White people,' one of them recently posted.

There has also been a fierce counterreaction from Whites, who seem to be reverting to type, the old familiar antipathy, directed at the 'other' side. There is the notion that it's all so unfair – that Whites have done enough and given up enough and tried hard enough and waited long enough and yet things are more painful than ever. It is self-righteousness mingled with self-pity that reminds me very much of how we were – and how we are, all over again. Because the anticipated escape from the gigantic prison we helped to build has not gone well, blame is heaped on the ex-prisoners. It is hardly surprising that the hatreds of the old South Africa are surfacing again, on both sides, and rumours of war multiply.

But to what purpose? When you look at the figures it is not deportation or pogroms or even the long-anticipated race war that will drive Whites into, or over, the sea. It is simply too late for that sort of thing. Demographics and disillusion may carry them away, whatever happens. It has been estimated that by 2030, in a group of one hundred young South Africans under the age of twenty-five, just one will be White. Whichever way you play it, I hear the music Oliver Tambo once told me that no one in his country wanted, or needed, to hear – the café de move-on blues.

Acknowledgements

I am most grateful for my three-month residency, in early 2017, as a Fellow of STIAS, the Institute for Advanced Study, at Stellenbosch University. The time and the peace this afforded, as I worked on early drafts of this book, was invaluable.

I greatly appreciate the help and advice given me by Bryan Rostron and Bill Nasson, whose subtle understanding of South Africa's complex and confusing history encouraged me to hope I might be moving in the right direction.

Some sections of Chapter 25 first appeared, in a slightly different form, in the *Guardian* newspaper.

Illustration Credits

p.4: Rhodes attacked, Cape Town, 9 April 2015 (*Rodger Bosch/AFP/Getty Images*)

p.8: Cecil Rhodes' statue being removed from University of Cape Town (*Roger Sedres/Alamy Stock Photo*)

p.33: Memento Park, Budapest (*Ferran Cornellà/Wikimedia Commons*)

p.40: Jan van Riebeeck, Cape Town, April 2015 (*Gallo Images/The Times/Adrian de Kock*)

p.63: Service protest (*Reuters/Siphiwe Sibeko/Gallo Images*)

p.69: Matjiesfontein station (*Education Images/UIG via Getty Images*)

p.84: Rock painting of Bushmen hunting, Karoo (*Yuri Biryukov/Shutterstock*)

p.111: Boer prisoners – British concentration camp, Bloemfontein (*Ann Ronan Pictures/Print Collector/Getty Images*)

p.112: Graveyard, Doornbult camp, Orange River Station (*The Heritage Foundation*)

p.119: Big Hole, Kimberley Diamond Mine (*travelview/Shutterstock*)

p.124: Honoured Dead Memorial, Kimberley (*Grobler du Preez/Shutterstock*)

p.126: Kimberley diggings, 1872 (*Ann Ronan Pictures/Print Collector/Getty Images*)

p.144: Koffiefontein's town sign (*Grobler du Preez/Shutterstock*)

p.154: Dr Hendrik Verwoerd, Orania (*Per-Anders Pettersson/Getty Images*)

p.168: The Rand Club, Johannesburg (*THEGIFT777/Getty Images*)

p.175: Vandalized statue of Gandhi, Johannesburg (*Alon Skuy/The Times/Gallo Images/Getty Images*)

p.179: Prime Minister J.G. Strydom, Krugersdorp (*Gallo Images/Foto24/Cornel van Heerden*)

p.182: Robert Broom and Mrs Ples, Cradle of Mankind, Sterkfontein Caves (*Ariadne Van Zandbergen/Alamy Stock Photo*)

p.194: Paintings being burnt, Cape Town University campus, 2016 (*Ashraf Hendricks/Anadolu Agency/Getty Images*)

p.199: Paul Kruger behind barbed wire, Pretoria, 2015 (*Gallo Images/Lungelo Mbulwana*)

p.209: Brooklyn Police Station (*Alexander Joe/AFP/Getty Images*)

p.211: Mandela at the Union Buildings, Pretoria (*J. Countess/Getty Images*)

p.213: Rabbit in Mandela's ear (*STR/AFP/Getty Images*)

p.223: Gallows, Pretoria Central Prison (*Associated Press*)

p.232: Happy's funeral, Tweefontein, 2013 (*Foto 24/Theana Breugem/Gallo, Camera Press London*)

p.249: Statue of King Shaka, International Airport, KwaZulu-Natal (*Rajesh Jantilal/AFP/Getty Images*)

p.254: King George V, Natal University, Durban (*Khaya Ngwenya/Foto24/Gallo Images/Getty Images*)

p.269: Horse Memorial, Port Elizabeth, 2016 (*Gallo Images/Foto24/ Werner Hills*)

p.276: Inspecting the Hottentot Venus (*Bibliothèque nationale de France*)

p.280: Plaque commemorating Hendrik Verwoerd being removed from the Stellenbosch University campus, May 2015 (*Ashraf Hendricks/Anadolu Agency/Getty Images*)

p.288: Hedge planted by Jan van Riebeeck in 1660, Cape Town (*Leoa's Photography/Wikimedia Commons*)

p.298: Noseless Rhodes on Devil's Peak, Cape Town (*Prosthetic Head/Wikimedia Commons*)